Popular Music and Multimodal Critical Discourse Studies

Also available from Bloomsbury

Music as Multimodal Discourse
Introduction to Multimodal Analysis

Popular Music and Multimodal Critical Discourse Studies

Ideology, Control, and Resistance in Turkey Since 2002

Lyndon C. S. Way

BLOOMSBURY ACADEMIC
LONDON · NEW YORK · OXFORD · NEW DELHI · SYDNEY

BLOOMSBURY ACADEMIC
Bloomsbury Publishing Plc
50 Bedford Square, London, WC1B 3DP, UK
1385 Broadway, New York, NY 10018, USA

BLOOMSBURY, BLOOMSBURY ACADEMIC and the Diana logo
are trademarks of Bloomsbury Publishing Plc

First published 2018
Paperback edition first published 2019

Cover image © tacktack/iStock
Series design by Louise Dugdale, cover design by Olivia D'Cruz

A catalogue record for this book is available from the British Library.

Library of Congress Cataloging-in-Publication Data
Names: Way, Lyndon C. S. author.
Title: Popular music and multimodal critical discourse studies : ideology,
control and resistance in Turkey since 2002 / Lyndon C. S. Way.
Description: New York : Bloomsbury Academic, 2017. | Includes bibliographical
references and index.
Identifiers: LCCN 2017027162 (print) | LCCN 2017029474 (ebook) |
ISBN 9781350016453 (ePDF) | ISBN 9781350016460 (ePub) | ISBN
9781350016446 (hardback)
Subjects: LCSH: Popular music–Political aspects–Turkey.
Classification: LCC ML3917.T9 (ebook) | LCC ML3917.T9 W39 2017 (print) |
DDC 781.6309561–dc23
LC record available at https://lccn.loc.gov/2017027162

ISBN: HB: 978-1-3500-1644-6
       PB: 978-1-3501-1899-7
       ePDF: 978-1-3500-1645-3
       ePub: 978-1-3500-1646-0

Series: Bloomsbury Advances in Critical Discourse Studies

Typeset by Integra Software Services Pvt. Ltd.

To find out more about our authors and books visit
www.bloomsbury.com and sign up for our newsletters.

For Ayla, Erim, Kerem, mum and dad

Contents

List of Figures

Acknowledgments

I thank my editorial team of Michal Krzyzanowski, John E. Richardson, and David Machin for their support in the preparation of this book. I give special thanks to David Machin who encouraged me to start this project and guided me through to the finish. Gurdeep Mattu at Bloomsbury deserves a shout-out for always offering positive and sound advice. I want to thank my friends at Izmir University of Economics including Aysun Akan and Ture Şahin who have helped in innumerable ways. I especially want to thank Yiğit Eygi for working through the music with me, Aytunç Erçifci for enjoying concerts as much as I do, and Levent Mercan for introducing me to some amazing music.

Previously published works in this volume:

The analysis of Grup Kızılırmak's *Çesmi Siyahim* in Chapter 7 is derived from Way, L. (2015), "Spaces of protest in Turkish popular music," in E. Mazierska and G. Gregory (eds), *Relocating Popular Music*, 27–43, London: Palgrave.

The analysis of Bariş Akarsu's "Kimdir O" in Chapter 8 is derived from Way, L. (2013), "Discourses of popular politics, war and authenticity in Turkish pop music," *Social Semiotics*, 23(5): 715–734.

The analysis of *Marsis* "Oy Oy Recebum" in Chapter 8 is derived from Way, L. (2016), "Protest music, populism, politics and authenticity: The limits and potential of popular music's articulation of subversive politics," *Journal of Language and Politics*, 15(4): 422–446.

The analysis of *The Ringo Jets*'s "Spring of War" in Chapters 8 and 9 is derived from Way, L. (2015), "YouTube as a site of debate through populist politics: The case of a Turkish protest pop video," *Journal of Multicultural Discourse*, 10(2): 180–196.

Preface

I have lived in Turkey since 2002. During this time, there have been two concurrent developments. On a personal level as a musician and fan, I have come to appreciate the diversity and depth of Turkey's music culture. Despite my constant attention, I continue to be pleasantly surprised. Like everywhere, Turkey has its fair share of chart music including the global genres of rap, dance, rock, and pop, a lot of which includes musings about relationships and love. It also has traditions of folk, arabesk, fantasy, and art music, just to name a few. And weaved within and between these genres of music is a tradition of music which subverts authority. By subvert, I do not only mean the commonly used meaning "to overthrow something established or existing," but the idea "to corrupt, criticize or undermine." It is here where my interest has gravitated.

The second development during my time in Turkey has been on a societal level: ongoing, dramatic changes socially and politically. My arrival in Turkey coincided with the Justice and Development Party (Adalet ve Kalkınma Partisi—AKP) first coming to power in national elections. Their time in office has witnessed many people becoming financially better off with many sectors in society seeing an improvement in their standard of living. This has come at a cost to not only other sectors of society, but also to basic rights including freedom of speech and freedom of expression. These negative changes have accelerated in recent years. Most mainstream media are now either pro-government or muted in their criticisms of the government due to perceived negative repercussions (more of this in the coming chapters). Alternative and new media are also regulated and controlled to an extent where again most oppositional voices are unheard.

Despite this dire situation, some music fills a void by speaking critically. And this is where this book begins. In this book, I examine how this happens. How music commodities with their visuals, lyrics, and sounds act as an alternative and subversive voice to what is on offer in other media. And it is here where I believe, despite all of music's shortcomings as a communicative act, hope lies.

Introduction

Songs are carried on the same breath as words, with their melody adding greater range and emotional impact and conveying a mood that transcends the barriers of language and culture. (Dr. Vaira Vike-Freberga, President of Latvia 1999–2007)

Music is, by its very nature, essentially powerless to express anything at all, whether a feeling, an attitude of mind, a psychological mood, a phenomenon of nature, etc. Expression has never been an inherent property of music. (Igor Stravinsky 1935)

There are a wide range of opinions on popular music's ability to communicate specific ideas, including politics, ranging from the most optimistic to those like Stravinsky's just mentioned. Though Stravinsky may have had reasons for making such a claim (Zbikowski 2015: 144), comments like his inform academia and everyday discussions about *what* exactly is the nature of relations between music and meanings, between music and politics. Can popular music be political? What types of music work best with politics? What types of politics work best with popular music? What influences can we witness? These issues are essential, explored, and considered in this book. However, the focus of this book is on *how* popular music is perceived to be political. That is, I consider what is it about a song, a video, a concert, a band, or any other musical commodity which conveys meanings. By answering *how*, questions about *what* become clear.

An example of what I mean ought to help. Let's consider the music video for Placebo's "Rob the Bank (alternate director version)."[1] Placebo is a British alternative rock group formed in London in 1994. To date, it has released seven studio albums, all of which have reached the top twenty in the United Kingdom, selling approximately eleven million copies worldwide. "Rob the Bank" comes from the group's seventh album *Loud Like Love* which was released on September 16, 2013. The video first appeared on YouTube on September 8, a few days before the album release.

Lyrics offer up a number of ideas such as the singer commanding listeners to "Rob the bank of England and America, Rob the bank of the entire Euro Zone." These commands or imperatives are simple, like the minimalistic musical sounds which accompany them. These could be construed as an act of defiance or revenge, considering the song was released in the wake of the economic crisis sparked by the actions of banks which then had to be bailed out by taxpayers' money. During this time, it was quite common to hear people and the media complain about the unfairness of these bailouts. Between commands to rob banks, the singer also tells the listener to do socially unacceptable actions like "make a joke out of dyslexia" and "pick your nose." Unlike the previous commands which challenge conventional economics, these question social norms. But typical of a lot of popular music, the social and political messages of the lyrics are not cut-and-dry, matter-of-fact, clearly articulated statements. To make meanings of the song even more confusing, the repeated choruses tell the listener "but take me home and make love." These lyrics are emphasized through musical choices. The phrase "but take me home" is sung a cappella, as opposed to the rest of the song where vocals and instrumentation vie for our attention. The phrase "and make love" is also emphasized by the singer drawing out the words, accentuating his emotions. Here we also hear a guitar solo characterized by a high-pitched wavering sound which contributes to emotional tension. What we hear then are lyrics and musical sounds which communicate not only subversion to economics and social norms, but also a highly emotional theme of love. This is a far cry from some sort of political manifesto delivered in a speech heard by the party faithful. However, unlike most political speeches and manifestos, it is heard by millions of popular music fans.

The visuals in the video also communicate a number of ideas. There are shots which show a man and woman in a ceremony resembling a wedding: white dress, veil, suit and tie, holding hands, and a flower girl. However, their surroundings of darkness, violence, and rubbish strewn floors suggest something else. There is an abundance of images which use protest-related symbols from Turkey's 2013 Gezi Park protests and the World Occupy movements, again suggesting politics of subversion. Twice we see a replica of a statue of David by Michelangelo wearing a gas mask and draped in a Turkish flag. David (of David and Goliath fame) has positive connotations, being a symbol of liberty, including the defense of civil liberties and freedom ('Michelangelo's David' 2014). The Turkish flag and gas masks place this defense for civil liberties in Turkey. Gas masks and surgical masks worn by characters in the video are similar to those worn by Gezi Park protesters against the overuse of pepper spray and gas by police. There is also a character whose pose and clothes look like one of the icons of Gezi Park protests, "the standing man." Newspapers blowing in the wind seem to reference media censorship. In Turkey this was brought to people's attention through a lack of coverage of the Gezi Park protests by news channels closely associated with the government. In the video, all this is shot in slow motion and slickly edited, representing protest as glamorous and sexy.

This close analysis of lyrics, sounds, and visuals also tells us something about the band Placebo and how it is an authentic "alternative" or "indie rock" band. After all, being against the authorities has been associated with some rock bands and types of rock since its beginnings, including indie rock. Musical sounds including a forceful beat and whining guitars make clear this song is indie rock. By telling us to rob banks and act against social norms, Placebo is telling us to engage in subversive activities. That makes them party to subversion. Likewise, showing protesters acting against the state in a romanticized way also suggests that Placebo is a part of this, an authentic anti-authoritarian indie rock band.

The focus of this book is not just answering what is subversive or political, but how this is achieved. This cursory examination of Placebo's "Rob the bank" unearths a collection of disparate ideas about the band, politics, economics, police actions, media censorship, anger, social values, and love. It is anything but a systematic and coherent argument. This look at "Rob the bank" also suggests that a close inspection of a musical commodity, such as a promotional music video, can be used to question not only what is being expressed in music which can be politically construed and used against, say, the banking system or the Turkish government, but also how this is done. This examination has also opened up a Pandora's box in terms of popular music, politics, authenticity, and various ways to examine relations between these. I intend to open this box even further throughout the following pages, offering insights into what others have said about these topics before using this information to explore the relationship further. To get started on such a task, I first outline some of the key issues and define some of the key concepts. Even this task is fraught with problems as popular music, politics, authenticity, relations between all of these, and how to understand these are all contested theoretical terrains.

What is music? Popular music?

The idea of music is difficult to explain. It is not a universal category agreed upon across time and place (Cook and Everist 1999). In some cultures, there is no hard-and-fast distinction between music, dance, and ritual; some cultures do not even have separate words for these activities (Frith 1996). Even within a given culture the category of what is music continually changes over time and between individuals. Just think how difficult it would be to get a consensus between a range of people even within your own community on offerings by Eminem, The Nihilist Spasm Band, or Behemoth in regard to what aspects of these are music, speech, or just plain noise. This blurring of definitions between speech, sound, music, and noise is noted by a number of scholars (Attali 1977; van Leeuwen 1999). Despite these cultural, historical, and taste-driven differences of opinions, for the most part, people in a given culture will share common ground on how they define music. Cook (1990: 223) observes that a music culture, or a shared opinion on what is music, "is a tradition of imagining sound as music. Its basic identity lies in its mechanism for constituting sounds as intentional objects, from the level of a single note to that of a complete work."

When we then try to define popular music (hereafter pop), again we find a variety of opinions. David Hesmondhalgh and Keith Negus (2002: 3) point out that "In studying popular music, we are dealing with an unstable, contested and changing category." Some, such as Theodore Adorno (1941), make distinctions between popular music and "serious" music, while some more contemporary scholars and fans make distinctions based on genre in the form of "pop" versus "rock." Even the word "popular" carries baggage with it. According to Raymond Williams (1988: 236), the predominant modern meaning of popular is "widely favoured" or "well-liked." But it can also carry with it negative connotations of "a strong element of setting out to gain favour, with a sense of calculation." Popular culture still carries meanings of not only "well-liked," but also "inferior types of work … and work deliberately setting out to win favour" (Williams 1988: 237). These negative connotations are used regularly in day-to-day conversations about pop.

With all this uncertainty in definitions, Graham Burton (2005: 147–148) offers six types of popular music definitions, including their shortcomings. Popular music is "the sum of its genres which attract large audiences and sales." This definition's weakness lies in deciding which genres are to be included and which excluded. Popular music is "chart music," though here we find that charts do not reflect consistent sales, but are based on the sales of singles and downloads, excluding other points of contact between musicians and fans. Popular music is the "experience of the everyday" on the radio, in shops, and other commercial venues. This definition, again, excludes a variety of music not in the mainstream which is not so easily available. Some define popular music as "the music of the young." However, sales of music to youth is a declining proportion of the total sales of musical commodities. Popular music is the "stuff of commercial mass production." This definition ignores the active role fans play in determining what is popular and leads to discussions about how many sales and how big an audience determines whether something is commercial. Finally, popular music is "of the people," as opposed to commercial interests. Here we run into trouble with who are "the people," a label notorious for its shifting definitions, used by different groups in society for a variety of purposes.

Each of these definitions offers some insight into how we may define popular music, though each has its own inadequacies as outlined above. For this reason, I keep my definition simple and lean on Raymond Williams's definition of what is popular. For this book, I use the term "popular music" loosely, defining "popular music" as any genre of music which is "well-liked." By "well-liked," I mean music which is accessible to an audience, whether that be 100 enthusiastic punk fans at a live gig in a pub, thousands at a concert, downloads—legal and otherwise, pirate copy CDs sold on the street or bought on the high road, or music listened to on the internet. By keeping my definition as loose as I have, I avoid the traps inherent in the above definitions of what is popular music and cast my web wide enough to include any genre of music enjoyed by fans.

Throughout the book I also refer to "music commodities." Here I mean musical productions and products associated with popular music such as posters, video clips, CDs, downloadable songs, and concerts. By naming these as such, I avoid the trap of labelling music a "thing," something musicologists are rightfully quick to criticize (see Chapter 3 for a fuller discussion). Instead, I focus my work on the roles of popular music in politics and, importantly, how this is done.

What is politics?

A scan through a number of dictionaries defines politics in terms of government actions, such as the *Cambridge Online Dictionary*'s "the activities of the government, members of law-making organizations, or people who try to influence the way a country is governed." But dictionaries also include definitions about power, control, and status, within groups or organizations. In both senses of the term then, politics is about power. However, Street (1988: 7) notes that "Politics is not just about power. Nor is popular music. They are both about how we should act and think." That is, politics in pop is about governments, activists, and musicians, but also about the pleasures and values pop communicates which affect the way we act and think. Street (1988: 3) notes politics in pop "affects or reinforces ... the politics of the everyday... being concerned with issues of power, equality and personal identity." These core elements are considered in scholarly work which examine pop and "the politics of pleasure," "gender politics," "protest politics," "populist politics," and "the politics of representation," to name just a few. In this book, I consider politics in both senses of the word. That is, I examine politics in pop which includes not only governmental politics, policies, and discourses but also politics in the wider sense including identity politics, power, and equality.

What are relations between politics, authenticity, and pop?

This is discussed in depth in Chapter 3. Here, it is worth noting that there is no real consensus among scholars as to what exactly are relations between politics, authenticity, and pop (Hesmondhalgh and Negus 2002: 7). Views range from the highly optimistic in terms of music's ability to represent and promote sociopolitical interests or particular cultural values (Lorraine 2006; Korczynski 2014) to views which are far more limited (Grossberg 1992). Sociologists have demonstrated how production, promotion, social, and consumption contexts constrain and influence potential meanings in pop (Frith 1988; Street 1988). Many researchers from various disciplines also note that much of pop's political power lies with listeners, meanings being ambiguous and open to individual interpretation (Hebdige 1979; Grossberg 1987; Street 1988; Huq 2002). Intertwined and inseparable from discussions on pop and politics is the issue of authenticity, this book adhering to the view that authenticity is the quality of "sincerity" or "playing from the heart" that listeners ascribe to performers (Moore 2002: 210). These issues are discussed in depth in Chapter 3 and then throughout this book in my analysis chapters which are concerned with how both politics and authenticity are articulated in pop.

How to study popular music and meanings?

Popular music and meanings can be examined in a number of ways, through the prism of popular music studies, musicology, sociolinguistics, ethnomusicology, and sociology, to name some of which inform this book and are discussed at length in Chapter 2. Most approaches tend to ask *what* is the extent to which popular music can articulate ideas about society, identities, and events. This book considers these issues by focusing on *how* this is achieved using an innovative set of methods from multimodal critical discourse studies (MCDS). MCDS can provide answers to these due to its attention to the details of how communication takes place, its interest in discourse, and how ideologies are naturalized and legitimized.

MCDS finds its roots in critical discourse analysis (CDA) which examines linguistic choices to uncover broader discourses articulated in texts. By discourses, I mean "complex bundle[s] of simultaneous and sequential interrelated linguistic acts," which are thematically interrelated (Wodak 2001: 66). These discourses can be thought of as models of the world and project certain social values and ideas which contribute to the (re)production of social life. Some scholars in CDA have pointed to the need to look more at how ideologies are communicated not only in political speeches and news reports, but also through entertainment like computer games and film (van Leeuwen 1999; Machin and Richardson 2012). These same scholars have also drawn on certain tools, approaches, and assumptions in multimodality to show how discourses and ideologies, as in language, can be revealed by closer analysis of images, designs, and other semiotic resources such as visual features, material objects, and architecture. The approach in this book is part of this multimodal trajectory, though also informed by various fields of musical study. This book views musical commodities as a means of communication used to articulate ideology. It is through the modes of lyrics, visuals, and musical sounds, I argue, that musical commodities communicate "multimodally."

The idea that musical sounds play a key role in meaning making is shared by a number of scholars across disciplines (Frith 1996; Cook 1998; Machin 2010). Music produces broad "unnuanced" emotions in us, as well as signaling more nuanced memories and emotions attached to individual people and relationships in our lives (Cook 1998). Therefore, music often brings with it particular affordances that are either difficult to express in more propositional linguistic texts or images, or, in some cases, impossible to express in other modes. In reference to music's roles in advertisements, Cook (1994: 38) notes "Music transfers its own attributes to the story line and to the product, it creates coherence, making connections that are not there in the words or pictures; it even engenders meanings of its own." Musical sounds matter. For example, imagine how Justin Bieber's "Sorry" would sound if the synthesized instrumentation, Bieber's smooth whispery voice, and upbeat dance tempo were changed into a soundscape of screaming guitars, triple speed tempo, and an angry growling voice like you can hear in Discharge's "State Control." Perhaps the illusion of a sincere apology Bieber tries to communicate would be more closely aligned to ridicule.

There have been various attempts to understand music's meaning-making potential in musicology (see for example Tagg 1979; Middleton 1990; Feld and Fox 1994; Leppert 1995). However, I believe a good place to start looking at music as a mode of communication is Theo van Leeuwen's (1999) investigation into meaning potentials of sound due to its emphasis on a detailed and systematic analysis. McKerrell and Way (2017) advance van Leeuwen's (1999) ideas and argue that musical sounds are a communicative mode, and that its semantic ambiguity and sonic presence lend it a particularly powerful affective role in communication. It is highly adaptable in multimodal texts, meanings communicated through the interplay with other modes and external contexts. These observations point to the importance of context in shaping the meaning potentials of musical sounds, an idea echoed in other work (see Goodwin 1993; Shuker 2001; Railton and Watson 2011). These observations also point to the importance of musical sounds in articulating discourses, even if they are less descriptive than written language.

Until very recently, there has been very little attention paid to the social semiotics of sound within multimodality. Much of the literature considers fairly static texts such as posters, paintings, or road signs. This is one reason why music has not been fully theorized in multimodality and is largely absent from many analyses. Musical experience has inspired a wide range of theories of how it makes meaning in people's lives. There has been an increase in interest in popular music in MCDS stemming from the work of van Leeuwen (1999) and David Machin (2010). This book places these kinds of observations within the context of Turkey, looking at how authorities seek to harness and control popular music and how music emerges as a site of resistance in certain venues and particularly across social media. The book aims to extend the work of van Leeuwen (1999) and Machin (2010) on how music communicates ideas, values, identities, and political stances, offering new conceptual ideas inspired by a variety of music oriented disciplines and real examples of popular music interacting with politics.

Turkey

This book's focus is on how popular music multimodally articulates meanings of politics and authenticity. I use Turkish popular music from 2002 until the present to illustrate how this is done. I chose this time and place because Turkey has seen massive political and social upheaval during this time, resulting in a very polarized political and social environment, as I discuss in detail in Chapter 4. The time period for my study coincides with Turkey's Justice and Development Party's (AKP) first electoral victory to parliament and its continuing grasp on power. With this upheaval, polarization, and shifting power situations has come opposition, some in the form of music.

AKP has won five consecutive federal elections since 2002. It has pursued a socially and religiously conservative agenda, symbolically and legally changing Turkey's secular laws and distancing itself from Western cultural practices. Under the stewardship of President Recep Tayyip Erdoğan and AKP, oppositional media have been closed, taken over by AKP-friendly owners, or their criticisms severely muted. These changes have resulted in Turkish media being deemed by Freedom House as "not free" ('Freedom of the press' 2016). Turkish pop has felt the effects of AKP's time in government. Music deemed to be subversive by the government faces obstacles not experienced by other music and musicians. There are dozens of examples of censorship, arrests, and exiles resulting from pop's politics. Live performances are canceled, distribution and sales of unwanted material are blocked, social media are tactically suspended, and musical videos removed while musicians are arrested or publicly harassed. It is in this context that music in Turkey since 2002 is examined.

What I look at in this book

The following is a chapter-by-chapter summary of the contents of the rest of the book. In Chapter 2, I introduce some of the core principles that underpin CDA, and especially its more recent "multimodal turn" in the form of MCDS. The chapter begins by introducing the concepts of discourse and ideology and shows how these are highly fruitful concepts for theorizing music as a form of communication. I then offer an overview of CDA and emphasize how power relations are reproduced through communicative practices. The chapter introduces the concept of recontextualizations which are important for highlighting the way that the representation of people, actions, ideas, and events are related to power. I then examine how MCDS has extended the analytical terrain of CDA into the analysis of music, noting the important contributions of van Leeuwen (1999) and Machin (2010).

Chapter 3 begins with a review of literature on the relations between popular music and meanings, with a focus on political meanings. This traces the study of popular music roughly in a chronological manner starting with Mathew Arnold and F. R. Leavis, Theodore Adorno, and then Raymond Williams. I then turn to more recent contributions to the study of popular music and politics by Simon Frith, John Street, Roy Shuker, and a host of other scholars from sociology, musicology, and popular music studies. These discussions focus on both the limits and potentials of popular music and politics. When studying these relations, researchers inevitably include examinations of how bands represent themselves and others. This includes the idea of representing themselves as authentic, that is, singing about politics sincerely. This area of study is explored according to the aforementioned authors and Alan Moore's (2002) and Philip Auslander's (1999) influential contributions to the subject.

In Chapter 4, I examine Turkish politics since 2002, when Turkey's political establishment changed dramatically with the election of AKP which is still governing the country and looks set to continue doing so for some time to come. AKP's socially and religiously conservative, Islamic, and economic neoliberal outlook along with the divisive character of Erdoğan has emphasized already existing ideological divisions throughout Turkey. The focus of the chapter is on both how AKP has wrestled control over most mainstream media channels and the implications for political expressions in Turkish music. These examinations illustrate how it is difficult to find discourses which are critical of the government in mainstream media and music. However, the chapter finishes with a discussion on how some popular music which is politically subversive has found outlets for expression which bypass the mainstream media, such as the internet.

But it is not just music of subversion which has harnessed the power of the internet. Chapter 5 investigates how political parties use the internet, mainstream media, and popular music to promote their policies and dominant discourses. Here I analyze musical election campaign advertisements available on the internet from the 2011 federal election campaign used by both the governing AKP and the main opposition party the Republican People's Party (Cumhuriyet Halk Partisi—CHP). First, I historically compare the two parties in the run-up to the 2011 election in order to highlight similarities and differences between the two parties. Then I analyze each video, detailing how choices in images, lyrics, and musical sounds reflect dominant discourses articulated by each party. These contribute to power relations in line with their distinct policies, but also division within Turkey. I illustrate how both parties are divisive, each advertisement articulating discourses which benefit those with interests closely associated with each political party and symbolically distancing those who do not agree.

Though most of the book examines musical messages on social media, Chapter 6 examines a live concert (though there is a recording of the concert available online). Live music has always been an important part of popular music in terms of marketing and authenticating musicians. Concerts are used to communicate ideas about musicians and their politics through a wide range of semiotic resources such as gestures, monologues between songs, selection of songs, and even choices of events. This chapter considers a number of concerts I have witnessed, with a focus primarily on a concert by Grup Yorum, a well-known politically radical group. This chapter reveals how discourses of a community of resistance which is knowing and correct are articulated alongside alternative politics. Though on first look, the politics articulated seem to be all-inclusive, a close examination of the concert reveals this is not really the case.

Music videos are a mainstay of popular music consumption in Turkey. The next chapter is dedicated to this form of musical activity. Chapter 7 looks at pop music as governmental policy criticism. Despite Turkish media and its government being intertwined to the extent where subversive discourses are all but silenced, some popular music videos question AKP government policies. These critique AKP's neoliberal economic policies, social and religious conservatism, corruption, and its foreign policies. Though I focus on the role of visuals in these videos, the roles of lyrics and sounds are also considered. We find government policies become articulated through a form of simplified popular politics, despite being presented as serious and authentic by a number of key signifiers. The sample reflects a number of genres and groups with a variety of political outlooks. What they have in common is criticisms toward AKP policies. Though a number of scholars have addressed the issue of subversion in music both as actual political challenge and as popular counterculture, this chapter assesses subversion in music in these terms in order to consider its likely place in political debate in Turkey's mediascape.

Chapter 8 examines music's place in social movements. Music has had a place in social movements from Black Rights to woman's equality to hippies and flower power. More recently the Occupy movement included videos posted on the internet of musicians both amateur and professional singing their support. During Turkey's 2013 Gezi Park protests, literally hundreds of songs and amateur videos appeared on YouTube during the first month of the protests in support of protesters. After the peak of the protests, a number of professional promotional videos visually and musically referenced the protests. This chapter uses some of these songs and videos as a case study to examine the limits and potential of popular music's articulation of the politics of this social movement. Past research has shown pop can articulate subversive politics, though these do not detail what that subversion means and how it is articulated. This chapter uses specific examples to demonstrate how musical sounds, lyrics, and images in online songs and videos articulate politics associated with a social movement. The discussion also considers how these authenticate musicians, protesters, and fans alike.

Chapter 9 examines the roles of social media in political debates. In popular music studies, it has been suggested that popular music songs and videos have been less than successful at communicating more than populist political sentiments. This chapter questions how fans interpret and use the politics of subversion expressed in music videos. Here I consider the comments posted below a sample of some of the videos examined in the previous chapters in the light of scholarly debates about the role of social media in public debate and protest. The chapter examines how fans deal with the actual events and issues represented in the videos.

In the final chapter, I review the key narratives of each chapter in order to offer a closing summation and final argument regarding the roles music commodities offer in the political arena and how this is achieved. I also consider recent events in Turkey, such as the attempted coup of July 15, 2016, and the subsequent state of emergency which led to the 2017 referendum and how these impact on freedom of speech and expression. I conclude on a positive note on how music and politics can work for a better world.

2

Approaches to the Study of Music and Meaning

When I was a teenager, I stood in the kitchen of my friends' house trying to convince him that The Misfits were good because they were being politically radical. He was doing the same for the band Crispy Ambulance. It was a heated debate as debates like these go, despite neither band being the pinnacle of progressive politics. Both of us were finding it difficult to describe why we felt both our bands were indeed saying something radical to us. In my case, I was hard-pressed to explain how The Misfits were radical with lyrics like:

1. I've got something to say,
2. I killed your baby today,
3. And it doesn't matter much to me,
4. As long as it's dead

Both my friend and I knew our respective bands were not "mainstream." The Misfits sang outrageous lyrics, looked scary, and sounded aggressive. I felt they were challenging norms of some sort or another, but neither myself nor my friend had the tools and theoretical knowledge to articulate our gut feelings that indeed our bands were politically radical. It was only later, when I was reading seminal books like *Sound Effects* by Simon Frith, *Subcultures: The Meaning of Style* by Dick Hebdige, and *Rebel Rock* by John Street that I realized pop can indeed be subversive and move people in ways political speeches and well-articulated arguments cannot. In this chapter, I look at such tools and theories which would have allowed me to explain why I felt The Misfits were politically radical. Furthermore, and more relevant to this book, these tools and theories allow me to approach music and meaning from a critical multimodal perspective.

Firstly, I consider and define what I mean by ideology and discourse. These concepts are crucial when unpacking the multitude of meanings loaded on to music, whether these are or are not intended by music producers. I also consider how others have approached the study of relations between music and meaning, especially political meanings. This informs my approach which draws upon multimodal critical discourse studies (MCDS). I consider how critical discourse analysis (CDA) and especially MCDS allow us to more precisely reveal the meanings carried by musical sounds, lyrics, and visuals. This last task includes not only considering what other scholars who use MCDS have uncovered in terms of music and meaning, but also outlines how I use MCDS throughout the book. The tasks I have just outlined are major works in and of themselves. It is not my aim to exhaust these, but outline how I will use these concepts throughout this book.

Ideology and discourse

Ideology is key to understanding issues of language, power, and politics across a large variety of communicative acts such as speech, broadcast news, and entertainment (Kress and Hodge 1979; Fairclough 1989, 2003). Here, I want to show how it is also a useful concept when considering meanings and music. Definitions of ideology are multiple (Williams 1988: 156). What I intend to do here is pick through concepts associated with ideology which are useful for the analysis of music.

Fiske (1989: 165) views ideology as "a way of making sense [of the world], the sense it makes always has a social and political dimension." This definition makes clear that ideology is social and political. Althusser (1971 in Fiske 1989: 174) believes ideologies are inescapable, being "deeply inscribed in the ways of thinking and ways of living." In fact both Althusser and Gramsci share the belief that ideology is all encompassing. However, while Althusser's ideas entrap everyone in ideology, Gramsci liberates society through the idea of "hegemony." Williams (1988: 145), summarizing Gramsci, writes hegemony,

> is not limited to matters of direct political control but seeks to describe a more general predominance which includes, as one of its key features, a particular way of seeing the world and human nature and relationships.

Various power groups in society vie for society's support. Hegemonic struggles are ongoing, winning, and re-winning the consent of the majority in society. In this sense, society is empowered. What's important in both the idea of ideology and hegemony is the central role of language. It is through language that hegemonic struggles for ideology are played out. Gramsci-inspired definitions of ideology emphasize the role of language, such as ideology is "a systematic body of ideas, organized from a particular point of view," that is, representations (Kress and Hodge 1979: 6).

Gramsci's ideas of ideology are found in more contemporary definitions. For example, Fairclough (2003: 9) defines ideology as,

> representations of aspects of the world which can be shown to contribute to establishing, maintaining and changing social relations of power domination and exploitation.

Fairclough's definition is useful for us. Here, ideology is redefined as "representations" of the world, such as those found in music commodities. The definition also encompasses the idea that representations are linked to "power, domination and exploitation." Finally, this definition includes "establishing, maintaining and changing social relations," acknowledging the struggle for various definitions of political issues.

The relationship between linguistic representations and ideology is one which has concerned scholars who use CDA and its precursor, critical linguistics. Gunther Kress and Robert Hodge back in the 1970s investigated the way ideology could be studied through the analysis of language. They found that ideology always "involve[s] language," and language choices (Kress and Hodge 1979: 15). In fact, if you track the importance of language in relation to power and politics in society historically, it is claimed that "the exercise of power, in modern society, is increasingly achieved through ideology, and more particularly through the ideological workings of language" (Fairclough 1989: 2). I argue that ideological workings are evident in not just language, but a whole host of representations, including those in music.

As is the case with the term "ideology," the term "discourse" produces a large number of definitions. These can be grouped into "formalist" definitions, which are associated with formal linguistics and "functionalist" definitions, associated with social semiotics. According to the *Cambridge Advanced Learner's Dictionary and Thesaurus*, discourse is "communication in speech or writing" and "a speech or piece of writing about a particular, usually serious, subject." Though the first of these definitions is most certainly a formalist's definition and the second slightly less so, this book takes a more functionalist perspective. Ruth Wodak's (2001: 66) definition is particularly useful noting that discourse is

> a complex bundle of simultaneous and sequential interrelated linguistic acts, which manifest themselves within and across the social fields of action as thematically interrelated semiotic, oral or written tokens, very often as "texts," that belong to specific semiotic types, that is genres.

This definition makes clear discourses are articulated through groups or "bundles" of communicative acts. These are ways of representing a "thematically interrelated" issue or idea. Multimodality is also suggested in this definition, discourse not restricted to only writing, but also "oral" and "semiotic" communication. Examples of discourses, according to Wodak, include unemployment, racism, and immigration restrictions. Music, I argue, is one such multimodal means of communicating discourses which project social values and beliefs beneficial to some parties at the expense of others. So, I argue that music, which I view as made up of musical sounds, visuals, and lyrics, are used by music producers and interpreted by fans to communicate ideological discourses, discourses which support and challenge political ideologies in Turkey.

How to study music and meaning

My examination of the relations between music and meaning generally, and music and politics more specifically, is informed by a large and diverse body of work on the subject coming from various branches of music studies including forms of musicology, sociology, and popular music studies. These approaches provide a rich array of knowledge. In the next chapter I examine some of the findings and ideas this work has produced. Here, I examine how some of this research has approached the subject. This in turn informs how and why I use MCDS.

Studying "the score"—some musicology before the 1980s

I begin here by considering a more traditional musicological approach which can be characterized as a popular practice in the past (before the 1980s) by some music scholars in the West who examined the scores of Western art music (Hesmondalgh and Negus 2002; Cook 2008). In some cases, analysis was limited to analyzing "the score," that is the written musical notes scribed on to paper with little consideration of context. For our purposes, this approach is useful in acknowledging the importance of analyzing musical sounds. However, it has been criticized for ignoring social and consumption contexts. Shuker (2001: 141), for one, criticizes applying musicology to the study of rock music first and foremost because its focus on the score severely limits the study of music to (literally) lines on a page. If we think back to my teenage experiences listening to the Misfits, this approach would recognize the aggressive music style scribed on to sheet music, but would miss most of the subversive meanings in its performance. This is because this approach ignores social, political and consumption contexts, and "the role of pleasure, the relationship of the body, feelings and emotions, and sexuality in constructing responses to rock music" (ibid.). There is also the problem that many readers are ill-equipped to deal with musicological terminology. Shuker believes analysis should consider context, consumption, and genre instead of a pure decontextualized text, while also studying "narrative structures and representations in popular music, particularly the ideological and contextual aspects of these" (ibid.: 141). To be fair, studying music as a decontextualized text is not characteristic of the many branches of musicology which have developed since the 1960s including new musicology, empirical musicology, critical musicology, and digital musicology, to name but a few (Cook 2008). On the whole, musicology has veered away from studying "the score" alone, recognizing the important roles musical sounds can play within social life (see Berger 1999; Tenzer and Roeder 2011; Tagg 2012; Moore 2013).

Sociology of music/popular music studies

For the most part, research on popular music is not as wholistic as Shuker's approach mentioned above. Since the 1950s, many studies of popular music have mostly concentrated on lyrics (Frith 1988; Shuker 2001). There have been criticisms of such a focus with Frith (1988: 107) arguing a content analysis of lyrics is too simplistic because "The words of all songs are given equal value, their meaning is taken to be transparent, no account is given of their actual performance or their musical setting." So, one ends up with questionable analytical results. For example, using "Spoonful" by Willie Dixon, Shuker (2001) describes how many in the 1960s thought the song was about drugs, something Dixon insisted was not the case. Alongside concentrating on lyrics, there has been a corresponding lack of analysis of musical sounds (Frith 1996). For the most part, music video analysis ignores musical sounds, and when it is examined, it is "usually relegated to the status of sound track" (Goodwin 1993: 4). This is a long way from the musicology described above which examined musical sounds, albeit in notation form. Though I believe a close examination of lyrics is essential for unravelling the meanings in music, I agree with Shuker's (2001: 148) observation that "popular music audiences listen primarily to the beat and the melody—the sound of the record—and make their own sense of the songs; accordingly, meaning cannot be simply read off from the lyrics." If we think back to the Misfits, a close examination of lyrics would reveal that they are outrageous and would rub many up the wrong way. However, meanings only become more subversive if the aggressive musical sounds and visuals are also considered alongside a social and historical context.

Calls for a detailed analysis of musical sounds are generally unheard across a variety of disciplines. The development of "New Musicology" which attempted to "walk away from an analysis of the score," and various types of cultural musicologies in the 1990s and throughout the 2000s, have retreated away from the analysis of musical sounds (McKerrell and Way 2017). In popular studies of music such as Dorian Lynskey's (2010) book on protest music, interviews and lyrics are used to discuss the protest potential of a wide range of pop, with almost no mention at all of musical sounds. The same criticism can be aimed at recent work on music videos, such as Railton and Watson's (2011) book.

There are some exceptions of scholarly work which have attended to music and sound. One such case is Shuker's (2001) analysis of songs and videos. Here, he analyzes lyrics, but also musical qualities and contextualizes his analysis in terms of genre, personal history of performers, their place in the history of popular music, and audience receptions. Andrew Goodwin's (1993) analysis of music videos also considers texts and contexts, performing a close textual analysis of videos' structures, forms, and narrative styles alongside sociocultural contextualizations. Both of these approaches can be characterized as wholistic which helps in the understanding of music's meanings, including those of the Misfits. However, I also believe an understanding of *how* meanings are communicated could be improved with a more systematic and thorough analysis of musical sounds. For example, in Shuker's (2001: 172) analysis of Duran Duran's "Hungry like the wolf" video, there are two sentences on musical sounds, but pages on the history of the band and the visuals. The analysis of The Who's "My Generation," the song, and the band's "mod" connections are explored. Lyrics are described in great detail, followed by a short description of tempo, use of voice (the stutter), and the role of instruments. Shuker's approach provides valuable insights, but the analysis of actual sounds provides a rather small proportion of the discussions as opposed to the material social context and visual style. Furthermore, his analysis shies away from this book's concern with popular music and politics.

Critical musicology

Some studies which use critical musicology include a deep reading of texts alongside contextual considerations. In their seminal book *Popular Music Studies*, David Hesmondhalgh and Keith Negus (2002: 4) characterize critical musicology as examining "the relationships of musical sound and social power." Typical of this approach is Ballantine's (2002) study of gender relations in South African 1950s pop songs. He analyzes songs' lyrics and sounds to argue that songs reflect the breakdown in gender relations under apartheid. Though lyrics are far from enlightening, musical accompaniment works against this "through their use of international and cosmopolitan idioms, and by suggesting alternatives to contemporary life through musical settings characterized by simplicity, gentleness and unity" (Ballantine 2002: 14). Other studies include examining the meaning potential in tempo variations in Brazilian popular music (Tatit 2002), combining a close reading of popular music with historical and social analysis to consider race and access to markets (Brackett 2002) and how feminist ideas have influenced women singing cover songs originally sung by men (Griffiths 2002). These few examples illustrate how some critical musicology indeed examines context and musical texts in some detail to expose relations of music and power.

Critical musicology is also useful for us, as it points to the importance of dimensions of music in meaning making, such as timbre and rhythm (Hesmondalgh and Negus 2002: 5). If we think back to the Misfits, it is many of the non-lyrical elements of their songs which carry meanings. Robert Walser's (1995) examination of Public Enemy's "Fight the power" exemplifies this. Here, he examines rhythm as "an embodiment of past experiences and identities." It is how the voice is used, not simply the words, where he finds "resentment of, and resistance to, years of oppression." Walser (1995: 204) also finds how "the emphatic repetition of the title serves as a rallying cry for collective struggle." Later, focusing this time on the beat, he (ibid.: 208) notes that "rhythm tracks built up of samples of earlier African American music conjure up collective black experience, past and present, while the rapping combines . . . the rhetoric of black preaching and the rhythms of black music." Studies like this emphasize non-lyrical musical elements of music as part of making meanings, even though some lack a systematic approach to this, an advantage seen when employing MCDS.

There are also more recent contributions to the study of music and politics which consider music multimodally. Ian Peddie's *Popular Music and Human Rights* (2011) edited collection offers an insightful survey of music which is engaged in human rights issues from around the globe. Some contributors examine the context, lyrics, and non-lyrical aspects of music which contribute to meaning. For example, Aaron Corn (2011) examines music's role in Australia's indigenous people's struggle for justice. He examines rhythm and chords, styles, and lyrics as ways of communicating meanings. Greene's (2011) examination of Nepal's heavy metal scene and LeVine's (2011) examination of Middle Eastern metal note how politics are expressed through voice style, emotions, and lyrics. These studies again point to the importance of examining musical sounds, though I prefer a more systematic and detailed analysis as to how these contribute to meanings.

Sociolinguistics

Sociolinguistics is useful for our purposes here, as it offers a systematic and detailed analysis of some aspects of music. This approach considers the social and political context of music while analyzing lyrics which articulate discourses of identity and politics. This is exemplified in Androutsopoulos's (2010) analysis of hip-hop songs performed by German-based groups of migrants. A thorough description of the social context of migrant hip hop and the use of language is performed. This is followed by an analysis of not only lyrics which contribute to expressions of identity, but also choices in migrant languages and even sound effects such as crowd sounds. Studies like this point to the importance of considering music as multimodal texts within contexts. In fact, the idea that music is multimodal is acknowledged in a variety of sociolinguistic studies. Visuals such as choices in dress, dance, hairdos, attire, jewelry, and graffiti, linguistic choices such as the use of English, adopted languages or local languages, as well as musical choices in beats, rhymes and sampling all contribute to expressions of identity and opposition (Hassa 2010; Lee 2010; Stylianou 2010). It is an approach like this which can reveal the subversiveness of bands such as the Misfits. It also points to the importance of considering music as multimodal communication, an idea essential to this book.

Cognitive linguistics

Here again is an approach which considers the multimodal nature of music in communicating meanings. In fact, in Lawrence M. Zbikowski's (2015) *Words, Music, and Meaning*, musical sounds are said to have a grammar, or a set of structures, which convey meanings. However, he notes the way music communicates is different than language. Not all thought involves a linguistic form, such as gesture, dance, and music. These modes communicate differently than linguistic communication as Zbikowski observes "in the main, language and music make use of different resources to achieve their expressive and communicative ends, a difference reflected in the structure and nature of their grammars" (ibid.: 147). Cognitive linguistics takes as a premise that language "is to direct the attention of another person to objects or concepts within a shared referential frame" (ibid.). Though music is not particularly good at this type of directing, "it is very good at representing through patterned sounds various dynamic processes that are important within human culture" (ibid.: 148). Chief among these are those associated with emotions and movement. He believes "a cognitive grammar of music offer forms—that is, specific sequences of patterned sound—to realize these [musical] functions" (ibid.: 148–149).

His approach, like many we are examining, notes the importance of social and cultural context in music's meaning-making potential. He states that music is analogical and

> analogical reference is shaped by context: whether we interpret a given dynamic process evoked by a sequence of musical sounds as a series of emotions, a pattern of bodily movement, or transformations performed on physical entities will depend on the context within which the analogy is drawn. In all cases, however, musical meaning begins with sonic analogs for dynamic processes. (Zbikowski 2015: 154)

In his analysis, there is a close description of notes and melody played, use of voice, and lyrics. He also considers how these work together, a type of conceptual blending not too dissimilar to MCDS. In fact, MCDS can benefit from Zbikowski's (2009, 2015) emphasis on musical sounds and context in meaning making. The approach in this book emphasizes these ideas along with a systematic analysis of lyrics, musical sounds, and visuals.

What is clear from the scholarship examined in this chapter thus far is that music is related to identities, the communication of ideas, and also social movements and subcultures. The approaches outlined so far for the most part suggest that the way to uncover these meanings is to consider music as a multimodal communicative act, and not just as written lyrics or notes on a page. I think that MCDS has much to offer here, a way of seeing the different modes as being harnessed together to articulate ideas. It is MCDS, with its roots in CDA, where I believe we can assemble a set of tools and concepts that allow us to both investigate how meanings are communicated and theoretically characterize these meanings.

Critical discourse analysis

The approach I take in this book is indebted to critical discourse analysis, a social science which is applied to the analysis of language in context (Fairclough 2003: 15). CDA examines lexical and grammatical choices made by text producers to reveal obvious and not so obvious discourses in texts while considering their social, historical, production, consumption, and/or political context. Analyzing language is important because language "is a version of the world, offered to, imposed on, exacted by, someone else" (Kress and Hodge 1979: 9). Its role in society is not only to communicate, but also to control (Kress and Hodge 1979: 6; Fairclough 2003: 34). So a close study of language "remains a central element of media [and cultural] analysis," used to reveal what are often hidden ideologies and world views (Fairclough 1995: 16). Through language analysis, we are able to examine "discourse as the instrument of power and control as well as with discourse as the instrument of the social construction of reality" (van Leeuwen 1993: 193). Scholars who use CDA presuppose that composing texts involves making lexical and grammatical choices which have political repercussions (Kress 1985: 3). CDA analyzes these choices to reveal ideologies within texts (Kress 1985; van Leeuwen 1993). In fact, Wodak (2001: 10) claims, "[o]ne of the aims of CDA is to 'de-mystify' discourses by deciphering ideologies."

CDA examines language to reveal broader ideological discourses such as what kinds of social relations of power, inequalities, and interests are perpetuated, generated, or legitimated in texts both explicitly and implicitly (van Dijk 1993; Kress and van Leeuwen 2001). These discourses can be thought of as models of the world, giving a clear sense of "what view of the world is being communicated through semiotic resources" (Abousnnouga and Machin 2010: 139). Like Michel Foucault, CDA practitioners believe these compositional choices have political repercussions (Kress 1985: 3). For example, naming a member of the Palestinian Liberation Organization a "freedom fighter" or a "terrorist" carries with it political significance.

We can think of language as constructed representations of events (van Leeuwen and Wodak 1999: 93). Let's consider a few lines from Green Day's (2016) song "Troubled Times" to illustrate this point. Green Day is credited with being political with songs like "American Idiot" and more recently chanting "No Trump, no KKK, no fascist USA" during its live performance of "Bang bang" at the 2016 American Music Awards. In "Troubled Times," language is used to represent aspects of Trump's 2016 American election campaign negatively. This was a common representation across many mainstream and less mainstream media. Here is the first verse and chorus:

1. What good is love and peace on earth?
2. When it's exclusive?
3. Where's the truth in the written word?
4. If no one reads it
5. A new day dawning
6. Comes without warning
7. So don't blink twice
8. We live in troubled times
9. We live in troubled times

Over the course of the song, Green Day tells us eleven times that "We live in troubled times." Though very little is given in the way of details of what is troubling and how this is happening, the verses give us some ideas. For example, the first two lines of the song ask, "What good is love and peace on earth, when it's exclusive?" In the context of Green Day's anti-Trump stance and visuals which show minority groups protesting and an animated character which resembles Trump yelling, one can assume that this line is referring to Trump's exclusive "love" of America and his attacks on minorities, women, and immigrants. Here, Green Day is using language as a way to represent or "recontextualize" Trump's election campaign announcements.

As we can see with the lyrics above, recontextualizations of social practices include activities, participants, performance indicators, times, places, tools and materials, dress and grooming, and eligibility conditions. All these elements of an activity, such as Trump's election campaign, are transformed into recontextualizations, "and what exactly gets transformed depends on the interests, goals, and values of the context into which the practice is recontextualized" (Van Leeuwen and Wodak 1999: 96). In our case, this is an anti-Trump music video.

There are four types of transformations we need to consider when analyzing a text which are very useful for looking at musical commodities. These are deletions, rearrangements, substitutions, and additions. Van Leeuwen and Wodak (1999: 96–98) note that not everything in a social practice can be fully represented, so some aspects are deleted. Whole aspects of an action or event may be deleted or more specific deletions such as passive agency which omits who performs an action. In the lyrics of "Troubled Times," the joy Trump supporters (both minorities and other Americans) felt during the election campaign is absent, as is who is responsible for our troubled times (passive agency). Rearrangement involves recontextualizing elements within a social practice in an order different from the order in which they actually occurred, so "they may be *rearranged*, scattered through the text in various ways which relate to the interests, goals and values of the context into which the practice is recontextualized" (van Leeuwen and Wodak 1999: 97). In "Troubled Times," the line "We live in troubled times" is arranged throughout the song, emphasizing this sentiment. Social practices are substituted by signs and the mode of representation used offers a range of possible ways of representing the activity. How social actors are named is a type of substitution. Activities are substituted through representations which may involve abstractions and generalizations. Here a loss of detail occurs though legitimation is gained. In "Troubled Times," the pronoun "we" is used repeatedly, a pronoun notorious for being vague yet grouping people in ways suitable to message producers. Here "we" represents those who believe that Trump is bad for America, suiting the aim of Green Day. And finally addition sees texts transform social actions so as to include reactions, purposes, and legitimations. Reactions are representations of the private feelings of participants. The purpose of social practices or parts of social practices can be represented in different ways depending on the recontextualization. These are added to the activities in discourse. Legitimations represent why social practices are as they are. This also is constructed in discourse. In "Troubled Times" the narrator adds negative reactions to the lyrics, as in "I wonder like a troubled mind." Here his private feelings are revealed, an ideological decision by Green Day to add negativity to an already pessimistic recontextualization of political events surrounding the American election campaign.

CDA practitioners believe that social, political, and historical context is essential in analyzing language. This is because CDA perceives discourse as a form of social practice or action, something people do to, or for, each other (van Leeuwen 1993). It is closely interconnected with other elements of social life, so one cannot be studied without the other (Fairclough 2003: 3). Van Leeuwen and Wodak (1999: 92) note this interdependence where "discourse constitutes social practice and is at the same time constituted by it." The importance of considering context can be witnessed in "Troubled Times." Without knowing Green Day's political stance toward Trump, many of the meanings of the song and video would be lost. For these reasons, both context and musical texts are analyzed in this book.

A key characteristic of CDA is its "critical" aspect. It is critical in the sense that scholars who use CDA have political commitments which are opposed to social inequality and the abuse of power (van Dijk 1993). It has been argued that all scholarly discourse and textual analysis are sociopolitically situated, selective, limited, partial, and thereby biased (Fairclough 2003; Richardson 2007). Choosing a critical approach provides "a scientific basis for a critical questioning of social life in moral and political terms, e.g. in terms of social justice and power" (Fairclough 2003: 15). So, research should question and not support unjust aspects of social life. Wodak's (2001: 2) definition of CDA highlights this political commitment:

> CDA may be defined as fundamentally concerned with analyzing opaque as well as transparent structural relationships of dominance, discrimination, power and control as manifested in language. In other words, CDA aims to investigate critically social inequalities as it is expressed, signalled, constituted, legitimized and so on by language use (or in discourse).

This concern with relations between language and power is echoed by CDA practitioners (van Leeuwen 1993; Fairclough and Wodak 1997). In fact, van Dijk (1998) highlights how CDA prioritizes a political commitment. He claims scholars start by identifying a social problem with a linguistic aspect, choose the perspective of those who suffer the most, and then critically analyze those in power, those who are responsible, and those who have the means and opportunity to solve such problems (cited in Wodak 2001: 1; Richardson 2007: 1). In this book, I have followed a similar line of thinking. I believe there is a problem in the abuse of power by AKP. This is manifested in most mainstream media, which it controls or it has scared into submission (see Chapter 4 for a full discussion). I believe that democracy and most people in Turkey are suffering due to this situation. I spend most of this book critically analyzing those in power and ways music offers an opportunity to solve such a problem.

Multimodal critical discourse studies

The above outlined key principles of CDA inform the analysis employed in this book. However, we rarely communicate monomodally. Even talking face to face with a friend involves not only spoken language, but facial gestures and hand movements at the very least. And, as mentioned previously, the anti-Trump lyrics of "Troubled Times" become far clearer with the help of visuals in the promotional video.[1] Figure 2.1 is a still taken from the video while the band sings, "We live in troubled times." Here, we can see references to Trump's controversial policies and statements such as a woman holding a sign that says, "No border wall," a person holding another sign which reads, "Against racist hate," and imagery taken from the women's rights movement. Furthermore, in the background of the image is a caricature of Trump with his arms in the air, in a pose which looks like he is orchestrating the troubled times. Here, it is the visuals which clarify the source of troubled times sung in the lyrics.

Due to the multimodal nature of communication, it makes sense that some scholars using CDA consider texts multimodally. As far back as 1996, Kress and van Leeuwen in *Reading Images* (1996) and *Multimodal Discourse* (2001) demonstrated how meanings

Figure 2.1 Troubled times

in texts are generated not just by written language but through other semiotic resources such as visuals, material objects, and architecture. Machin (2013) describes these two works as groundbreaking because they introduced the idea to linguists that non-linguistic modes also create meaning. These books also emphasize that communication historically has been moving from monomodal to multimodal, partly due to technology. Machin (2013: 348) believes their work points "to the possibility of a social semiotic approach to different forms of communication that allowed not only deeper analysis, but as in linguistics, a more systematic level of description. And this is where its strength lies."

MCDS, with its origins in CDA, assumes linguistic and visual choices reveal broader discourses articulated in texts (Kress and van Leeuwen 2001). A mode can be thought of as a socially agreed-upon channel of communication, rather than a channel of human perception (McKerrell and Way 2017). So, I consider the modes of most music commodities to include lyrics, visuals, and musical sounds.

Analyzing texts multimodally can reveal how various semiotic resources, or modes, play a role in articulating ideological discourses (Kress 2010; Machin 2013). This has the advantage of revealing the way each mode works to articulate discourses "on a particular occasion, in a particular text" (Kress and van Leeuwen 2001: 29). Though most work in MCDS has concentrated on visuals, some scholars have analyzed material aspects of war monuments (Abousnnouga and Machin 2010), sound (Roderick 2013), color (Zhang and O'Halloran 2012), and clothing (Bouvier 2017), to name just a few. In practical terms, MCDS gives us a chance to take advantage of CDA's systematic analysis, that is, by "taking the power of description so useful for drawing out buried ideologies in linguistic-based CDS to be applied to other communicative modes" (Machin 2013: 348).

Machin and Mayr (2012) argue that the task of MCDS is to draw out the details of how broader discourses or the "scripts," the "doings" of discourse are communicated and how the different modes play different roles. According to Machin (2013: 353), "What is of foremost importance in MCDS is the way that different kinds of semiotic resources can be used to communicate the scripts of discourses in this process of deletion, addition, substitution, and evaluation, that is recontextualizations." Analyzing music commodities using MCDS allows us to critically consider the communicative roles of each mode, say lyrics, images and musical sounds, in recontextualizing events, issues and politics.

Critical multimodal research is sparse (see multimodal special edition of *Critical Discourse Studies* (2013) for some very good critical examples). It is the aim of this book to analyze music commodities critically. This is done by closely following an approach used by a number of groundbreaking scholars (Kress and van Leeuwen 1996, 2001; van Leeuwen 2005; Machin 2007, 2010; Abousnnouga and Machin 2010). This approach views features in texts as communicating discourses, comprising identities and values. Though textual features are analyzed to uncover their meaning potential, rigid connotative meanings are not assigned to these. Instead, analysis considers the important role of cultural conventions and metaphorical associations which work alongside features of texts to construct meanings. My approach to analyzing music rests on these MCDS foundations.

MCDS's approaches to the study of music and meaning

MCDS considers music commodities as "multimodal ensembles" (Norris 2004), where a combination of modes, such as lyrics, visuals, and musical sounds, each plays a role in communicating discourses. Much of music's power lies in its multimodality, that is, its lyrics, visuals, and musical sounds. The music industry, governments, and artists have always relied on visuals such as posters, films, and album covers to enhance and make specific the meaning potential in musical sounds. The role of MCDS is to examine how this happens.

There has been a very small amount of work using MCDS on songs and music video. These studies demonstrate how music commodities can communicate ideas, attitudes, and identities, through cultural references and through specific meaning potentials (van Leeuwen 1999; Machin 2010). Much of this research leans on groundbreaking work on music and meaning, resulting in an approach developed by van Leeuwen (1999) and Tagg (1982, 1983, 1984) and furthered by Machin (2010). In van Leeuwen's (1999) *Speech, Music, Sound* he identifies six major domains of sound which music producers manipulate to generate meaning potentials. "Perspective" refers to a metaphoric social distance and hierarchy created by the "closeness" of sounds. The domain of "time" is manipulated, adhering (or not) to regularity. How sounds "interact" in terms of sequentiality and simultaneity have meaning potential related to relations of power. Melodic continuity, patterns, pitch movement, range, and level determine "melody's" role in representing the environment, actions, and interactions of people and emotions. The dimensions of "voice quality and timbre" generate meanings associated with rough versus smooth, tense versus lax, breathiness, soft and loud, high and low, and vibrato versus plain. Finally, "modality," which is the act of assigning a degree of truth to a representation, is considered (ibid.: 156). Here, pitch range, duration variation, dynamic range, perspective depth, degrees of fluctuation, degrees of friction, absorption rate, and degree of directionality are examined. As is the case with all social semiotics, these domains do not dictate what listeners hear but identify experiential meaning potential of the sounds listeners experience (ibid.: 94). David Machin's (2010) *Analysing Popular Music* focuses these more general ideas of music and sound and adds some of his own to perform a number of multimodal examinations of a wide range of popular music songs, album covers, videos, and music in film and television.

MCDS has also been used by scholars to examine politics in music. I have applied some of Machin's (2010) ideas and van Leeuwen's (1999) categorization of sounds to a wide range of political popular music videos (Way 2012, 2013, 2015, 2015a, 2016a, 2016b, 2016c, 2017). These studies demonstrate how music commodities work multimodally to articulate not only political discourses, but also discourses of authenticity. Machin and Richardson (2012) analyze two pieces of music associated with two pre-1945 European fascist movements. Through an analysis of melody, arrangements, sound qualities, rhythms, and lyrics, they demonstrate how semiotic resources communicate discourses of a machine-like certainty about a vision for a new society based on discipline, conformity, and the might of the nation including unity, common identity, and purpose. McKerrell (2012) analyzes the role of lyrics, context, performance, reception, and mediatization of a song in the press to demonstrate how cultural performance can construct sectarian difference in the Scottish public imagination. Later, McKerrell (2015) examines the construction of social semiotic space and social distance in sectarian YouTube videos. Some of this work focuses on a specific musician and how their politics are articulated. For example, Power, Dillane, and Devereux (2012) explore how the singer Morrissey has represented the struggles of the proletariat in a detailed textual reading that reveals a counterhegemonic stance on the issue of social class. This is illustrated through a semiotic, musical, and contextual reading of a Morrissey song, examining the harmonic and melodic structure, tempo, and instrumentation and the visuals in the accompanying video, as well as a sociohistorical and political contextualization of the era and the performer himself.

The examination of music using MCDS has become more sophisticated as more work is done in the field, some incorporating more ideas from other music disciplines (see Way and McKerrell's (2017) edited collection). For example, Matthew Ord's (2017) musical knowledge is combined with MCDS when examining musical production values as a mode of communication. He considers the contribution of recording techniques such as echo, reverb, and panning to the construction of countercultural meanings in folk-rock recordings of the 1960s and 1970s. Johnny Wingstedt's (2017) examination of advertising jingles is also heavily influenced by musicology, making for a more sophisticated analysis. Speech alongside a wide range of musical resources such as meter, period, melody, harmony, instrumentation, tempo, rhythm, voice character, genre, and style is considered. Here he demonstrates how they work alongside context to articulate ideas, attitudes, and discourses about social actors and also audiences. Van Leeuwen (2017) also critically analyzes advertising jingles as well as audio logos of a range of IT corporations, ringtones, advertisements, and news themes. Here, he analyzes how sounds and music are used to convey corporate identities and values by considering melody, timbre, instrumentation, and other musical properties and their meaning potentials. He shows how ringtones provide very similar melodic motifs and timbres for personal use, thus connecting corporate and personal identities and values into listeners' everyday sonic experience.

Advances have also been made on the analysis of more overtly political musical commodities. John E. Richardson (2017) examines the ways that music represents and constructs antagonistic political identities. He critically examines fascist music and reveals three ways in which recontextualization occurs in fascist song—through appropriation, interpolation, and ideological realignment—and explores the functions that this, and the performance of song and music more generally, serves to fascist cultural projects. Way (2017) critically examines subversive articulations in a protest song which not only enables musicians to express social concerns in the public domain, but also shapes musicians' narratives of authenticity about themselves, their fans, and others. Political issues in music examined using MCDS also include domestic violence in Spain through a musical government public information campaign, the delegitimization of the working class in musical choices in a Swedish reality show, and musical challenges to colonial and racist discourses in Guatemala's Mayan rap scene (Barrett 2017; Eriksson and Machin 2017; Filardo-Llamas's 2017). This book aims to harness the good work so far in MCDS and advance the study of politics in music even further.

This section has revealed a number of issues about MCDS. First, each of the studies examined here is multimodal in nature, though which modes are analyzed vary from study to study. This section also demonstrates that MCDS is indeed critical, reflecting scholars' political commitments which are opposed to social inequality and the abuse of power. Finally, this section exposes how little work there is on music and meaning from an MCDS approach. This book aims to contribute to this small but growing corpus of literature.

This book's approach to using MCDS

In this book, I analyze musical political campaign advertisements, concerts, songs accompanied by cut-and-paste visuals shared on social media and professional promotional videos from Turkey since 2002. I consider what politics are being articulated and how this is done. To do this, I examine in detail the modes of lyrics, visuals, and musical sounds, harnessing the analytical potential of MCDS. Though most of my work analyzes videos, I use the word "visuals" to mean any visual material associated with music such as posters, digital images cut and pasted into a fan-made collage on social media, moving images on a professionally made promotional music video, and concert visuals which may include imagery projected on screens, body movement, lighting, and colors. I also examine the meaning potential of musical sounds and their interrelationships with lyrics and visuals. In the spirit of CDA/MCDS, I do not analyze all these music commodities in the same way, but I tailor my analysis to each individual project, depending on my research needs. As Wodak and Weiss (2005: 125) claim, scholars who use CDA must ask "[w]hat conceptual tools are relevant for this or that problem and for this and that context?" Due to this flexibility, CDA offers a framework which can be tailored to reveal the ideologies buried in music, depending on which aspect of recontextualizations best reveal the ideological work at play. So, in one analysis I may concentrate on the representation of social actors, while in another, I may examine the representation of actions or the role of metaphors. The bottom line is there is no set "methodology" I use throughout the book. Instead, I metaphorically dip into a CDA/MCDS toolbox and use which tools best reveal discourses. Saying that, what follows is a description of the "tools" I use the most in the book. These are described under the headings of the three modes I examine throughout the book. I illustrate points with examples taken from a video in support of Gezi Park protests called "Dans Et" by Istanbul group Dev, an indie rock duo formed in Istanbul in 2008.[2] The lyrics to the song are below. With the exception of lines one and two, the lyrics are repeated throughout the song.

1. Dawn has been broken, you aren't in your place
2. It became the night time, if I ask where you are
3. Tell me whose hero are you
4. You're someone's nightmare again
5. I wish you come into my dream, too
6. You are even afraid of the dark
7. If I asked you to save me, you'd flee

8. You only, You only . . .
9. Dance, while your hands in your pocket
10. Dance, your head is not in the right place
11. Dance, I wish you take me too

Lyrics

I examine how participants or "social actors" are named and their actions represented, following the influential work of Fairclough (2003) and van Leeuwen (1996). It has been shown how analyzing social actors is central to revealing discourses (Wodak, de Cillia, Reisigl and Liebhart 1999; Bishop and Jaworski 2003). Who is included and who is excluded in representations is ideological and considered in my analysis. Lexical choices used to represent social actors are also examined, including pronouns, as individuals or groups, personally or impersonally and the use of titles. These choices are ideological. For example, pronoun choices, which are common in lyrics, promote "us" and "them" divisions by representing and constructing groups and communities (van Leeuwen 1996; Fairclough 2003). In Dev's lyrics, no social actors are specifically named. It is through the multimodal video text that we are able to identify the "you" and "your" as police and "I" and "me" as a protesting narrator. This use of pronouns sets up two groups which suit the aims of Dev to represent sympathy toward protesters and opposition to the authorities. Participants can also be named as groups which may be homogenized, ignoring differences while naming actors as an individual grants readers a "point of identification." Impersonal representations of social actors dehumanize them, while personal representations emphasize their human qualities. And the use of titles such as "President Erdoğan" connotes a degree of formality, power, and status while informal namings such as "Tayyip" do not.

At another level, recontextualizations of social action are examined following van Leeuwen (1995). How social actions are recontextualized "encode different interpretations of, and different attitudes to, the social actions represented," a significant factor in articulating discourses (van Leeuwen 1995: 81). There are a number of ways actions are recontextualized. For example, material and transactive activations (somebody doing something to somebody) connote great power (ibid.: 90). In Dev's lyrics, police are never activated in this way. Instead, we find police "are not in your place," "are even afraid of the darkness," and "flee." These omit positive representations of power and all suggest wrongdoing and cowardliness. In fact, actions such as the police "are not in your place," lack detail and context, making the representation quite abstract. However, it represents the police negatively, legitimizing Dev's anti-authority and pro-protester stance. Throughout this book's analysis, these concepts and how they are used to legitimize will be explored.

I examine the role played by metaphors. Popular music tends to rely on metaphor, possibly more so than other communicative modes (Way 2015). Though aesthetically pleasing, metaphor is also a powerful representative strategy, "a functional mechanism which affects the way we think, act and experience reality" (Lakoff and Johnson 1980 in Flowerdew and Leong 2007: 275). In Dev's lyrics, police are represented as "Dance, hands in your pockets." Here, police obeying government orders and not supporting protests are recontextualized in a commonly used metaphor of "keeping your hands in your pocket." This simplifies what must have been a very difficult situation for many officers who had to weigh up following orders which they may not have agreed with or losing their jobs.

Representations of place and people in places are also revealing. These are powerful, affecting our understanding of places, reinforcing myths, and providing listeners with a sense of identity (Forman 2002). Representations can be in the form of band names such as Ladysmith Black Mambazo and Cypress Hill, but also in lyrics and visuals. Of course, this is genre related, as we will see in later chapters. For example, Kanye West singing about country streams and flowing prairie grass sounds as strange to us as Garth Brooks singing about life in New York slums. In song, analysis of settings are "highly revealing about the world being communicated" (Machin 2010: 92), and "can be used to understand broader social relations and trends, including identity, ethnicity, attachment to place, cultural economies, social activism, and politics" (Johansson and Bell 2009: 2). But these representations also suggest authenticity. Urban dwelling is an important part of authenticating bands within rock genres (Connell and Gibson 2003: 37) and movement is associated with "freedom and adventure." On the contrary, rural settings are part of authenticating folk and country, with rural spaces echoing mobility (Connell and Gibson 2003: 82). Dev's lyrics do not point to urban nor rural settings. Instead, settings of "night," "dawn," "nightmare," "dream," and the "dark" are represented in the lyrics. Nightmarish, dark, and mysterious settings are common in heavy metal, including "Enter sandman" by Metallica, a band known to span the gap between heavy metal and indie music. Representing such settings, like Metallica, serves to authenticate Dev as metal-influenced indie rockers. They also suggest a discourse opposed to the police. Darkness has the universal meaning potential of evil, a lack of clarity, and untruths. With negative representations of police alongside settings of darkness and night, negativity surrounds the police. Though these representations of settings lack detail, they serve to authenticate Dev and legitimize a negative stance toward the police.

Obviously, each analysis in this book is unique and does not examine every aspect of the lyrics. Instead, I examine representations in lyrics which reveal dominant discourses in each musical commodity. Most of the lyrics analyzed in this book are in Turkish. These have been translated into English. Though best avoided, translations are commonly used in CDA (e.g., van Leeuwen and Wodak 1999; Wodak and Weiss 2005; Flowerdew and Leong 2007). To overcome any bias, I had all lyrics and comments translated by three individual translators. I then examined the translations. If any discrepancies were found, I first went back to the original text and did an additional translation. I then consulted with the original translators. If we could not agree on a phrase or a sentence (which was very rare), it was not used in the analysis.

Visuals

Whether in the form of posters, CD sleeves, clothes and dance at a concert, cut-and-paste fan made videos shared on social media, or professionally produced promotional

Figure 2.2 Dancing protester's demand image

music videos, imagery is an integral part of popular music. In my analysis, all these are considered under the heading of visuals. In the visuals, as with the lyrics, I also examine the representation of social actors, social actions, places, and people in places. For the most part, the visual analysis mirrors the lyrical analysis. This is not new, with scholars applying, for example, social actor analysis to visuals (Kress and van Leeuwen 1996, 2001; van Leeuwen 2005; Machin 2007). Visual analysis follows the work of Kress and van Leeuwen (1996, 2001) and Machin (2007). These scholars define three broad categories of visual representations of social actors; positioning, kinds of participants, and actions. How viewers are positioned in relation to participants inside images through gaze, angle of interaction, and distance is considered. One important distinction made here is between "demand" and "offer" images. In demand images participants directly address viewers, creating symbolic interaction, suggesting power and demanding a response (Kress and van Leeuwen 1996: 127–128). This can be seen in Figure 2.2 which is an image of a dancing protester taken from Dev's video. Here, the woman is empowered, symbolically addressing the viewer. Alternatively, participants in "offer" images do not gaze at viewers, omitting contact and the power to address. These images are offered as information available for scrutiny (ibid.: 124). This can be seen in Figure 2.3. Here, both a protester and a police officer do not gaze at the viewer. There is no symbolic interaction between viewer and the characters in the video, especially the police officer, his head being covered with a helmet.

The "kinds" of participants are examined considering three criteria. Participants may be represented individually, drawing viewers metaphorically close thereby humanizing them as opposed to group shots which may create homogenous "types" or anonymous groups (Machin 2007: 118–119). If we contrast Figure 2.2 with Figure 2.4, it is clear we are metaphorically much closer to the protester than the police, creating more empathy and sympathy toward her. Participants can also be categorized culturally and socially, these being either positive or negative depending on context. In the case

Figure 2.3 Police and dancer's offer image

of our images, the close metaphoric interaction with protesters categorized by clothing and accessories is a far more positive representation than police who dress the same, move the same, and whose faces are hidden by full faced masks. Whether participants are included or excluded visually is also considered. Finally I examine in detail how actions and agency are visually represented, analysis closely following lyrical analysis (see the section titled "Lyrics" for details). In the case of Figure 2.3, we see a protester blowing smoke into the face of a police officer, a metaphor for "giving the police exactly what they gave the protesters." This action with agency (someone doing something to somebody) is a very empowering image. In contrast, Figure 2.4 sees the police dressed the same and moving robotically together, as though unthinkingly obeying orders. In

Figure 2.4 Police as unthinking robots

both cases, these images articulate ideological discourses which are positive toward protesters and negative toward authorities.

I also consider a variety of composition choices such as those which connote relations between elements of images following the work of Kress and van Leeuwen (1996) and Machin (2007). Compositional choices concerning salience are considered, expressed through visual devises such as potent cultural symbols, size, color, tone, focus, and foregrounding. Image organization is also examined, including the positioning of elements and framing which contributes to an image's internal "flow" (Kress and van Leeuwen 1996). In Dev's video, there are compositional choices which suggest commonality between the band and protesters and difference between these groups and the police. The band, protesters, and police share the same location, a gray smoky background creating a type of "integration" connoting closeness between the groups (van Leeuwen 2005: 112). However, the protesters and the band also share a similar indie rock dress code of T-shirts and jeans, aligning the band with protesters, while the police share none of these. Again, these choices reveal discourses articulated in the visuals.

Music

My approach to analyzing musical sounds closely follows the work of Theo van Leeuwen's (1999) *Speech, Music, Sound* where he identifies six major domains of sound which contribute to music's meaning potential (see the section titled "Visuals" for full details). This seminal work has the distinct advantage of offering the framework for an in-depth and systematic analysis of sounds. Though many of the approaches examined in this chapter refer to musical sounds and visuals, van Leeuwen's approach offers unparalleled detail and systematic analysis. This approach also emphasizes the crucial role of context in defining the meaning potential of sounds. Though this emphasis is shared by a number of approaches outlined above, it is lacking from other approaches, such as some traditional musicology.

To illustrate the importance of context in analyzing music sounds, I refer again to Dev's "Dans Et." One key discourse during the time of the Gezi Park protests seen in most foreign and Turkish alternative media was the police were unthinkingly obeying orders from the government. We have noted how this is articulated in the visuals and lyrics above. In the context of these, musical sounds also play a key role in articulating this discourse. Police obedience is connoted through instrumentation and timing. In the first verse, the guitars and vocals are dominant. But at the beginning of the second verse, drum sounds rise in the hierarchy of sound. The drums are sparse with minimal reverb, sounding like the drums used in a military march. Furthermore, they are very regular in timing. Van Leeuwen (1999: 58–63) notes how this can have the meaning potential of rigidity, "to stand at attention," and align itself with regularity like the time of the clock. In the context of police dancing like robots in unison, the discourse of police unthinkingly obeying the commands of the elite is articulated.

Van Leeuwen's work is informed by a range of highly respected music scholars such as Philip Tagg and Nicholas Cook. His work on music and sound has been the bedrock of almost all examinations of music and meaning from an MCDS approach. This work, such as that by Machin (2010), is also considered along with much of the good practice and knowledge accumulated by previous work examined above from other music disciplines. As such, my method gives me a "hindsight" advantage of employing what works best to reveal discourses articulated in music commodities.

Putting it all together

As I have been stating throughout this chapter, music is a multimodal medium. Above, I have described how I analyze each mode and the importance of considering political, social, and historical contexts in order to ascertain the meaning potential in music commodities. My approach to analyzing music commodities considers all these aspects of music and context. Modes in each musical commodity take on unique roles. Sometimes, all three modes articulate the same discourses. Sometimes, modes articulate similar, but not identical, discourses. Many times, musical sounds need the more focused meaning potentials of images and lyrics to be understood in their context. In all cases, it is the multimodal package of meaning which needs to be considered in order to define meanings.

Though a multimodal package, a systematic, detailed analysis of each mode is essential to reveal how discourses are being articulated. So how do I marry up a systematic analysis of individual modes with the idea of music being multimodal with meanings dependent on context? My answer is it depends on the artifact being analyzed. In all circumstances, I examine political, social, and historical contexts. Without these, meaning potentials are too wide. At times, my analysis is divided into headings of the discourses articulated in the musical commodity being analyzed. This is particularly useful when all three modes articulate the same or very similar discourses. As such, a sense of how each mode works with the other modes to articulate discourses is prioritized. At other times, I examine each mode one at a time and examine how each mode articulates a specific set of discourses. This approach of prioritizing modes I find useful when each articulates different discourses. To ensure a sense of how the artifact works multimodally, I refer to the other modes when indeed they work with the mode being examined. Following in the spirit of CDA/MCDS, I am flexible in my approach, asking, "[w]hat conceptual tools are relevant for this or that problem and for this and that context?" (Wodak and Weiss 2005: 125).

As mentioned above, my approach to analyzing musical commodities is not only based on just good practice in terms of methods, but also informed by findings from a multitude of work done on music and meanings done before me. These findings inform my discussions on what these relations are and how this is done. It is here we turn to next.

3

Difficult Relations: Music, Politics, and Authenticity

Political ideas in an array of genres of music are not new. Europe of the 1920s saw music along with art and architecture "used as central parts of communicating fascist ideology" (Machin and Richardson 2012: 331). Popular music's relations with politics are as old as the industry itself, from Billie Holiday's "Strange Fruit" (1939) to Kate Tempest's "Europe is Lost" (2016). Careers such as Bob Dylan's and The Red Skins are seen by many as based on politics and music. Whole books, such as Lynskey's *33 Revolutions per Minute*, are devoted to protest songs which are described as "a song which addresses a political issue in a way which aligns itself with the underdog" (ibid.: ii). Popular music which is seen as political not only enables musicians to express social concerns in the public domain, but also shapes musicians' discourses about themselves and their fans.

This chapter considers what studies of music and meaning have been able to make of relations between popular music, politics, and authenticity. Though this is by no means exhaustive, it allows me to look at the main findings, positions, and thoughts on the subjects in order to theoretically ground my study. The chapter explores music's relations first with politics and then with authenticity. I trace the study of popular music and meaning, with a focus on politics, roughly in a chronological manner. I start with a very brief introduction to Mathew Arnold and F. R. Leavis who are credited with being some of the first scholars to consider popular culture and popular music as an academic area of study. Their influences can be seen in much popular sentiments about popular culture even today. I then consider influential thinkers on popular music and politics including Theodore Adorno and the Frankfurt School and then Raymond Williams. Again, these scholars' influences can be seen in both popular thought and academia. I then go into greater detail outlining more recent contributions to the subject from sociologists, popular music studies, and sociolinguistics. This survey of scholarship helps define the limits and potential of popular music in relation to politics.

Songs not only enable musicians to express social concerns in the public domain, but also shape musicians' personal narratives of authenticity about themselves, their fans, and others. As discussed in greater detail later in this chapter, and as I will demonstrate in the analysis of chapters which follow, discourses of authenticity are socially, historically, and genre dependent, intimately linked, and inseparable from music commodities. Just think of how Dev's video discussed in the previous chapter articulated discourses which were against police actions. These discourses also serve to authenticate the band as being anti-establishment, a key component to being a rock and/or indie rock performer (Hibbett 2005). In cases like Dev's, authenticity is more clearly articulated than any obvious political stance, a theme examined throughout this book. Authenticity is considered leaning on the disciplines mentioned above, as well as Philip Auslander's (1999) and Alan Moore's (2002) influential contributions to the subject. The aim of this chapter is to make clear *what* relations are between music, politics, and authenticity. This knowledge is then used to inform my analysis chapters which explore further what those relations are and *how* politics and authenticity are articulated in musical commodities.

Beginnings: Popular music's role in society

The "Culture and Civilization" tradition of examining popular culture may be a good starting point for our discussion on music and politics. Though not concerned specifically with popular music, Mathew Arnold in the late nineteenth century studied relations between culture and society in *Culture and Anarchy* (1960). Here, he set up a dichotomy between "culture" and "popular culture." Culture, he claimed, was "the best that has been thought and said in the world" (ibid.: 6). This includes literature by Shakespeare and music by Beethoven. Popular culture, which is synonymous in his writings with "anarchy," is the "disruptive nature of working-class lived culture" of the 1860s when working-class urban men got the right to vote (in Storey 2001: 14). These concepts are highly political. Culture, he thought, could be used to educate and civilize the working classes while popular culture was something to be discouraged. In the 1930s, F. R. Leavis continued this line of thinking. Here, Leavis and his colleagues saw a cultural decline, a "standardization and levelling down" of culture (Leavis and Thompson 1977: 3). Again, Leavis prefers "high culture" over popular culture. Leavis attacks many forms of popular culture, saying they are addictive. For example, popular fiction is "a form of compensation . . . is the very reverse of recreation, in that it tends, not to strengthen and refresh the addict for living, but to increase his unfitness by habituating him to weak evasions, to the refusal to face reality at all" (ibid.: 100). Here, again, popular culture (including popular music) is seen negatively, as a disruption to mainstream society.

   Popular culture's negative role continues to be represented in some forms of Marxist critique, such as the Frankfurt School. Possibly the most well known and outspoken scholar within this tradition is Theodore Adorno (1941, 1991). For the most part, Adorno's *On Popular Music* (1941) attacks popular music while indicating that "serious" music offers a positive role in society. Adorno (1941) believes that "authentic culture," such as serious classical music and avant-garde music, has a critical function to play in society. These offer an implicit critique of capitalist society and suggest an alternative, utopian vision of society expressed through their "form" rather than commanding through "content." Unfortunately, "serious" music's critical function, in many cases, has been usurped by the cultural industry which has packaged and commodified it. Adorno (1941, 1991) criticizes popular music, which is firmly in the hands of the same cultural industry. Unlike Leavis and Arnold, it is not criticized for causing anarchy, but for serving listeners standardized fare with unique selling points, or pseudo-individualization. This promotes consumption which is always passive, and endlessly repetitive, confirming the world as it is, a kind of "social cement." Like those noted above, Adorno (1941, 1991) believes popular music is political. Unlike those noted above, Adorno believes popular music supports an unfair status quo, rather than threatening it.

Culturalism, which began in the 1950s, emphasizes human agency in popular culture, and popular music, unlike previous ideas of music and politics. Culturalists believe active production of meaning is at the heart of popular culture, not passive consumption. There are a large number of names which fit under this culturalist umbrella, such as Richard Hoggart, E. P. Thompson, Stuart Hall, and Paddy Whannel, but possibly the most well known is Raymond Williams. Like other culturalists, he believes cultural texts reveal the "structure of feeling" or shared values and beliefs of a society. Put another way, through an examination of cultural texts, we are able to uncover dominant discourses of a given society. What cultural products are widely distributed, archived, and held in esteem are selected, where "there will always be a tendency for this process of selection to be related to and even governed by the interests of the class that is dominant" (Williams 1963: 313). Furthermore, though most offerings of popular culture given to the public are aesthetically wanting, Williams and culturalists, in general, believe meaning is generated by how fans use popular culture products. This theoretical positioning emphasizes the importance of social, political, and consumption contexts in the making of meanings. And it is these ideas which are echoed in this book's approach which emphasizes a close textual reading in context.

Though this review barely scrapes the surface of what these earlier scholars have said about popular music and politics, we now consider how some of these ideas are incorporated into more modern ideas of relations between music and political meanings.

Relations between music and political meanings updated

A difference of opinion

There is considerable debate about how to characterize relations between popular music and meanings which have produced no real consensus among scholars (Hesmondhalgh and Negus 2002: 7). Some scholars have been highly optimistic as regards the ability of music to represent and promote sociopolitical interests or particular cultural values (Lorraine 2006; Korczynski 2014). Some scholars seem to "sit on the fence" in regard to pop and politics such as Shuker (2001: 238–239) when he notes:

> the issue of the political role of popular music is hardly an "either-or" argument. For every case of a performer, genre, text, or consumer constrained and regulated by gender expectations, capital, pressure groups, and the State, there are counter-

examples of the successful use of the music to raise political consciousness and finance for political issues, causes, and movements. In terms of cultural politics, popular music is a site of cultural struggle, with constant attempts to establish dominance, exploit cultural contradictions, and negotiate hegemony.

Other scholars, however, have pointed to its limitations (Hesmondhalgh and Keith 2002: 5). The Frankfurt school and their heirs believe "popular music [i]s essentially manipulated by the market and consequently devoid of oppositional cultural possibilities" (in Shuker 2001: 235). In some studies, skepticism of music's role is blamed on academics' optimistic readings of its political potential (Grossberg 1992: 168). This skepticism is based on Grossberg's "commonplace observations" that see many listeners derive pleasure from political songs and bands without either subscribing to their politics or even being aware of them. This sentiment is echoed in Huq (2002), who argues that academics overrate the politics in rave culture in the traditional sense, instead of considering its concern for the politics of pleasure. In any case, optimistic or pessimistic, there is a large body of work which has examined these relations, which we now turn to.

Social and institutional context in meaning making

My study of music, politics, and authenticity is greatly indebted to John Street's seminal *Rebel Rock* (1988) which examines relations between music and politics in great detail. It is many of his observations which contextualize my observations. Music is political, "when they [governments, political activists and musicians] employ it to convey a particular message or elicit a certain response" (ibid.: 2). But it is political in other ways as well. According to Street (1988: 3), music is also political "because it affects the way people behave. It may make little difference to the way they vote, but votes make little difference to the way politicians behave. What it affects or reinforces are the politics of the everyday. Its concerns are with our pleasures and our relationships, and the intuitions that inform both."

Politics in pop are a result of its making, marketing, and distribution. Political discourses in pop cannot be separated from the industry that produces it. Musicians are a part of this industry. Their politics, which they may choose to represent in song, are a result of their experiences as individuals, citizens (victims, supporters, or opponents of governments), and workers (subjected to exploitation and abuse). Street (1988: 128) notes, "in all these roles, they have questions to resolve or ignore, decisions to take or avoid, commitments to make or abandon. The consequence of each contributes to the politics of pop." These decisions and their consequences are magnified in Turkey, where being too outspoken against government actions and policies can result in censorship, being publicly chastised, a jail term, or even exile.

A musical commodity is the result of decisions made not just by musicians, but by record executives, lawyers, accountants, producers, engineers, publicists, sales personnel, radio programmers, disc jockeys, music journalists, and many more before listeners get to hear anything. As Street (1988: 6) observes, "A single is not a piece of pure art; it is the result of countless choices and compromises, using criteria that mix the aesthetic, the political and the economic." Production and promotion by large corporations, along with social and consumption contexts, constrain potential meanings in pop. Though constrained, the music industry does not necessarily control music "unless the stock market is offended" (ibid.: 107), resulting in political discourses being a part of some pop.

Some scholars believe the role of the recording industry may be more powerful than what Street claims. Steve Capple and Reebee Garofalo (1977) have argued in the past that the recording industry plays a large role in determining the politics of pop. Referring to what they perceived as depoliticized 1970s rock music, they claimed "that the control of musical production by a few major labels led to the erosion of oppositional or anti-materialist" music and the co-optation of musicians into an entertainment business which had become "firmly part of the American corporate structure" (in Hesmondhalgh and Negus 2002: 145). However, Garofalo (1986: 83) later reassessed the scale and certainty of this critique by acknowledging that "there is no point-to-point correlation between controlling the marketplace economically and controlling the form, content and meaning of music." This much more nuanced position is echoed in the work of Street (1988) and Frith (1981). Acknowledging that indeed politics in music is far more than just a musician's ideas independent of any social and industrial context is helpful in understanding what politics are articulated and how this is done. This may also go a long way in explaining why political discourses in music are indeed as vague as they are in most circumstances, as I reveal in later chapters.

The institutional context of music making is essential in understanding relations between music and politics. Simon Frith (1981) maps this out in great detail. His sociological study was conducted over thirty-five years ago and details have changed, but many of the ideas still ring true. Frith's (1981) meaning-making process can be divided into three steps: who records, what is recorded, and what reaches the public. Who records is determined by artist and repertoire (A&R) personnel, managers, and bands. The dialectic between these interests aid in constructing the politics in pop. Record companies want bands that will turn a profit, so conservative choices in terms of band sounds and stereotypes are exploited.

What is recorded is determined in the studio by bands, record producers, and engineers. Again, it is in the interests of the industry and also the band to produce something that sells. In the industry, the emphasis is on the single. Frith claims "this emphasis on the single makes clear what's at stake in the studio—a sound that can be fitted into the appropriate radio selling-slots" (Frith 1981: 113). Again, these choices favor conservative sounds, ones which resemble other bands that sell well.

The final step in Frith's meaning-making process is music distribution. Though a large part of music is distributed by digital means unlike during the time of Frith's study, many of the same priorities remain. Distribution is determined by musical gatekeepers such as radio station music directors, disc jockeys in clubs and pubs, concert promoters, and now YouTube recommendations and Spotify. The single from the studio is aimed at radio, music video, and digital playlists. Frith (1981: 117) says, "To sell a record, companies must, in the end, get a sound to the public—to do this they have to go through a disc jockey, the most significant rock 'gatekeeper.'"

What was true back then still holds true today, with radio being an important source for hearing new music. Disc jockeys are paid to please the public, granting them a degree of independence from record companies. However, record company representatives attempt to persuade programmers that their products fit station's format and audience needs. They also limit the choices available to radio stations. Street (1988: 124) notes radio stations stick to well-proven formulae and "records are chosen on the basis of technical quality, non-offensiveness, previous success and so on, all of which serve to maintain the status quo." Though rare, distribution in some countries like Turkey are also influenced by government actions. With mainstream broadcasting mostly in the hands of the government and government-supporting conglomerates, distribution is a major stumbling block for musicians known to oppose the government (see Chapter 4), musicians like most of those represented in this book.

What types of politics work with what types of music?

Most scholars agree that music commodities have the potential to articulate political discourses, though its compatibility with all types of politics is far from universal. When dealing with political issues, most pop songs such as Pussy Riot's "Punk Prayer" and hip hop from around the world rarely deal with other countries' politics, keeping to the local (Terkourafi 2010; Street 2013). Saying that, there are exceptions where music attempts "to address and transform both local and global political discourses" (Hess 2010: 169). Examples of this can be seen in Greek rap act Imiskoumbria which "both critique[s] and celebrate[s] the arbitrariness of contemporary Greek culture, articulating in the process, a systemic critique of global power relations as they manifest themselves at a local level" (ibid.: 170–171). In Turkey, Saian's "Feleğin çemberine 40 kurşun" tackles injustices both in Turkey and globally through lyrics and visuals (Way 2016b). But these are more the exception than the rule. Pop also does not necessarily express conventional politics well (Frith 1988; Street 1988). Instead, music is more compatible with political ideas such as nationalist struggles (some black music), the politics of leisure (youth cults and gay disco), gender, race, class, sexuality, and the environment (Frith 1988: 472; Shuker 2001: 230–231). That is, music is particularly well at representing discourses which are part of "the shaping of social identities" (Shuker 2001: 231).

So, not all politics can be expressed in music. Likewise, "not every style of music or every form of musician" can be associated with politics (Peddie 2011: 53). In short, genre plays a large role in fans' expectations about pop and politics. Street (1988: 6) notes how "rock, soul and folk musicians can talk about politics, and country singers about marriage and children, in ways that are denied to most pop musicians." Rock's politics can include being anti-establishment, something pop bands have more trouble with, though pop stars like Justin Bieber seem to go against this trend. Indie rock may include noncorporate and noncommercial ideals (Hibbett 2005; Machin 2010). Alternatively, American hip-hop politics may include black rights and tackle racism (Fraley 2009: 43). Global hip hop expands Fraley's restricted politics to include "youth protest and resistance around the World" (Williams 2010: 67) which challenges the status quo (Lee 2010: 139).

Music and populist ideas

Though the politics of identity are indeed paramount in much of the analysis which is to come, I want to explore in more depth the nature of the politics in political songs. Scholars have noted that pop which is deemed political tends to be highly populist rather than about specific issues (Street 1988; Way 2016a). The word "populist" needs clarification here. By populist, I mean "representing popular interests and values" (Williams 1988: 238), including a universal "appeal to the people and anti-elitism" (Laclau 2005: 7). Populism "pretends to speak for the underdog ['the people'] whose political identity is constructed by opposing it to an elite" (De Cleen and Carpentier 2010: 180). According to Laclau (2005: 74) and De Cleen and Carpentier (2010), "the people" is not a prefixed natural category, but a signifier that acquires meaning through a diversity of discourses. Its meaning changes and are fought for by different groups (Laclau 2005: 74). For example, De Cleen and Carpentier (2010) identify how "the people" are constructed differently by Belgian extreme right-wing political groups and those opposed to them. This discursive construction is in conjunction with "the formation of an internal antagonistic frontier separating the 'people' from power" (Laclau 2005: 224). If we think back to the Dev music video, it too articulates populist politics multimodally, pitting "us" protesters and sympathizers against the authorities, in this case the police. Though studies which examine political discourses in music suggest lyrics are generally ambiguous and the way they are performed, and marketed, plays a big role in how they are perceived, populism is one discourse common in pop. This is revealed through a close reading of a number of music commodities in the chapters that follow.

The role of fans in politics and music

Despite an array of perspectives on the role of audiences in the meaning-making process of music, almost all recent accounts agree fans do indeed play an important role. Here, we can turn to Street again as a starting point. Political pop brings together the public and the private world of fans. Using his personal experience with Elvis Costello's "Pills and Soap," Street (1988) claims it was a private pleasure for fans to listen, but it was also tied to the world of politics. He links the song with his despondency at Margaret Thatcher's electoral win, claiming the song was successful by "the way private feelings are tapped by the song [and] are linked to the public world which shapes the listener's experiences. Bringing together the public and the private, the individual and the collective, is precisely the way in which pop seems to work" (ibid.: 7). This is possible through "ambiguity in the words and the importance of the much less defined sounds" (ibid.). Comparing socialist-leaning Billy Bragg and The Redskins, he illustrates how it is "uncertainty and ambiguity" in Bragg's performance and lyrics which prove to be more potent (ibid.: 67). The Red Skins lyrics are those of certainty and action with vocals which sound like "they belong to a political meeting" preaching to the converted. But pop's audience is "the politically confused who need to be convinced" (ibid.: 66). Billy Bragg deals in gradualism, not revolution, illusions in performance, "his audience share[ing] in his illusion that there is a drummer and bass," community through imagination, the mixing of uncertainty and ambiguity. Street (1988: 66–67) notes how "Bragg tries to engage his audience, not lecture them . . . His music draws together the personal and the political." From this comparison, Street (1988: 67) concludes that "socialism and rock can be linked, but it is an alliance marked by compromise, by a recognition that the relationship between audience and popular music is importantly different to that between political activism and political change."

Public perceptions and reactions to popular music and their fans also contribute to meanings in music (Shuker 2001). In fact, at times it is precisely these perceptions and reactions which make pop "political." Taking the example of punk in the late 1970s, the hostile reaction "help[ed] to politicize the musicians and their fans" (ibid.: 217). In cases such as these, social concerns become exaggerated, creating a moral panic where "the perceived threat to social harmony was by no means as ominous as many regarded" (ibid.). This case study highlights the important roles fans and others play in relations between music and politics.

The importance of consumption contexts on a social level is echoed by Street (2013). On August 17, 2012, Pussy Riot's well-publicized performance in a Moscow church and its aftermath were both criticized and defended in broadcasting, political, and celebrity circles. Street (ibid.: 48) observes that "Whatever view one takes, the fact that a group of musicians can ignite feelings among presidents, pop stars, diplomats, academics and clerics is worthy of note. Perhaps more significantly, the feelings they provoked were not about matters of moral behaviour (the traditional focus of pop-inspired discussion), but about political rights, the abstract principles that found constitutions." A more recent case of this was Beyoncé's 2016 Superbowl fifty performance of "Formation." Though she used imagery in her "Formation" video which draw upon discourses associated with the Black Lives Matter campaign, it was her performance which caused much debate. This featured backup singers who were dressed in black, with black berets and afros—reminiscent of the dress style of members of the Black Panther Party in the 1960s. They performed black power salutes, arranged themselves into the letter X for Malcolm X, and one performer held up a sign which read "Justice for Mario Wood," the 26-year-old shot twenty times for not dropping a knife for San Francisco police officers. This multimodal performance received mixed reactions. Former New York Mayor Rudy Giuliani said on Fox News that "I think it was outrageous . . . . the halftime show I thought was ridiculous anyway." Alternatively, Black Lives Matter activist Erika Totten said Beyoncé's message accomplished exactly what the movement is supposed to. He said, "Our goal is to disrupt the status quo and bring the message wherever the message may not be heard." Here again is a case which highlights the importance of consumption context in politicizing pop.

There are a host of other views which view consumption as essential for music's making of meaning. In his classic study, Dick Hebdige (1979) demonstrates how music and other cultural artifacts are used by some as part of a self-imposed exile from mainstream culture. The idea of "using" pop to be political can be seen in Lawrence Grossberg's (1987) examination of rock. He argues that pop's politics are not in the music per se, but played out in the activities associated with different tastes of music. Settings and which medium music is experienced also contribute to meanings, as does how music fits into fans' lifestyles (Frith 1988; Zbikowski 2015). This is illustrated by

Zbikowski's (2015) example of Harburg and Arlen's "Over the Rainbow." He argues that "Over the Rainbow" functions one way while performed by a cabaret performer in a nightclub and quite another way when it is performed by an amateur singer at the funeral for a friend. Though he acknowledges there is overlap in meaning between the same songs which are performed pretty much the same way, he believes "there will also be significant differences, many of which reflect the multivariate ways the musical utterances actually function within these social and cultural contexts" (ibid.: 149). A striking example of this I have witnessed was in the Gezi Park protests. Here, protesters would chant in unison "Jump jump who doesn't jump is Tayyip." In the context of the protests, this was a rallying cry to create a communal bond, articulate difference between protesters and Erdoğan, and to uplift spirits among protesters. Later, it was incorporated into Marsis's "Oy Oy Recebaum." Here, it still carries the meaning of protest and difference, but much of its meanings and how it functions have changed significantly (see Chapter 8 for a full discussion).

This chapter up to now has examined a lot of ground on the representation of politics in popular music, exposing some of its limits and potential. This knowledge is essential so as not to overstate or understate the political role music plays in Turkey. I now turn to two specific sites where pop and politics meet, two sites examined in my analysis chapters: pop and political parties and social movements.

Pop and political parties

There are plenty of examples of political parties which use popular music. In fact, political parties from all sides of the spectrum use it. In 1983, the British Conservatives were sung to by Lindsey de Paul, Bruce Springsteen's "Born in the USA" was a part of Ronald Reagan's 1984 campaign, and D:Ream's "Things can only get better" was an integral part of Tony Blair's 1997 campaign. Labour sponsored a tour by Billy Bragg and used his voice in a Party Political Broadcast in an attempt "to capitalize on the youth vote" (NME February 23, 1985). White supremacists organizations like the National Front in the United Kingdom have used Oi music to attract new recruits. More recently, in his successful bid to become president in 2016, Donald Trump used Aerosmith's "Dream On," Neil Young's "Rockin' in the free World," and REM's "It's the end of the World as we know it (And I feel fine)," much to the dislike of the musicians.

The links between popular music and politicians can be traced to 1930s America (Street 1988: 48). It was the Democrats who traditionally have used popular music more than the Republicans because "its traditional constituency among the underprivileged and the exploited inclines the party towards the use of popular music" (ibid.). However, since the Republican Party adopted more populist politics under Reagan in the 1980s, it has also used popular music. Relations started as a way to exploit musicians' political connections and personal interests to appeal to young voters. In the 1970s, US law changed, and rock concerts became a legitimate way to raise money for campaigns. Record companies and powerful radio figures volunteered groups to perform. This arrangement benefits politicians who borrow the power of popular music to bring people together. At the same time, it also benefits record executives who "wanted to purchase influence in the political establishment" (Street 1988: 50).

Unfortunately for musicians and politicians, music and party politics do not always live up to expectations. Street (1988: 50) observes that "What happens is the politics and the music are reduced to their lowest common denominator." When musicians use their concert audience to support a cause, again limits become obvious. Street (ibid.) claims musicians find that "concerts given as part of an anti-nuclear campaign or to help the miners tend to attract people who care more about the music than the cause." The result is a mismatch for both politician and musician. Despite these limitations, popular music can be used to attract the attention of an audience to a cause or a partisan message. This is evident in Turkey, where popular music promotional advertising videos are an integral part of election campaigns. Most recently, this was seen with videos released which support and oppose the 2017 referendum which aimed to increase the powers of President Erdoğan. Whether the politics are progressive or not, relations between political parties and popular music are an uneasy one, with benefits uncertain for both (Frith 1981). Despite these limitations, it seems unlikely political parties, whether in Turkey or elsewhere, will stop using the power of popular music in their campaigns to win votes.

Pop in social movements

A social movement may be defined as "central moments in the reconstitution of culture" (Eyerman and Jamison 1998: 6). Social movements take on many forms such as the civil rights movements in the United States; anti-nuclear demonstrations in the United Kingdom; the Gezi Park protests in Turkey; identity movements about ethnicity, race, sexuality; and the Occupy movement across the world. Many scholars believe that popular music plays a significant role in social movements, though the nature of this is again a topic of debate. Frith and Street (1992) believe pop and social movements are not necessarily compatible with one another due to pop's ephemeral character. Elsewhere, however, Street (1988: 51) demonstrates how social movements depend on popular music to provide a "sense of solidarity and community which movements need." In fact, Street (ibid.) asserts that popular music provides a whole list of advantages which social movements utilize:

> It [popular music] is easily transmitted, everyone can remember a tune . . . . It is also much harder for the authorities to control music than it is for them to control the written or spoken word: in a song, the meaning is opaque; and in mass singing, the crowd gains strength in harmony. Furthermore, pop musicians share with political movements the preference for a politics organised around a cause rather than an ideology or an electoral campaign.

These advantages of pop form the basis for relations between popular music and social movements, relations which are of mutual benefit to both activist and musician. For a closer look at these relations in the context of the United States, I turn to Eyerman and

Jamison's (1998) *Music and Social Movements*. They are optimistic in terms of music's role in social movements, calling songs and singing "powerful weapons in the hands of social movements" (ibid.: 43). Though they concentrate for the most part on folk music, they acknowledge that "even mass-produced popular music" such as rap, rock, and soul have also been used in social movements.

Memory plays a key role in music associated with social movements, according to Eyerman and Jamison (1998). Music is easy to remember, more so than, say, a speech. Many protest songs may not be the most sophisticated, created, and chosen for ease of remembering, lending "themselves to shared performance," such as "Jump, jump, who doesn't jump is Tayyip" sung in Gezi Park protests. Historically, this can be seen in the Weavers in the 1950s who wrote "zipper" songs with repeating verses, "so constructed that you have to zip in only a word or two to make an entirely new verse" (ibid.: 66). Later, songs which accompanied the American civil rights movement "were simple but emotive, geared to being sung collectively" (ibid.: 102). Memory also works in another way. Eyerman and Jamison (1998: 1–2) believe "musical and other kinds of cultural traditions are made and remade, and after the movements fade away as political forces, the music remains as a memory and as a potential way to inspire new waves of mobilisation." Here, the role of memory includes songs being a way to remember past social movements. And songs associated with previous social movements carry with them the cultural capital which can be "remade" and used in other political movements.

This process can be illustrated with the song "We Shall Overcome," which has its roots as a spiritual, but has been used and remembered as part of the labor movement, the civil rights movement, and now has been adopted by a range of movements around the world, including anti-abortion activists' sit-ins (Eyerman and Jamison 1998). This same remembering was seen in the late 1960s and early 1970s when rock took folk and other genres to shape a new kind of opposition, drawing from the social movements of the early 1960s (ibid.: 108–109). And it is noticeable today in US rap music which keeps the message of the civil rights movement alive, though organized movements are absent.

Eyerman and Jamison (1998) expand the functional roles of music in social movements to more than just attracting an audience. It is used for recruitment and commercial purposes. It can also act as a source of empowerment, education, and "consciousness-raising" (ibid.: 78). In US civil rights movements, it has been a source and sign of strength, solidarity, and commitment. It has helped "to build bridges between classes and status groups, between black and white supporters, and between rural and urban, northern and southern blacks" (ibid.: 98). Music can create and articulate a sense of community, by the act of singing and listening together. Eyerman and Jamison (1998: 173) recognize such a community may well be "imagined," but "since it affects identity, it is no less real for that." I noticed such a role in Gezi Park where protesters would jump up and down in a synchronized style, similar to a group dance. Together, protesters would sing "Jump, jump, who doesn't jump is Tayyip." Here, differences among protesters were momentarily forgotten and a sense of community was shared, a community bound by opposition to the government.

Music also plays a "truth-bearing" and "knowledge producing" role within social movements. This is done by music acting as a symbolic representation of the individual and the collective. It symbolizes what movements stand for, what is virtuous, and what is evil. This is communicated cognitively and emotionally, linking the past with the present. Music in social movements is a "process of connecting a selected or 'usable' past with the present" (Eyerman and Jamison 1998: 29). Songs with a history of protest "are powerful weapons in the hands of social movements" (ibid.: 43). Again, this recycling of culture was seen in Gezi Park where peace signs were painted on pavements and songs such as John Lennon's "Imagine" were sung in the park. This recycling was done multimodally, where music, symbols, and images from the past helped to represent the present and it is here where a close reading of cultural texts can reveal how this is done.

Music's representational role is not limited strictly to participants in a social movement. Music "can serve an educative function for more than the participants and their immediate public . . . . In this light, art and music—culture—are forms of both knowledge and action, part of the frameworks of interpretation and representation produced within social movements and through which they influence the broader societal culture" (Eyerman and Jamison 1998: 23–24). This greater societal role occurs when music permeates the wider community. It is when after social movements have "faded away as active political forces, that the music has defused into the broader culture and changed popular mores and tastes" (ibid.: 78).

In fact, Eyerman and Jamison (1998) claim social movements also affect music and musicians. It is a two-way reciprocal relationship. They claim that "by combining culture and politics, social movements serve to reconstitute both, providing a broader political and historical context for cultural expression, and offering, in turn, the resources of culture—traditions, music, artistic expression—to the action repertoires of political struggle" (ibid.: 7). So, not only does music spread ideas from social movements into society, social movements help shape music and musicians altering what indeed they may have created had there been no social movement. For example, the socialist movement between 1930 and 1950 provided a context for the making of American folk music and brought folk songs into popular culture. Folk of the 1960s was "intimately and intricately connected to the political campaigns and struggles that were taking place. The music and the politics fed into one another in complex and variegated ways" (ibid.: 13). In Turkey, I believe that Gezi Park and AKP more generally have deeply affected many musicians and shaped what they write and sing about.

As is the case with politics and music in general, different social movements attract different genres of music. In fact, it is not just "progressive" or "left" politics which have courted popular music (Street 1988; Eyerman and Jamison 1998). Street (1988) examines how the United Kingdom's racist Right in the late 1970s was courted by Oi bands such as Screwdriver and The 4skins while other groups like Sham 69 and Bad Manners attracted racists, even when they denounced racism. The National Front favored Punk, New Romantics, and Oi music, with various arguments about their origins being white and their content and style being the sound of "white working-class frustration" or an all-white "contemporary version of classical and Aryan music" (Street 1988: 53). All the same, the music served a peripheral role in the racist Right movement "used to reinforce or identify opinions already established by other means" (ibid.: 55). In fact, this role is given to pop and social movements of any ilk. Street

(1988: 59) observes that "Music contributes to the fight, but is not a part of it." Its power is defined and limited by sounds, references, and images, a far cry from facts and figures and coherent arguments, as I explore in later chapters. In the United States, country music is most linked to right-wing social movements. Street (1988) notes how country music has provided a medium for right-wing views on Vietnam, Darwinism, bussing, federal government, taxes, and race. Country has been appropriated by the Right because country emphasizes the voice making lyrics easily comprehensible. Country also works with a sense of history and a sense of community which is stronger than rock.

But popular music is mostly associated with more progressive social movements and causes such as the Wobblies and the American Socialist Party, Rock Against Racism, workers' rights, nuclear power, Nicaragua, famine, apartheid, racism, black civil rights, and critiques of the military, the Vietnam war, official authority, conventional morality, industrial society, and technology (Street 1988; Eyerman and Jamison 1998). Progressive social movements such as these attract a wide variety of music types. Though Eyerman and Jamison (1998) include rockers such as Jimi Hendrix and Janis Joplin, soul artists such as James Brown and rap music, for the most part folk music has been associated with progressive social movements in the United States. This preference may be due to its form. Eyerman and Jamison (1998: 122) claim, "The quiet sounds of folk music perhaps encouraged focus on text as a prime source of meaning, while the open-ended nature of the protest lent itself to a poetic, or at least more emotive form of political communication."

This assessment of folk's compatibility with social movements does not answer how other forms of pop have become associated with social movements. Here, Street (1988, 2013) has an answer. Music and musicians must be perceived by fans and social movements as legitimate in terms of their political commitment. This is not found in lyrics alone, but is how musicians represent themselves multimodally. According to the Socialist Workers Party, "Good music is music made from the results of struggle and suffering, and away from the world of 'capitalist enterprise' " (in Street 1988: 58). So, musicians who are represented with political commitments like Gil Scot Heron are valued because of their lyrics and personal political commitments while the Clash are legitimized through their choice of singing at benefits and singing about unemployment and riots. In later chapters, I examine how groups legitimize themselves through representations of being politically committed.

Though the above two cited studies are confined to Western social movements and music, scholars differ somewhat in their view on relations between the two, reflecting differences in local contexts. In Australia, aboriginal music is seen as having a powerful role in the indigenous struggle for justice (Corn 2011). Some musicians are credited with "celebrat[ing] the strength shown by Indigenous Australians in the face of state oppression, and paved the way for reconciliation with non-Indigenous Australians" (ibid.: 18). This view of music's role in social movements is very optimistic and shared by LeVine (2011). He considers Middle Eastern metal and the region's struggle for human rights. LeVine claims underground music's political role is one of "avatars of change or struggles for greater social and political openness. They point out cracks in the façade of conformity that is crucial to keeping authoritarian or hierarchical political systems in power" (ibid.: 56–57). Other scholars are less optimistic. Greene (2011) and Muktuavel (2011) assess Nepal's heavy metal scene and its human rights movement, and the neo-folklore movement of occupied Latvia in the 1980s against Russian occupation respectively. Greene (2011) observes that politics in songs are underdeveloped, drawing "on a partial control of the facts at hand, and rarely articulat[ing] a coherent plan for social action" (ibid.: 28). All the same, he points to the multimodal potential of music noting a sense of community is articulated through the raw emotions of voice and sounds which create a shared emotional intensity "that helped to galvanise resistance, much more than well-articulated verbal arguments or formulations of rights" (ibid.: 28). Muktuavel (2011: 89) claims neo-folklore acted as musical accompaniment to the politics; that is, the movement "was strongly supported and uplifted through singing" (ibid.: 89).

This section has revealed that there are certainly a wide range of music styles which become associated with an array of social movements. Though most scholars agree that music plays a role in social movements, what that role is seems to differ across social movements and among scholars. This lack of certainty is reflected in all aspects of relations between music and politics we have thus far examined. With a close reading in context, MCDS, I believe, can help define music's roles in terms of what politics are being articulated and how this is done. I now turn my attention to the issue of authenticity, an issue also intertwined with music and politics and again an issue with much contested terrain.

Authenticity in pop

It is not only political ideas which are communicated through images, sounds, and lyrics, but also discourses about music producers themselves and fans. Think back to our discussion about Dev and how representations of place and the authorities not only multimodally express subversion to authority but also authenticate Dev as legitimate indie rockers. Ideas of authenticity emerge as an important theme, closely intertwined with politics and genre. To understand authenticity is central to understanding the often deeply emotional connections we have to music. Discourses of authenticity are thought to be constructed in and through semiotic resources in music commodities. Much has been written on the subject including its usefulness (see for instance Redhead and Street 1989; Moore 2002; Burns 2007). Though the idea of authenticity generates considerable debate, recent studies have found it useful to view it as the quality of "sincerity" or "playing from the heart" that listeners ascribe to performers (Moore 2002: 210). How this is assigned is socially, historically, and genre dependent by music producers and fans alike.

Musicians, record companies, and their managers use semiotic resources such as musical sounds and visuals including looks and styles to articulate authenticity as part of a group's "discursive package" (Goodwin 1993: 8; Auslander 1999: 74). These packages are ideological, based on culturally and genre-determined conventions. They are "a result of industrial practice: the music industry specifically sets out to endow its products with the necessary signs of authenticity" (Auslander 1999: 70).

Notions of authenticity have their roots in the Romantic tradition where artistic creativity was seen as coming from the soul, as opposed to something which emerged from society (Machin 2010). These beliefs contribute to the dichotomy of authentic verses "establishment." Authenticity is dependent on "the inauthentic other," such as authentic rock versus inauthentic pop (Auslander 1999: 71). Auslander (1999: 69) observes that

> The ideological distinction between rock and pop is precisely the distinction between the authentic and the inauthentic, the sincere and the cynical, the genuinely popular and the slickly commercial, the potentially resistant and the necessarily co-opted, art and entertainment.

Though these distinctions are a dominant discourse about some popular music among many fans, including rock fans, rock is not the only popular music which is considered "authentic." Different semiotic resources are used based on genre and subgenre to connote authenticity. So, a tightly choreographed dance routine may signify authenticity in a soul-influenced pop group but would be disastrous for a rock group. Rock's authenticity is determined by live performance and being anti-establishment (Frith 1981; Auslander 1999: 70). Rock musicians can represent themselves as authentic by articulating anti-establishment political discourses, like Dev does in "Dans Et." But even within the genre of rock, there is divergence. There have always been "many forms of rock authenticity," varying between its many sub-genres and across time (Grossberg 1992: 202). In fact, Grossberg (1992: 209) notes that "Rock must constantly change to survive; it must seek to reproduce its authenticity in new forms, new places, in new alliances. It must constantly move from one center to another, transforming what had been authentic into the inauthentic in order to constantly project its claim to authenticity."

Grossberg's observations are noticeable in rock as well as other forms of pop. Gilbert and Pearson (1999: 164–165) observe that 1980s authentic rock entails singers to speak the truth of their (and others') situations by representing the culture from which they come as well as the presence of specific instruments. Indie rock positions itself against the inauthenticity of mainstream (including 1980s) rock and pop. Here, authenticity is about purity and non-corporate ideals not found in "high-tech manipulations of large scale production" and "defined in opposition to the commercially influenced" (Hibbett 2005: 64; Machin 2010). This aversion to large-scale production is a commonly heard bragging right of indie bands and labels. For example, Sub Pop Records claims it "recorded cheaply and quickly" seventy-five singles, albums, and EPs between 1987 and 1989. Contrast this with the eleven months it took to record Pink Floyd's *The Wall*.

Though concerts and playing live have always been a crucial part in notions of rock authenticity, Auslander (1999) acknowledges a post-rock authentication process. Here, it is the video which is of utmost importance in a three-way authentication process between the video, the performance, and the recorded song. He observes that "While the video authenticates the sound recording by replicating the live production of the sound, live performance authenticates the video by replicating its images in real space" (1999: 93). There is also something Auslander calls "authentic inauthenticity." This is when recording artists admits they do not live up to rock's standards of authenticity. In this way, musicians subvert rock authenticity, defining themselves against traditional rock authenticity and authenticating themselves as something post-rock. An infamous example of this is the Pet Shop Boys' Neil Tennant's statement, "It's kinda macho nowadays to prove you can cut it live. I quite like proving we can't cut it live. We're a pop group, not a rock and roll group" (in Goodwin 1993: 268).

Alternatively, American hip-hop authenticity is articulated through lyrics which reveal personal truths, representing a geographical background linked to lived experiences in predominantly black urban neighborhoods (Fraley 2009: 43). Global hip-hop authenticity is about "keeping it real" by linking global criteria of hip hop with the local (Pennycook 2007: 103). Terkourafi (2010: 7) observes that hip hoppers around the world establish their authenticity on two levels.

> At one level, they address local issues and social realities and . . . at another level, they enter into a dialogue with the whole of hip hop culture, acknowledging its supra-local origins and drawing cultural capital from them . . . . At both levels they claim authenticity through both *form* (music samples and language varieties used) and *content* (topics and genres referred to, and attitudes expressed).

Depending on the context, these two levels of authenticity are achieved in a variety of ways. For example, vernacular speech is seen as authentic in migrant German rap (Androutsopoulos 2010: 20), English language in French rap authenticates it by referring to rap's origins (Hassa 2010: 57), while local languages in Egyptian rap are seen as authentic because they are local (William 2010: 71). Local or regional issues such as pan-Arab issues in Egyptian rap authenticate musicians as Arab rappers (Williams 2010: 83), while accent and dialect play a role in a variety of contexts (Brunstad, Royneland, and Opsahl 2010: 230; Stylianou 2010: 196). These examples not only illustrate the importance of context, but also how discourses of authenticity and politics are multimodally articulated.

Despite genre-dependent variations in criteria for authenticity, it is the notion that musicians are sincere and singing from the heart which musicians and genres all have in common. And it is this notion which points to active listeners who make decisions about authenticity (Moore 2002; Hibbett 2005; Machin 2010). Authenticity and inauthenticity are known by fans based on how "we judge people's sincerity generally" (Frith 1996: 71). One factor in fans determining the legitimacy of political intervention by a musician, such as Pussy Riot, is "to do with the authority and/or legitimacy attached to any given performer" (Street 2013: 50). And this legitimacy is "not simply there in the music; they are there because the way we think about music puts them there" (Cook 1998: 14). These judgments are based on not only musical sounds, "but also of prior musical and extra-musical knowledge and belief" (Auslander 1999: 76). Fans' "extra musical knowledge" contextualizes musical sounds and images which authenticate musicians and fans alike. Authenticity is created through listeners responding to choices music producers make in terms of musical sounds, images, and styles, things I examine in depth in this book.

But authenticity is not just about musicians. Music commodities also express ideas of authenticity about fans and others multimodally. Moore (2002) identifies three levels in which authenticity can be articulated and experienced. There is *first person authenticity* which is most commonly referred to in the aforementioned studies. This type of authenticity "arises when an originator (composer, performer) succeeds in conveying the impression that his/her utterance is one of integrity, that it represents an attempt to communicate in an unmediated form with an audience" (ibid.: 214). This can be achieved through a wide range of semiotic choices such as vocal style, facial expressions, and instrumental choices. *Second person authenticity* "occurs when a performance succeeds in conveying the impression to a listener that that listener's experience of life is being validated, that the music is 'telling it like it is' for them" (ibid.: 220). This authenticates listeners by articulating a place of belonging which distinguishes the music from other cultural forms. In many of the Gezi Park protest videos, including Dev's "Dans Et," we see the band authenticating themselves as indie rockers, but we also see the idea that protesters and fans are also legitimate. They are represented as powerful and correct, legitimating the protest, "telling it like it is." *Third person authenticity*, according to Moore (ibid.: 218), "arises when a performer succeeds in conveying the impression of accurately representing the ideas of another, embedded within a tradition of performance." For example, Eric Clapton, a white Englishman, is renowned for authentically playing country blues music associated with blacks in the Mississippi Delta in America. Though for the most part, the analysis in this book examines first person authenticity, second person authenticity is also referred to when appropriate, especially in Chapter 8.

A final note

This chapter has outlined *what* we know about relations between music, politics, and authenticity. We know that these relations are not easily compatible. The work examined in this chapter points to what types of politics work best with what types of music. It also reveals the importance of authenticity which is intertwined with politics and music. We know that music can represent political issues, not so much like a logical speech, but more like an emotive cry, expressed multimodally in lyrics, sounds, and images. We know that issues of authenticity help determine not only what politics can be expressed in what music, but also how audiences may respond to such musical expressions. Some scholars are far more optimistic than others concerning relations between music, politics, and authenticity. In fact, these are highly contested terrains to say the least. All the same, MCDS has much to offer to the examination of music, politics, and authenticity. The strength of MCDS is its detailed systematic analysis of the modes used in communication. With this approach we can clarify *what* the politics are and discourses of authenticity articulated in song and importantly *how* this is done across the modes of lyrics, visuals, and sounds. I do this in the analysis chapters which follow. But before I take on such a task, MCDS demands a thorough understanding of the political, social, and historical contexts surrounding texts. In this way, the meaning potentials of communicative resources are revealed. So, before I begin my analysis of a variety of musical commodities which have been available in Turkey since 2002, the next chapter examines the contexts in which these musical offerings emerged.

4

Turkey under the Stewardship of AKP

When I was in Canada, I saw one of Billy Bragg's concerts in Toronto as part of his North American tour which promoted his 1991 album "Don't Try This at Home." He expressed outrage at the US president of the time, George Bush. Between songs, he joked and made negative remarks about the president. On the back of his guitar, he showed us a sticker which read "Eat Bush," which we all laughed at for its two very different meanings, though he claimed it was there to insult the president. He told us that "Unlike Tracy Chapman who talks about revolution, here we are a revolution." All the while the police and authorities did nothing in Toronto or anywhere in North America to stop his concerts or any of his activities. Fast forward to Izmir, Turkey, in 2015. There is a general election campaign in full swing while Duman, a band which is known for its stance against the Justice and Development Party (AKP), play outdoors to a large and enthusiastic crowd. A campaign bus for AKP drives close to the event. One of the members of the band makes a gesture toward the bus and many members of the crowd, myself included, yell abuse at the bus. My friend standing next to me and a host of others tell us who are yelling and abusing the bus to "keep it down" for fear of being arrested. In the meanwhile, there is an ongoing campaign by the youth branch of AKP to ban Duman from playing in a number of places and universities around Turkey. The contrast between the two times and places could not be more obvious. Unlike in the West, where opposition to politicians is tolerated, and at times expected, in Turkey, bands are shunned, told they are traitors, their songs get no airplay, instruments are smashed by police, and musicians are jailed and exiled for expressing opposition to AKP.

Despite these hurdles, some bands continue to express their opposition. Some, such as myself, would say this is welcome in a country where opposition in mainstream media has been either silenced through direct government takeovers or pressured into turning a blind eye to AKP and its faults. Music offers a way for musicians and fans to express themselves, though what they are able to express and how this is done are directly related to social and political circumstances. For example, Duman cannot be as blatant and obvious about their opposition to AKP as Billy Bragg was to Bush without the risk of jail and the likes. This is partly to do with contemporary deep ideological divisions in Turkey which have been exasperated since 2002 when AKP came to power. This chapter examines in depth what are Turkey's current social and political contexts in which music is played, performed, recorded, and distributed. This examination aids in better understanding and focusing the meaning potential of lyrics, visuals, and sounds in music commodities, whether opposed or supportive of AKP.

To understand why it is the case that musicians face such strong opposition by authorities, we need to examine AKP and its policies which are represented and opposed by musicians, as well as those policies which affect musicians. This chapter begins by historically contextualizing AKP's rise to power, seen by many as a reaction to more established political perspectives in Turkey, such as Kemalism. I then examine AKP's policies which are represented in music, that is, policies which have affected aspects of Turkish culture such as ideological divisions, perspectives on religion, and economics. I also examine AKP's relations with mainstream media and the music industry, relations which directly affect musicians, what they can sing about, and how they can do this. The chapter finishes with a discussion on how some popular music which is politically subversive has found an outlet in the form of the internet to carry its messages of subversion.

The demise of Kemalism

Before AKP came to power in 2002, the dominant ideology throughout Turkish political history was, in one form or another, known as Kemalism. It has its roots in the Turkish national independence war from 1919 to 1922, when Turks and Kurds fought against the occupying forces who had carved up the remnants of the Ottoman empire after the First World War. Kemalism, or "The Kemalist modernization process," spearheaded by Mustafa Kemal Atatürk (the founder of the modern Turkish Republic), aimed to modernize Turkey by creating a homogeneous, secular, and Western society. Kemalism views Mustafa Kemal Atatürk as the symbolic leader and hero of Turkey, a champion of secularism, modernization, and closeness with Europe (Mango 1999). In 1920, Atatürk set up a new political assembly and the Turkish Republic was established in 1923.

The nation-building process crucially involved homogenization policies based on Turkish language, culture, and being Muslim. In the 1924 constitution, "citizenship" referred to Muslim Turks. The Kurds and other Muslim minorities were considered Turkish provided that they did not identify themselves with their ethnic origin (Yıldız 2001). A rebellion in 1925 by some Kurds broke this uneasy alliance. Soon after, Atatürk began to put less emphasis on Muslimness as the most important common tie between the people of Turkey with different ethnic and linguistic origins and began to stress Turkishness as the most important component of the new republican citizenship (Yeğen 1999). These policies ignored Kurds and all other non-Turkish ethnic groups or simply tried to assimilate them into the new nation state (ibid.: 555). In an effort to create an imagined homogeneous community, the elite saw assimilation necessary for "uncivilized, uneducated and backward Kurds" (ibid.: 563). A cycle of uprisings followed by more severe and more restrictive measures during the Republic's first fourteen years, resulting in over 45,000 deaths, the Kurdish language being banned, many Kurds forced to leave their villages, and Kurdish name places replaced in the name of Turkish nation building (Ensaroğlu 2013; Pusane 2014).

The multiparty era began in 1950, though all parties carried on Kemalism in various forms, including the principle of secularism. This emphasis "resulted in the supremacy of the laic [secular] bourgeoisie in the social hierarchy" (Öncü and Balkan 2016: 35). When religious-oriented parties were elected, military intervention soon followed, such as the military coup of September 12, 1980. Today, Turkey's political opposition still are Kemalist oriented. For example, the main opposition party, the Republican People's Party (CHP), embraces a Western outlook and secularism, while the smaller Nationalist Movement Party (MHP) emphasizes the Turkish nation and state.

After the 1980s military coup, Turkey embraced neoliberalism and globalization along with most of the world (Öncü and Balkan 2016: 35). This included "privatization, financialization, the management and manipulation of economic crises, and the redistribution of state assets" (ibid.). Bahçe and Köse (2016: 63) observe that "Turkey has been a pioneering country in the implementation of neoliberal reforms since 1980. Beginning with the coup d'etat in September 1980, the neoliberal programme has been implemented by subsequent governments without any disruption."

Until further reforms took place in the late 1990s, Günlük-Şenesen and Kırık (2016: 76) characterize Turkish politics up to this point as "military supremacy over civilian politics" where military involvement "in the political process spans from constitution writing (1961, 1982), to the creation of new institutions" creating "the semi-politicization of the army and partial militarization of politics." In 1999 and then in 2001, governments introduced democratic reforms aimed at the protection of fundamental rights, strengthening the rule of law, and limiting the role of the military.

However, progress was very slow and limited. This was because between 1989 and 2001, there were thirteen coalition governments, none of which lasted very long (Bahçe and Köse 2016: 65). It is this unstable political climate that saw the rise of the Islamic/neoliberal AKP. The financial crisis of 2001 also played a key role. Başlevent and Kirmanoğlu (2016: 88) note how "AKP was believed to be the recipient of a substantial amount of protest votes by those who were adversely affected by the gloomy economic conditions that existed in the aftermath of the 2001 economic crisis." The result was three parties who had formed the previous coalition government were "wiped out" while AKP swept to power winning "the election thanks to an effective and critical campaign against the ruling coalition" (Boratav 2016: 5). It is at this point we see the start of a new era in Turkish politics, an era under AKP which has deeply affected Turkey socially, economically, and politically.

The era of the Justice and Development Party

AKP is an economically liberal and socially conservative political party founded in 2001 by members of existing Islamic and conservative parties including the Islamist Virtue Party and the Motherland party. It won its first national election a year later in 2002. With the exception of its June 7, 2015, short-lived minority victory, AKP has won a majority in each national election. Unlike administrations before it, AKP brands itself as an alternative to Kemalism. According to Uzgel and Duru (2010), AKP represents itself as a bridge between Islam, democracy, and neoliberalism. It appeals to a wide spectrum of the population including big business interests, the religious poor, and Kurds (until recently). I now turn to AKP's relations with these aforementioned groups, relations which are the subject of much music opposed to the government. In fact, much of the music I analyze later in this book opposes relations I outline below. By being aware of AKP's relations with these groups in Turkey, we can better understand the meaning potential of lyrics, visuals, and sounds in music commodities. For example, without the contextual examination of AKP's close relations with big business, music which expresses opposition to this, such as Mor ve Ötesi's "Şirket" (Way 2016b) or Grup Kızılırmak's "Çeşme Siyahim" (Chapter 7), is lost on fans.

AKP policies which musicians oppose in music

AKP's relations with big business

AKP claims that its brand of Islam supports the success of businessmen, Islam being represented as anything but an obstacle to economic growth and modernization. Boratav (2016: 5) notes how Recep Tayyip Erdoğan, as mayor of Istanbul, had worked closely with various business groups (usually with roots in Islam) to such an extent that these groups "were influential in local AKP branches." Moreover, "organic links" with conservative/Islamist business groups and associations have always been a driving force in AKP. This thinking informs its policies which include an aggressive program of privatization of many of Turkey's services and monopolies, with financial benefits to business groups close to AKP. At the same time, it discriminates against companies it does not agree with. The Agency on Public Procurements and Tenders is manipulated by the government in favor of itself and its supporters. Here, according to Boratav (ibid.: 7), public procurements are used to "discriminate in favour or against; to reward or exclude particular domestic and external groups, firms, corporations and business-people . . . Big business groups (e.g. Koç and Doğan Holdings), which did not fall in line with the government on political and other issues, were confronted with tax inspectors or other authorities and sometimes had to deal with court cases."

Though favoritism occurs, it is economic liberalism that is driving the economy. This is made clear on its official website where the market economy is "favored," privatization is "an important vehicle for the formation of a more rational economic structure," and globalization should "be carried out with the least cost" while the state should remain "outside all types of economic activities." It uses "globalization" discourses in order to make a more AKP- and business-friendly environment. According to Uzgel and Duru (2010: 24), AKP has privatized most public/state institutions including interests in communication, transportation, industry, and energy without regard to its benefits. Though privatization is not unique to Turkey, the rate of such privatization is unprecedented (Karip 2013). Since AKP came to power, "economic policies became increasingly neoliberal, leading to further consolidation of this mode of capital accumulation. By the end of this journey, Turkey had completed its transition from a mode of capital accumulation driven by import-substituting industrialization to a regime based on global flows of goods and capital, popularly known as neoliberalism" (Öncü and Balkan 2016: 30).

AKP has overseen the transformation of the economy into a neoliberal model in ways previous governments could not achieve, due to their precarious positions as minority governments. With AKP ruling since 2002, it has been able to continue and advance its economic program of "massive privatizations, bringing a great deal of flexibility to labour markets, restructuring of public administration, deregulation of the social welfare and public health systems and alleged 'de-politicization' of the monetary and fiscal policy-making" (Bahçe and Köse 2016: 65). As is the case in other countries which have embraced neoliberalism, AKP has reduced the social security rights of its citizens resulting in a kind of a charity state (Uzgel and Duru 2010: 24). By 2013, AKP had made Turkey a very attractive place to do business. Boratav (2016: 5) notes how

> flexibility of the labour markets was realized as far as it was politically possible. Trade unions had effectively disappeared from wage-determination. Sub-contracting had become pervasive and had even spread extensively into the public sector. Contractual employment within public administration and market-based provision of public services expanded significantly. Privatization of state-owned enterprises (SOEs) was to a large degree completed and extended into public land.

These massive economic changes have not come about without practices of corruption. Though previous governments have also been accused of similar actions, there has been a "substantial expansion of corrupt practices within the ranks of political leaders" in AKP's time in government (Boratav 2016: 8). For example, the graft probes of December 2013 involved contractors and politicians including Erdoğan himself, in accusations of bribery. Boratav (ibid.: 8) describes the corruption as "far beyond tolerable levels" and "corruption of astronomical magnitudes starting from Erdoğan." The government managed to represent the corruption as a "coup attempt" while legislative and parliamentary rules were changed to protect the government and its politicians. In the meantime, a scapegoat in the form of supporters of the Gülen Movement was identified as responsible (ibid.: 8; Karatepe 2016: 47).

AKP's relations with religion and the poor

AKP has represented itself as the voice of the religious poor, and especially those who share their interpretations of Islam. There is a common oppositional discourse in Turkey which sees AKP exploiting religion and the uneducated poor in order to gain votes. Some music, such as Duman's "İyi de bana ne" (Way 2012) and many songs by Grup Yorum (Chapter 6), targets these issues by representing opposition in song to religious conservatism and injustices toward the poor. Here, I investigate these relations to reveal what it is musicians are opposed to.

With the success in some sectors of Turkey's economy, there has also been record unemployment and poverty in others (Sümer and Yaşlı 2010: 17), especially the laboring classes (Bahçe and Köse 2016: 70). For those who have suffered financially, AKP has used its self-made financial crisis for its own ends. It promotes its prestige by distributing fuel, food aid packages, and sometimes refrigerators to the poor during election times, representing itself as looking after those who have suffered under AKP financial policies. Alternatively, some within the lower and middle classes have seen a rise in their living standards which "has translated into electoral success for the incumbent party" (Başlevent and Kirmanoğlu 2016: 88).

One aspect of society which involves AKP, Islam, and the poor is the construction industry and the state-run Housing Development Administration of Turkey (TOKI) which oversees the building of houses by AKP and its supporters. Though its official aim is to construct homes for low-income groups, it has also built non-residential buildings such as mosques and hospitals, "giving the appearance that TOKI is more than just a public agency created to solve a housing problem" (Karatepe 2016: 49). AKP uses TOKI to appear to be acting in the interests of Islam and the poor by providing mosques and houses for those who can afford them within the laboring classes. Many of these projects involve displacing large numbers of people from areas which are then regentrified by AKP associates for huge profits, while the displaced fend for themselves or are offered housing in far less desirable locations at far more money. Opposition to such moves is represented multimodally in Grup Yorum's concert analyzed in Chapter 6. However, TOKI and its effects are a win-win situation for AKP. As Karatepe (ibid.: 59) notes, the "handover ceremony of TOKI houses has been designed for electioneering or propaganda of Islamic conservative politics." Furthermore, TOKI is represented as a success and families on low to middle income become bound to AKP financially by owing large sums of money and otherwise. The result is TOKI "promote[s] their [AKP] hegemony" (Sönmez 2015: 16).

TOKI is also used by AKP to gain votes by benefitting its close business associates and some in the laboring classes while disadvantaging others. Unlike other neoliberal governments, AKP has expanded the role of its housing authority, building more than 600,000 homes since it came to power. This is directly linked to its economic development program which has seen AKP and the construction industry becoming "inextricably enmeshed" (Karatepe 2016: 47). Laws are amended or passed in order to make construction easier for both companies closely associated with AKP and projects with direct links to the government (ibid.: 49). Patronage between construction companies and AKP through TOKI contracts have rewarded companies and expanded the financial base of the party. This has resulted in the rapid growth of pro-government companies at the expense of others (Sönmez 2015: 82). With these companies rooted in Islam, TOKI has benefitted AKP and its conservative politics. In the meantime, "environmental havoc, drastic socio-economical changes" are dismissed "for the sake of the stability of the construction undertakings" (Karatepe 2016: 49).

Though religion is an intricate part of the TOKI program, religion is also used by AKP in much more direct ways. In recent years AKP has pursued a socially and religiously conservative agenda, symbolically and legally changing Turkey's secular laws and distancing itself from Western cultural practices. Boratav (2016: 6) observes that starting from 2007, there has been "the gradual Islamization of the AKP's discourse and policies and the consequent reactions, including mass protests leading to the

Gezi uprising of June 2013." There are countless examples of such practices, changes occurring at an ever-increasing rate, especially since the failed July 15, 2016, coup attempt. For example, rules on wearing the Islamic headscarf in public institutions which was previously banned have now been relaxed. The headscarf is reviled by many secular Turks, thought of as a symbolic threat to Turkey's secular politics. Also, AKP members do not drink during public functions while they openly talk against alcohol consumption. This has coincided with significant alcohol price increases and the tightening of laws pertaining to licensed premises. AKP emphasizes its Islamic roots and future. On its website, AKP claims, "Our party considers religion as one of the most important institutions of humanity." Religious references are used regularly as in "May Allah be the beloved and assistant of our nation?" In February 2012, Erdoğan caused controversy by telling reporters AKP was bringing up a new generation of even more religious AKP politicians ("Erdoğan dindar" 2012). By emphasizing Turkey's Islamic and non-Western traditions while de-emphasizing its European ambitions, many secular Turks are concerned (Mango 1999) and this is played out in some music we examine later. This emphasis on Islam has benefitted not only big businesses associated with AKP, but also a "new Islamic middle class faction that have benefited economically, socially, and culturally" (Öncü and Balkan 2016: 35).

AKP's relations with Kurds and other minorities

When AKP first won the parliamentary elections back in 2002, it did so with promises including more equality and freedom for all oppressed groups (Günlük-Şenesen and Kırık 2016). Kurds, religious Turks, and a host of other minorities such as Alevis who felt alienated by Turkey's secular elites welcomed such an initiative. Though indeed many religious groups and people have benefitted from AKP's time in office, not all promises concerning Kurds and Alevis have materialized as obviously as many would like and AKP has continued to marginalize groups it claimed it would help. These issues fuel a whole host of musicians and their music, some of whom merely sing in the Kurdish language (Nudem Durak) while others are more radical, supporting the idea of Kurdish autonomy (Grup Yorum). In most cases, such actions involve arrest and jail sentences. Here, I examine relations between the state and Kurds, relations criticized in song and analyzed in later chapters (Chapters 6 and 7).

Kurds are the largest minority in Turkey with estimates ranging from eighteen to twenty-five million out of a population of some seventy-eight million people. AKP have appealed to this sector of the population, originally claiming they were the victims of secularization forced on them by Kemalist modernization, thereby ignoring identity problems. AKP's solution to this interpretation of the Kurdish problem was using Islam as the glue which binds everyone in the nation (Yavuz and Özcan 2006; Pusane 2014). Although there were some improvements in relations in 2003 and 2004, resulting in permission to use Kurdish names, "Return to Village and Rehabilitation" projects and the release of some political dissidents, little else materialized. In 2007, AKP renewed its strategy in order to appeal to the Kurdish vote (Yavuz and Özcan 2006; Pusane 2014). In 2009, after AKP won its second parliamentary election, the "Democratic Opening" program was introduced with the aim of disarming the PKK. Steps such as the establishment of a Kurdish language broadcast channel and the return of some PKK fighters to Turkey were seen as victories by some Kurds. This process continued until 2011 when it lost its popular appeal. After AKP's third victory, the government renewed its efforts by conducting a dialogue with Kurdish political parties and the PKK (Pusane 2014). This gradually reduced the number of clashes between the PKK and the military and helped establish a conflict-free period. However, these improvements were put under pressure prior to Turkey's June 7, 2015, parliamentary elections when the political rhetoric saw a breakdown in relations, a stop to the peace process, and accusations of broken promises, each group accusing the other of being a problem, not a solution. This was seen by many as an attempt to attract voters (Köylü 2015).

Government policy changed due to a change in Kurdish politics. Until 2015, Kurdish politicians ran as independent candidates in order to bypass the 10 percent threshold rule in Turkish politics which prohibits political party representation in parliament unless a party achieves more than 10 percent of the popular vote. In 2015, the Kurdish-rights-oriented People's Democratic Party (Halkların Demokratik Partisı—HDP) decided to run as a party in the hopes of surpassing this. It reached out to other oppressed groups, including women, lesbian, gay, bisexual, and transgender (LGBT) individuals. As the election approached, polls indicated a significant shift in votes from AKP to HDP. Many long-term Kurdish AKP supporters switched alliances, seeing AKP's peace attempts as a failure (Tremblay 2015). This was disastrous for AKP's hopes of securing a fourth consecutive parliamentary majority.

HDP achieved 13 percent of the popular vote at the expense of an AKP majority. This deeply and negatively affected AKP's plans to change the constitution from a parliamentary democracy to a presidential one, a plan which required a majority and a move many describe as anti-democratic (Keleş 2015). Despite calls for a coalition government, AKP and Erdoğan seemed to many to be uninterested. In the meantime, armed conflict within Turkey intensified. A second election was called on November 1, 2015, and AKP was rewarded with its fourth majority, though HDP managed to keep 11 percent of the popular vote and its place in parliament. Since this election and up to the time of writing this book, AKP has unleashed a civil war in the southeast of Turkey, with promises of militarily defeating Kurdish fighters and refusing to start peace talks, while jailing many HDP parliamentarians, including its leaders. It is on this backdrop that Kurdish musicians and musicians with Kurdish sympathies produce music opposed to such relations while risking arrest and jail.

AKP policies which directly affect musicians

AKP's relations with the media

Music was an important part of the Gezi Park protests including live performances which accompanied other forms of protest all over Turkey. In Izmir, I was part of the Çapulcu Muzik Orkestra, which followed our band leader and his trumpet around the center of town with our guitars, drums, flutes, singing, and clapping. Recorded music also played a role with over 140 songs and music videos posted onto YouTube during and immediately after the protests. Most are amateur cut-and-paste visuals edited onto music and lyrics recorded in studios by one-off bands, university music groups, and more established groups, while others are professional promotional videos by well-established bands. Despite this high number of musical offerings, not one, professionally produced or not, has ever appeared on mainstream media, as far as I am aware.

This case of omission is to do with Turkey's history of close relations between media and politics (Özguneş and Terzis 2000: 414). Relations can be characterized in terms of Hallin and Mancini's (2004) "Mediterranean or Polarized Pluralist Model." Turkey has a politically oriented press, high political parallelism in journalism; the state plays a significant role as owner, regulator, and funder of media as it oversees a high degree of ideological diversity and conflict in society. There are also differences between Turkey and this model, echoing Papathanassopoulos's (2000: 505–506) assertion that "each national system still differs in many respects when compared to others . . . since media organizations reflect the differences between political systems, political philosophies, cultural traits and economic conditions." An examination of both the role of the state and the corporate media culture is important to understand how Turkey has experienced "an erosion of press freedom and legitimated bad practice" (Christensen 2005: 196; Finkel 2005: 24).

Before the introduction of commercial media in Turkey (officially in 1993, but unlicensed broadcasting began in the mid-1980s), broadcasting was monopolized by the state-run Türkiye Radyo Televizyon Kurumu or Turkish Radio and Television Institute (TRT), where the state wielded enormous power over content (Finkel 2000: 155). The early years saw this relation turn on its head with some critical, investigative journalism (ibid.) and challenges to oppressive "legal norms established earlier on under the monopoly of state control" (Karaman and Aras 2000: 46). However, according to Christensen (2005: 183), the media honeymoon was short-lived with the Turkish business world focusing on the economic and political possibilities of media ownership. Governments at the time were unable or unwilling to curb the powers of media owners, "while at the same time hindering, via restrictive legislation, the ability of journalists to engage in critical reporting" (ibid.: 183).

Owners of these large conglomerates had little experience in the media world. They used their media companies for ulterior motives (Tunç 2003). For example, Christensen (2005: 187) recalls how the most powerful media conglomerate at the time, the Doğan Media Group, was involved in forcing two ministers to resign after they publicly spoke out against the interests of the media group. Large media owners' search for profit and political influence included the virtual elimination of unions. With no government policies to protect workers, media owners gave media workers a choice between a job or a union. With ownership concentration as high as it is, finding another job is very difficult, resulting in journalists towing the corporate line (ibid.: 191).

The rights of media workers have come under even more pressure since AKP. In 2005, a new Turkish Penal Code (TCK) was introduced by AKP which further eroded the rights of media workers. Miklos Haraszti, from "Operation in Europe Representative on Freedom of the Media" (OSCE), was highly critical of the changes, citing twenty-three of the most problematic aspects of the new code in relation to their possible effects on freedom of the press "including: the increase in penalties for crimes committed through print or mass media; a lack of provisions 'securing the rights of journalists to report and discuss' public interest issues; restrictions on access and disclosure of information; and overly vague and subjective 'defamation' and 'insult' provisions which put free and open discussion of public affairs at risk" (in Christensen 2005: 194).

Though the TCK was amended, addressing seven out of the twenty-three points raised by the OSCE, legislation brought in by AKP has resulted in a media sector which is far from critical. As Christensen (2005: 195) notes, "The potential 'chilling effect' of these articles on the practice of journalism is clear: under these legal guidelines, it would be virtually impossible for investigative journalists to, for example, expose political or military corruption, or to implicate a public official in criminal activity, without running the risk of themselves being convicted of a crime."

Despite these repressive measures, Turkey has an impressive number of media outlets. It has approximately 180 newspapers. There are also around 1,100 private radio stations and 14 state-run TRT stations. Television broadcast numbers are also impressive. There are 24 national, 16 regional, and 215 local television stations, with TRT controlling 11 of these. Though numbers are excessive, Turkey's media are dominated by TRT and five private media conglomerates. This almost monopoly is a result of Turkish media policies since 1993 which introduced private broadcasting and actively pursued a private conglomerates policy "to promote the formation of media conglomerates with a secure capital-holding base and to minimize the number of dominant media players in the public arena" (Özguneş and Terzis 2000: 10). A smaller number of players means it is easier to control. According to the European Journalists Association, Turkish media are heavily dominated by large multi-sector groups controlling newspapers, radio, and television channels.

Turkey's media experience heavy censorship and state control (Chistenssen 2005: 182). TRT has been accused of being a mouthpiece for the government, it literally being a department within the government. Likewise, relations between the private media conglomerates and Turkish politics are very close. Though Turkish media conglomerates achieve low investment returns on their media interests, they "use the media to manipulate other economic or political interests" resulting in a "notorious interlocking of interests between the media, politicians and the businesses" (Özguneş and Terzis 2000: 414). The resulting mediascape is one of tight political and big business influence and control, even more so than in nations where governments are not as close to the media, like Britain and North America.

This relationship has taken on greater significance with AKP gaining more control over media than any of its predecessors (Jenkins 2012: 1). This can be seen as early as 2003 when the Uzan Group, which founded Turkey's first private broadcaster Star TV, "was seized by the Turkish state following the filing of criminal charges against most of the members of the Uzan family" (Christensen 2005: 187). This wrestling of control of the media by the government has continued, and has increased in pace over recent years. The Doğan Media Group (DMG) was the largest media group in Turkey before 2011. It was outspoken in its criticism of AKP. A quarrel between Erdoğan and the owner of the group, Aydın Doğan, resulted in Erdoğan publicly threatening Doğan for his critical and "unresponsible journalism." Erdoğan subsequently excluded Doğan from any government contracts and dispatched tax inspectors to DMG. The government found DMG guilty of "tax evasion" and imposed a fine reported to be between 3.7 and 4.9 billion Turkish lira (well over one billion pounds sterling). There were secret negotiations. The result was the DMG paid a small percentage of the fine, had to sell off some of its media assets, and has since turned a blind eye to AKP. The assets sold included *Milliyet* and *Vatan* newspapers, each sold to pro-AKP media interests. Kanal D Romanya and Star TV were both confiscated by the state and then sold to Erdoğan's friend Ferit Şahenk, who is the owner of the AKP-friendly Doğuş Media Group.

AKP continues to put pressure on existing media to become less critical while acquiring media outlets and initiating its own communication channels, resulting in a receding plurality of voices with most supporting AKP (Sümer and Yaşlı 2010: 17). Another example of this can be seen in the case of (now) pro-government *Sabah* newspaper. It was established in 1985. After a number of takeovers, it was sold in 2007 to Çalık Holding, whose chief executive officer is the son-in-law of Erdoğan. In 2013, *Sabah* was sold to Zirve Holding owned by the Kalyon Group ("Turkey clashes" 2013). Kalyon's founder, Hasan Kalyoncu, is a longtime personal friend of Erdoğan's and contributed to the establishment of AKP ("Hasan Kalyoncu Kimdir" 2008; Demirkaya 2013). This close relationship has benefited the Kalyon Group by winning numerous government contracts, including the metro line and the Taksim pedestrianization project which led to the Gezi Park protests of 2013.

News coverage of recent events reflects media ownership patterns which are skewed as noted above. This can be seen in coverage of the 2013 Gezi Park protests where close ties to the government have been blamed on the underreporting of the protests (Işik 2013). This biased reporting is represented in The Ringo Jets "Spring of War" (see Chapters 8 and 9). And since the protests, the government has tendered huge fines on television channels which opposed their views, such as Ulusal Kanal, Halk TV, Cem TV, and EM TV. According to Mehmet Özgenç from the government's media watchdog RTÜK, the fines were given because "These channels are encouraging the violence of the people" ("RTÜK'ten Halk TV" 2013).

Since 2014, Turkey's press has been deemed as "not free" ("Freedom of the Press" 2016). In 2016, Turkey was ranked 151st out of 180 countries in Reporters Without Borders' world press freedom index. These very low marks reflect an ongoing trend since AKP gained control of power. The number of jailed journalists is one of the highest for any country in the world. This is partly to do with Erdoğan's intolerance for insults. As of March 2016, more than seventy people, most of these journalists, have been prosecuted for "insulting" Erdoğan since his election to president in August 2014. A newspaper's (Cumhuriyet) editor in chief, Can Dündar, who described the process of arrests as a "kind of deterrence policy," was arrested and is now in exile for crossing swords with Erdoğan. In the run-up to the June 2015 elections, the World Association of Newspapers and News Publishers (WAN-IFRA) called on the Turkish government "to urgently recognize the importance of plural voices within the media and to provide the conditions for independent sources of information" ("WAN-IFRA calls" 2015). Furthermore, after the July 15, 2016, attempted coup and the state of emergency, many more journalists have been arrested and jailed and news institutions have been shut (Öğret 2016).

AKP's relations with the music industry

Throughout Turkey's history, musicians who oppose the government have been targeted by the authorities resulting in bans, jail terms, and exile. This continues under AKP and has accelerated since the 2016 coup attempt (see final chapter). To appreciate the conditions Turkish music is performed, recorded, produced, and listened to, here I outline AKP's relations to the industry.

Turkish music production is a multi-million-pound industry involving both major global record companies and independents. The majors dominate the market while independent music production is confined to local record labels and distribution. The dominance of the majors has been enhanced by the political and economic liberalization of the 1980s and 1990s, including broadcasting and the market in general which saw an increase in foreign investment. These government moves, similar to what was experienced globally, drove a wedge in the music market between the local and the global, between "down-market local cassette production and the glamourous, cosmopolitan world of Turkish pop and rock CDs" (Stokes 2003: 300). Stokes notes how Polygram, in collaboration with Turkey's RAK, was instrumental in this division and "signed up nearly every major pop and rock star for a global market by the mid-1990s" while less-known groups remained with more "national" labels (ibid.: 300). Though the technology has changed, there is still a distinction between music which is more local and that aimed at the global.

Many of the groups (though by no means not all musicians) examined in this book remain locally produced and distributed. Music which is guaranteed to get no airplay in Turkey is shunned by the majors. Moreover, musicians deemed to be subversive by the government face many obstacles and governmental controls at the levels of production, distribution, and performance with censorship (Bülent Ersoy, Dev), arrests (Grup Yorum, Fazıl Say), and exiles (Cem Karaca, Ahmet Kaya). Recently, modernist composer and pianist Fazıl Say has faced official censorship, charged and jailed in 2003 and again in 2013, and all members of Grup Yorum were jailed in the winter of 2017. At the production level, not only is subversive music for the most part confined to local record companies, government music policies have also had more direct detrimental effects. For example, the government has tried to eliminate modern musical institutions affecting modernist composers such as Kamran İnce and Aydın Esen negatively. In the meantime, musicians and genres positioned against modernism such as arabesk music performers Orhan Gencebay and Nihat Doğan who openly support AKP policies are granted their support (Way and Gedik 2013).

Live performances as well as recordings are also subjected to scrutiny and censorship by the government. Authorities can refuse to grant permission for concerts. When granted, concerts may be canceled at the last minute despite being organized and paid for by the band and its supporters, financially punishing musicians and fans. These actions are usually accompanied by band members being arrested for spreading "propaganda." I experienced this in 2016, when a Grup Yorum concert in Izmir was canceled at the last minute, inconveniencing fans while the group was arrested (see Chapter 6 for more details). Also Grup Yorum band member Seçkin Taygun Aydoğan was jailed recently for six years due to his involvement in a protest concert held in Istanbul.

Furthermore, for a recording to be officially released, it must first get a "bandrol." This is a sticker issued by the Turkish Ministry of Culture which indicates the product's manufacturer has paid the required tax. However, this branch of the government uses bandrol to censor music. Solomon (2005: 6) notes how the government tightly controls and refuses their issuance, "among the reasons for this censoring of recordings may be language objectionable to the government for its political content, such as song lyrics perceived to advocate violence, political views the government would rather not see expressed, such as advocating Kurdish cultural rights, or simply the presence of swear words."

Another obstacle facing subversive music is its lack of access to broadcasting. Though there are abundant broadcast outlets, these are tightly controlled by the government and big business, many closely associated and politically aligned to the government (see above). So, broadcasters shy away from music and content which may offend the government, self-censoring being widespread in Turkish media. When music and content are deemed to be other than what the government wants to hear, broadcasters are shut down. For example, in 2016, Yön Radio, a folk music radio station, was shut down by the government along with a host of Kurdish broadcast outlets. In the meanwhile, mainstream music television and radio channels play a key role in distributing government-friendly music. As Barış (2010) notes, "*Kral TV* and *Number One TV* are music channels which broadcast, rank and promote music-clips and in this way to a certain extent manipulate the music market in Turkey."

The role of the internet as alternative media in Turkey

With mainstream broadcast media and the music industry under tight direct and indirect control of the government, bands which express opposition to AKP are forced to look elsewhere to be heard. Almost all the music examined in this book is not heard on mainstream television or radio. However, it is widely available and, in some cases, enjoyed by millions through the internet. For example, a recording of the Grup Yorum concert I examine in Chapter 6 has had over 3.5 million hits. This is despite members of the group sitting in jail as I write. Here, I argue, is a case of music on the internet serving as an alternative media.

Alternative media come in many forms such as blogs, vlogs, fanzines, graffiti, student radio, and newspapers. Most definitions of alternative media include comparisons to mainstream media in terms of scale, participation, and commercial aspects (Dowmunt 2007: 1). Definitions also include the idea of radical, dissonant, subversive, oppositional, and/or progressive content (Atton 2002, 2004; Dowmunt 2007). Atton (2002: 14) offers a wider definition of alternative media which links it to social change, claiming definitions "begin with the presence of radical content, most often allied to the promotion of social change." His model also considers how media are organized within their sociocultural context including "media's capacity to generate non-standard, often infractory, methods of creation, production and distribution" (ibid.: 3–4). Defined as such, alternative media means more than the politically subversive, but also artistic and literary media such as video, music, zines, and hybrid forms of electronic communication. Atton (ibid.: 27) offers six criteria, three related to "products" (politically, socially, and/or culturally radical content, form, and reproductive innovations/adaptations) and three to "process" (alternative distribution, social relations, roles, and responsibilities and transformed communication processes). Media are not deemed "alternative" using these as a fixed set of criteria, but are considered as "hybrids," each artifact considered "alternative" based on a mix of the above. Downing, Ford, Gil, and Stein (2001, xi) agree, noting that alternative media's commonality "is that they break somebody's rules, although rarely all of them in every respect."

If we consider this more inclusive model of alternative media, then we can say songs and music videos on the internet in Turkey are alternative media. Though Turkish mainstream media shun subversive music, musicians can articulate alternatives to those offered in the mainstream in official and nonofficial music videos distributed on the internet. As such, these videos are an "alternative medium" in terms of both content and the use of alternative distribution (Atton 2004).

Despite most of these videos being consigned to the internet, AKP still puts a lot of effort into controlling the internet and social media. It has temporarily closed down Twitter and Facebook on numerous occasions and for various reasons. In the case of any crisis, these are the first casualties, such as immediately after terrorist attacks or scandals. Turkey has attracted international criticism when it temporarily banned access to Twitter and YouTube when information was leaked which linked Erdoğan to graft allegations against government officials. The government also controls social media through scare tactics. Following 2013's Gezi Park protests many users were detained because of their posts on social media in support of demonstrators. Furthermore, the government demanded the names of Twitter users who offended the government (Burch and Ozbilgin 2013) while people are constantly being arrested for insults aimed at Erdoğan posted on social media. Songs and music videos have also been targeted. Videos and related posts which are posted on YouTube and other social media sites which criticize the government are constantly being removed. I witnessed this on a number of occasions when collecting Gezi Park protest videos. Many no longer appear on the internet, one group (Dev) claiming it had to re-post them several times. Other videos are allowed, though comments about the videos are blocked. These observations call into question some scholars' ideas of the internet as a bastion of democracy (Von Hippel 2005; Jenkins 2006), or claims of social media's highly optimistic roles in social movements (Howard and Hussain 2011). In Turkey, it too suffers the wrath of government actions. All the same, social media in Turkey is far less controlled than other media, offering an outlet for more political music. In this sense, it can be considered an alternative to mainstream media and offers an alternative space for subversive voices to be expressed and listened to. And it is songs and videos which represent opposition to AKP and its policies outlined in this chapter and affected by AKP media policies and relations that are distributed via the internet which make up the bulk of music analyzed in this book.

5

Political Parties and Pop

Election campaigns in Turkey are colorful affairs where flags and banners of political parties hang everywhere and anywhere vying for voters' attention (see Figure 5.1). Vans and buses painted in the colors associated with each party drive through crowded urban streets blasting out their political messages with the accompaniment of music. When I first experienced this in the run-up to the general election in 2007, I was amazed at just how different election campaigns were to those I had experienced back in the United Kingdom. In the next general election of 2011, I was more discerning and I noticed differences in political parties' choices of music. On the streets, I heard Islamic rap, rock-inspired music, and a variety of songs with roots in more Turkish traditional sounds.

Figure 5.1 A typical pre-election street scene

It is not just in the streets where you can hear music used by political parties in Turkish election campaigns. The two main political parties also produce musical political advertisements which are played on mainstream television, before and after live rallies and found on the internet. It is here again I noticed choices were being made in sounds and visuals. And it is here, through a close reading of these musical advertisements, where we can see what political discourses are being articulated and how this is being done. What follows next is a brief explanation of the importance of the 2011 general elections before I analyze these musical offerings.

2011 Election campaign in context

National parliamentary elections in 2011 were critical in terms of the Justice and Freedom Party's (AKP) power projectory. Since 2002, it had increased its share of the popular vote, and was to do so again in 2011. This is a first in Turkish multiparty politics. The economy was improving for many Turks so it "put its economic record at the centre of its campaign" promising new construction projects like canals, airports, hospitals, and even a new city ("Turkey ruling" 2011). The campaign also took on a more nationalistic feel. Letsch (2011) observes that "During the election campaign Erdoğan adopted a harsher and more nationalistic tone which, critics say, has alienated many Kurds." Despite confidence going into the election, AKP had everything to fight for. AKP's elite pinned high hopes on winning a large majority in order to change the constitution. Due to AKP party bylaws which state that a person can run for parliament for only three consecutive terms, well-known members of the party including then Prime Minister Recep Tayyip Erdoğan would not be eligible for nomination in the following 2015 general election. And partially because of this bylaw, AKP wanted to bring in constitutional change which would see Turkey's parliamentary system transformed into a presidential one. If AKP could win 330 seats or more in the election, it would be able to change the constitution, placing Erdoğan as president in a presidential system, a possibility the opposition parties were united against (Esen and Ciddi 2011).

The official opposition, The Republican People's Party (CHP), also had a lot to play for. The election was the first to be contested by the CHP's new leader Kemal Kılıçdaroğlu, who replaced Deniz Baykal in 2010. Kılıçdaroğlu, the party's popular mayoral candidate for Istanbul in the 2009 local elections, was elected as the new chairman of the party by an almost unanimous vote (Esen and Ciddi 2011). He wanted a shift in both membership of the party's elite and focus to revitalize its chances at the polls. Upon assuming office, Kılıçdaroğlu shuffled the Central Executive Council replacing the old guard with younger and more progressive members and tried to "portray a more reformist image against the AKP government" (ibid.). To do this, Kılıçdaroğlu's CHP moved "from the party's rigid secularist positions" and "formulated a populist platform, largely aimed to incorporate the socioeconomic groups excluded from the AKP's neo-liberal agenda (farmers, unemployed workers, retirees, and state employees)" (ibid.). It campaigned for lower petrol prices for farmers, more jobs, higher retirement wages, a reduction of subcontracted labor, and a minimal family wage benefit.

The results of the June 12 election were as expected. AKP won a majority, though slightly smaller than in 2007. It won 49.9 percent of the popular vote, giving it 327 seats in the 550-seat parliament. The result fell short of giving AKP the power to submit proposed constitutional amendments to a national referendum and well short (forty-one seats) of the two-thirds majority needed to rewrite Turkey's 1982 military constitution without having to consult parliament. The bottom line was it could not put amendments to the public without consulting the opposition, all of which were united against a change to a presidential system. CHP came second with 25.9 percent of the popular vote, gaining 135 seats in parliament. The Nationalist Movement party (MHP) took 13 percent and fifty-three seats while the pro-Kurdish Peace and Democracy Party (BDP) took 5.8 percent of the vote winning thirty-six seats (though they had to stand as independent candidates due to Turkey's 10 percent minimum rule for parties to be recognized as such in parliament—see previous chapter).

The two musical advertisements

The AKP musical advertisement has received over one million hits on YouTube over two separate links, while the CHP song received 275,000 hits. In this chapter, I examine how the two main parties—the ruling AKP and main opposition CHP—used these musical commodities to target their voters while excluding those who do not fit their target voters' profile. I look at how places, social actors, and actions are represented in lyrics and visuals and how musical sounds contribute to these representations. I argue that despite the parties and these musical advertisements being presented as speaking to and for all Turks, on closer examination we see how they are divisive tools in Turkey's already polarized society.

AKP's "Biz hepimiz Türkiyeyiz/we are all Turkey"

This is AKP's campaign song and video prepared for Turkey's 2011 parliamentary elections.[1] Reflecting AKP's dominant ideologies of the time, the video articulates discourses of unity among potential AKP voters who are religiously and socially conservative alongside positive connotations of the AKP government. In the lyrics, metaphors play a role connoting a common dark past while unity is evoked, though within the confines of socially conservative and religious discourses. In the visuals, people who were socially excluded and discriminated against in the past and now make up a large part of AKP's voter base are represented positively alongside traditional Turkish symbols and musical instruments suggesting social conservatism, prosperity, and the importance of religion. Music plays the role of supporting the discourses articulated in the visuals and lyrics. I now look in much greater detail how the modes of lyrics, visuals and sounds in these two advertisements articulate discourses which benefit the political parties but do little to promote unity in a divided Turkey.

Lyrics to AKP's musical advertisement

Lyrics play a key role in this video. Here are the first few lines:[2]

1. We passed the same path
2. We drank the same water
3. Our summer is one, our winter is one
4. We are the wind of the same mountain

"We" are united

Unity is a dominant discourse drawn upon in almost every line of the song. This is achieved through a variety of strategies, such as the use of pronouns. Fairclough (2003: 149) identifies pronouns which promote "us" and "them" divisions and construct groups and communities, such as, "we," "our," "they," and "theirs." But the groups and communities constructed using these pronouns in political discourse are vague, referring to various combinations of party, nation, government, and residents, used to serve politicians' purposes (Fairclough 1989: 148; Billig 1995: 106). In AKP's lyrics, "we," "us," and "our" are used extensively, as in "we suffered" and "let's remain together." Using "we," "our," and "us" makes the song accessible to many, a common strategy in popular music used to keep songs "highly accessible to all" (Machin 2010: 87). For example, referring to the use of "we" in Public Enemy's "Fight the power," Machin (ibid.) observes that "this use of collective pronouns serves to point out that this is not just his voice, but that he speaks for many." Using "we" connotes a vocalist is speaking for many and also to the many, as with Bob Marley who uses "we" extensively throughout his work "to address a range of listeners" (ibid.). So, "we" in AKP's lyrics signifies the vocalist is a singer for the many, a united "people," as well as suggesting the song is addressing a range of listeners (voters), being accessible to all who are interested. This message is emphasized by "we" appearing eleven times in the lyrics, alongside "us" a further three times. This is a clear case of overlexicalization, where a lexical item appears more than would normally be expected in a text used to emphasize, in this case the discourse of unity (Kress 1985).

The use of pronouns are instrumental here in connoting unity, emphasized by their sheer number of utterances. Other lexical choices and how actions are represented further emphasize unity. There is an abundance of word choices such as "the same" as in "We passed the same path," "together" as in "We sing together," and "one" as in "Our summer is one" all suggesting unity. Furthermore, the idea of doing things together is represented. For example, "we passed the same path," "we drank the same water" (repeated twice), and "We sing together." Though these actions are vague and metaphorical for the most part, they suggest unity in action.

In fact, the use of metaphors is a powerful tool used to represent aspects of the world in certain ways (Lakoff and Johnson 1980). Flowerdew and Leong (2007: 275) note that metaphor "is not only a matter of language usage or poetic license, but a functional mechanism which affects the way we think, act and experience reality." They can have specifically political roles, strengthening, reproducing, or subverting relations of power.

Mottier (2008: 184) notes how "metaphors classify and order reality, social and political classifications and ordering . . . [they are] the vehicle through which power operates." In the first two examples above, metaphors are used to connote unity, a politically motivated representation in the context of this video. Like most music, particulars are absent and abstraction prevails (Machin 2010). There is no detail as to who "we" are, what path we have passed, and what water we have drunk. However, actions and metaphors like this alongside lexica like "together" emphasize the idea of unity.

Up to now, we have seen how the use of pronouns, word choices and representations of actions all suggest unity. But the unity it is suggesting is selective. This is seen in its representation of a common past of suffering. Representing common suffering is a well-known strategy to bring different people together, more so than common happiness (Renan 1992). AKP consistently refers to a secular past more broadly in its political discourse, a past it represents as one where "the people," including religious people, were discriminated against by Turkey's elite (Way 2017). This discourse is part of AKP's success in creating a wide coalition of support within Turkey, including several classes of society who have felt a sense of being socially excluded and discriminated against by the secular elites of the past (Özbudun and Hale 2010: 78). In lines like "Same path we passed," a common history is connoted, a history of hard times suggested by the idea of having to pass paths as opposed to sing and dance which is represented in the present. "Our summer is one, our winter is one" also metaphorically draws upon a discourse of longevity of unity, but also hardship. On the one hand, "our summer" connotes togetherness through the pronoun "our" but also pleasant times suggested by "summer." On the other hand, "our winter" suggests the opposite, togetherness during the cold, difficult hard times.

These lines vaguely refer to the plight of religious people in Turkey's secular past. When Mustafa Kemal Atatürk founded the Republic and governments which followed, they, with the backing of the military, discriminated against religious critics who challenged Turkey's secular stance. This was done to ensure the secular nature of the Republic at the expense of the rights of those with strong religious affiliations. Discrimination took on both symbolic and legal forms. For example, women were forbidden to wear the headscarf at state universities and state-run institutions such as hospitals. Since AKP came to power, many of these laws have changed, resulting in a change of fortune for the religiously pious who display their religious affiliations.

Though there are representations of a dark past, a present and future full of hope is also represented in lines such as "Songs are the same, ballads are the same, we sing it together." Here, unity again is suggested in lexical choices such as "we," "same" and "together." But unlike the past when we passed paths in the winter, now we sing "songs" and "ballads" connoting a time of celebration, having fun and/or expressing feelings. Positivity replaces the negative past as "we" sing, dance and celebrate in the success of AKP's Turkey.

Though "we" are united, Turkey is divided

Up to now in the analysis, I have analyzed the lyrics and found various strategies used to communicate unity. If the unity being suggested was all inclusive, then we might say that the musical advertisement is a positive thing, bringing a polarized society together by promoting unity amongst a very heterogenous society. Many would say, this is something a polarized society like Turkey needs. However, I want to examine the lyrics from a more critical perspective. In doing so, we can see that the unity being suggested is not unity for all in Turkey. In fact, it is a very selective unity, a unity of people likely to vote for AKP. By including those likely to vote for AKP, the lyrics exclude those not likely to vote for them, perpetuating the idea of a polarized society.

An exclusive unity is connoted in a number of ways, including how place is represented. Representations of place are powerful, affecting our understanding of places, reinforcing myths, and providing listeners with a sense of identity (Forman 2002). In the lyrics here, the Turkey mapped out is far from inclusive. It is a case of an "invented geography," echoing Connell and Gibson's (2003: 39) observation about (Western) folk music's preoccupation with rural areas. Here, rural settings are suggested through lexica like "paths," "wind," "mountains," "private gardens," "our land," and "roses." These lexical choices reference a large part of AKP's voting population who are conservative rural dwellers and internal migrants from the rural east. Turkey has seen mass migration from rural to urban centers over the past eighty years which peaked in the 1980s, though the migration continues steadily with many settling in the large cities and especially Istanbul ("UNICEF in Turkey" 2010). It is many of these rural dwellers and migrants who tend to be religiously and socially conservative, who were subjected to discrimination in the past, and make up a key demographic of AKP voters.

It is also cultural references which further map out not only parts of Turkey, but also its religious and traditional past. This can be seen in the line "Halays are one, Horons are one." Halay and Horon are traditional Anatolian folk dances. Though the Halay is performed throughout the country, the Horon comes from the Black Sea coastal region, an area renowned for its conservatism. Both are performed at special occasions such as weddings, suggesting celebrations and positivity. They are traditional folk dances, one from a very conservative part of the country, both drawing upon discourses not of modernity and the West, but of a traditional past steeped in religious and social conservatism.

Finally, and possibly most importantly, religion is represented as part of a discourse of unity. This draws upon AKP discourses which see Sunni Islam as the "glue" which binds Turkey's population as one. On December 11, 2005, Erdoğan claimed, "Religion is cement and it is our most important unitary element. It has been like that through our history" ("Başbakan Erdoğan" 2015). But Erdoğan is not referring to all religions here. This is indicated by Erdoğan's well-publicized religious piety based on his interpretation of Sunni Islam and making such statements at political rallies while grasping a Koran and not other religious texts. AKP has used this strategy to attract not only religious Turks, but also Turkey's large religiously conservative Kurdish population.

In the song, the lines "Hearts are the same, prayers are the same" and "We are one of god's creatures" not only draw upon religious lexica such as "prayers" and "god," but also exclude by presupposing that people in Turkey conduct religion in the same manner. Presuppositions are "a taken-for-granted, implicit claim embedded within the explicit meaning of a text or utterance" (Richardson 2007: 63). These are powerful ideological tools which enforce ideologies without questioning them (Fairclough 1995: 14; Richardson 2007: 187). Though approximately 90 percent of Turkey's population consider themselves Muslim, not all consider themselves to be actively religious. Many are secularists who have varying degrees of commitment to religion. Furthermore, there are other religions and factions of Islam in Turkey such as Alevis, Shias, Sufis, Christians, and Jews to name but a few. To refer to the same prayers and God excludes all those who do not value Sunni Islam as AKP does. It is lines like these which exclude as much as include and shape not only the song's exclusiveness, but add to the polarization already seen in Turkish society in general.

Visuals in AKP's musical advertisement

The visuals in the musical advertisement also articulate a discourse of unity. This is evident by the large cross section of people represented. However, there are also many groups excluded. Furthermore, actions which are represented visually articulate discourses of social and religious conservatism, excluding many from AKP's Turkey. There is also a discourse of the power of Erdoğan. Singing, dancing, and being happy can be seen throughout the video, with almost all shots depicting Turks from many walks of life acting in unison. This is all done under the protective eye of Erdoğan, evident by his appearance at the end of the video. A closer look at the strategies used in the visuals makes these discourses more evident.

"We" are united in happiness and religion

Like the lyrics, visuals articulate a discourse of unity. The unity may be read as even more inclusive than the lyrics. There is a fairly even mix of males and females from all ages within the voting population of Turkey. There are also people represented from a variety of backgrounds such as Turks, Kurds, Alevis, and a variety of orientations such as socially conservative, religiously conservative, and people who are represented as less so. Throughout the video, clothes associated with various folk traditions can be seen such as an Aegean traditional hat, Sufi dancers' clothes, pink head covering and scarves, both linked to Turkey's southeast where many conservative Kurds live. Folk costumes not only identify visually various groups within Turkey who the "we" are in AKP's Turkey, but also draw upon a shared history back to the time of the Ottomans, connoting a historical legitimacy of AKP. Socially conservative clothes are worn, such as women wearing baggy clothes and a headscarf, and men with short hair wearing a shirt and sometimes a tie and/or jacket.

Equally telling is who is not represented. As van Leeuwen (1996) notes, exclusions are an important part of discourses. Here we do not see men wearing casual clothes or sports clothes. Likewise there is an exclusion of women wearing short skirts or revealing outfits. In the context of AKP's social conservatism, these exclusions reveal who are excluded from AKP's Turkey.

Figure 5.2 is a montage of Turkish people who are included in AKP's Turkey. This is a group shot which has the meaning potential of de-emphasizing the individual and emphasizing the importance of a team or group (Machin 2007: 118–119). In this case, it is both the group and individuals who are emphasized. Togetherness is connoted by common actions. Here, everyone is represented singing, playing, or dancing together to the music. Commonality is further signified through color. Van Leeuwen (2005: 12) notes that images can "rhyme" through sharing a same color which can signal that they "have some quality in common. What the quality is depends on the color and its significance in the context." In Figure 5.2 we can see that all images have the same background color of an opaque yellow. This yellow is a color in Turkey associated with AKP. In fact, the yellow animated lines which separate people in the image is AKP's yellow used in their lightbulb logo. Here the yellow lines act as a metaphorical glue which binds people together, reminiscent of AKP's discourse on the role of religion. All the same, the lines also represent separation (van Leeuwen 2005: 13). So, in one "box" we have a Sufi dancer, in another box there is a religiously conservative woman, in another a middle-aged man. Each person acts as a metonym for a different section of the Turkish population, this way spreading its appeal across sections of Turkish society. Taken as a whole, the image suggests it is these groups within Turkey who make up a united Turkey.

Most of the images in the video are individual shots, making it easier for viewers to have a point of identification with the subjects by humanizing and sympathizing with them (van Leeuwen 1996). Figure 5.3 is one such example. Here a woman is dressed in religiously conservative non-revealing clothes and a headscarf. This image represents a segment of AKP's core voters. In fact, religious conservativism is connoted in many of the other images. For example, while the vocalist sings "We are one of God's creatures" the visuals reveal a traditionally dressed woman moving her right hand to her chest and softly stooping. This is a traditional Turkish move of salutation with religious

Figure 5.2 AKP's Turkey

Figure 5.3 Conservative unity

connotations by putting one's right hand to one's chest. It is these details in the visuals which exclude while unity is suggested.

All the same, discourses of unity and happiness are dominant. How subjects are represented plays a role in this. In Figure 5.3, the woman is in a "demand image." She directly addresses viewers creating symbolic interaction and suggesting power (Kress and van Leeuwen 2001: 127–128). This positive positioning of viewer to subject is seen throughout the video, adding to the feel-good factor of the video and AKP. Positivity is further connoted with her smile. A smile takes on a variety of meanings depending on context and in some cases "there may be a kind of smile that invites us in or allows us to share the joy of a moment" (Machin 2007: 111). Here, her smile indicates she wants us to share in the joy of being a part of AKP's Turkey. Furthermore, the vertical angle of interaction between the camera and the subject is at eye level, signifying equality between viewer and subject (ibid.: 114). As an equal, she is inviting us to join her and AKP.

The woman is swinging her hand with her palms up. This is a common gesture in Turkey used for emphasis while talking. Here the woman and the following few shots show a cross section of people doing this motion while singing, "We are the roses of the same garden. Let's do it again, again, again." The hand movement adds emphasis to both a united AKP discourse and a continuation of AKP in power. The discourse of unity is further emphasized through the use of written text in the image. Superimposed text reads, "We are the roses of the same garden." In fact, throughout the video, superimposed text on the visuals repeatedly displays the words "same" and "we" (aynı biz), "all together" (Hep beraber), and "one" (bir) all reinforcing the idea of unity.

A conservative Turkey

Social conservatism is represented in a number of ways visually. One such way is by excluding various groups, as noted earlier. It is also connoted symbolically through the visual representation of musical instruments. There are two people who play a nylon string classic guitar. Though this is a Western instrument, it has been adopted by a vast array of Turkish musicians, including folk singers and musicians who play traditional music. As such, the guitar suggests the past and tradition, unlike an electric guitar would with connotations of rock and possible subversion (Way 2012). However, traditional Turkish instruments related to Turkey's past are represented far more often. The oud and zither—popular instruments in Ottoman society—are seen. The shrill pipe, folk drums, and bağlama are also traditional Turkish instruments which are still popular in the Anatolian region. Using these instruments in the visuals, instead of Western and modern instruments, draws on a romanticized past of Turkey's pre-Republic times, a time when Turkey looked East, not West, something notable in AKP discourses. These instruments can also be seen as antagonistic toward the Kemalist modernization project. When Kemalists were establishing the Republic after the collapse of the Ottoman Empire, much traditional music was banned and the folk tradition was tightly controlled and even made up (Gedik 2010). By representing instruments associated with banned music from the past, AKP suggests opposition to Kemalism and policies such as these.

Another way social conservatism is articulated is through gender roles. Many of the shots include male and female couples, reinforcing conservative social norms. In Figure 5.4, the man and woman are middle aged. Though the woman is not covered, her hair is drawn back in a conservative style while baggy clothes suggest modesty. Likewise, the man wears a plain white-colored T-shirt with short smart hair. Though not obviously religious, the small details suggest conservatism. They first sing to each other for a few seconds before, in unison, they sing to the camera. These choices naturalize the idea that a happy, singing, united, heterosexual couple praise AKP together. In other shots, men are seen in the background clapping along to women moving their hands and singing in the foreground. Their actions of singing and moving together connote unity. They also have the meaning potential of men encouraging "their women" to support AKP. Considering AKP's stance on women, it is hardly surprising men would be represented in this "knowing" and encouraging role.

All under the watchful, approving eye of Erdoğan

The final two shots of the clip make clear that it is AKP under the guidance of a strong confident Erdoğan which unites all these people. The last shot shows AKP's symbol of a lightbulb with "AKP" written below it. This is preceded by a close-up of Erdoğan with the written text of "Together we are Turkey" (Figure 5.5). The written text again draws on an exclusive unity, the "we" representing the approximately 40–50 percent of Turkey's voters who give their support to AKP. In this image, Erdoğan's dress suggests he is one of "the people." He wears clothes like his people, a white shirt and no tie. Facial

Figure 5.4 Gender

hair and haircut again are similar to the men depicted in the video. The background of the image is the same color, again connoting commonality. As such, the image suggests unity with his people, a discourse of "the same path" associated with AKP.

Yet he is different. He does not sing and dance and smile at the camera, like his people. Instead he looks on with approval, empowered by his lack of action. Here

Figure 5.5 Powerful Erdoğan

the camera looks up to Erdoğan, suggesting power (Machin 2007). Abousnnouga and Machin (2010: 144) examine war monuments and find that most of the subjects do not symbolically demand anything of their viewers, but look off to the horizon. This has the meaning potential "of wanting the public to see the soldiers [in the monuments] as part of a different world, one of the glory of God . . . metaphorically [looking] to the future and high ideals." Here Erdoğan gazes in a similar manner, looking thoughtful, full of high ideals and looking into the future. He looks up, almost as though in prayer. Facial expressions make clear he is proud of his "flock" who have been singing and dancing in honor of his party. It is he and AKP which are responsible for unity in Turkey.

Musical sounds which emphasize

Though musical sounds in isolation carry a range of meaning potentials, visuals and lyrics focus meanings. In this video, musical sounds also articulate a discourse of unity and positivity around AKP, but also suggest social and religious conservatism. The song is a popularized genre of traditional Turkish art music called Fantazi (Fantasy) music, steeped in tradition and conservatism. This genre dates back from at least the earliest years of Turkey's Ottoman past, a time of religious and social conservative values. Stokes (2010: 15) notes that for most Turks in the 1980s, "identifying with art music often involved a conservative political orientation, hospitable to the recuperations of the Ottoman past and Islam in public life that were being promoted by the dominant conservative parties." Today, links between forms of art music and these traditions continue. AKP choosing this genre for their campaign song suggests ties and importance to conservative politics and Islam.

An emphasis on unity

Like the visuals and lyrics, unity is a dominant discourse notable in the sounds. For instance, vocal and instrumental arrangement plays a role. Singing and playing the same notes at the same time suggests social unison by emphasizing collective experiences and a sense of belonging to a community while de-emphasizing individuality (van Leeuwen 1999: 79). The song's vocal arrangement starts with a single female voice. With each line, more and more people join her, all singing the same notes. Instrumentation is increased as the song goes on, again each instrument playing the same notes as the vocals. The visuals parallel the sound with people visually joining the singing and playing as the song progresses. Here a community of people is represented in sound, singing, and playing as one, united in their support for AKP.

Emphasizing positivity around AKP

The introduction also suggests positivity and confidence. The woman's vocal style is key to this. Her voice which starts the song and is salient throughout the song is smooth, loud, and open-throated. Smooth sound is valued and related to a sense of an ideal, connoting positivity (van Leeuwen 1999: 132). Her loudness resembles a "call" to join her, while her open-throated style suggests confidence and a lack of tension and constraint (van Leeuwen 1999: 130). Vocal pitch also plays a role in not only positivity, but tenderness. The vocals at the beginning are high pitched with little pitch movement (see Figure 5.7). Van Leeuwen (1999) observes that small melodic movements at a high pitch give a sense of "tenderness." As noted in the lyrical analysis, common sufferings from the past are represented. Tenderness in the melody connotes sympathy for the represented plight of voters in the past as well as sympathy toward AKP governance.

Positivity surrounds conservatism

Instrumentation suggests not only unity as described above, but also a conservative tradition. Instruments heard are those found in traditional Turkish art music. This has a history back to the traditional Anatolian and Ottoman times. These were religiously and socially conservative times, with laws enforced by pious Sultans. The tambour with strings, oud, folk drum, tambourine, and reed flute are all instruments from this time and can be heard in the music. The meaning of the song would be very different if a distorted electric guitar was used or samples and a techno beat. By choosing these instruments, the video references tradition and conservative values, appealing to those who share such values and excluding those who do not.

Melodic choices play an important role in articulating discourses. But before I examine these in depth, I want to explain how melodic progressions and pitch are represented in this book. Western music notation is based on an eight-note scale, note one (and eight) being the name of the scale, or root note. Music in scholarly work tends to be represented by musical notation such as in Figure 5.6. Throughout this book, I have chosen to not represent music in this way, but to use a simple graph where the vertical axis represents notes on the scale (one and eight being the root note) and time represented along the horizontal axis. Representing melodies as such, I believe, is an easy way to "see" a melody, whether the reader is someone who can read music in traditional music notation or someone who cannot.

Figures 5.7 and 5.8 represent the verses' two melodic lines respectively, functioning to signify positivity toward AKP. One and eight represent the root note of B. Machin (2010: 107) observes that the first and fifth are notes which "anchor the melody to the scale" and "allow the music to feel 'easy' or 'rounded'." The first line of the song starts on the fifth (F#) and then moves up to the high first (represented as eight on the above chart). It makes small moves between the sixth and seventh and then finishes back on the fifth. This melody relies heavily on the first and fifth. With lyrics and visuals which connote unity and praise for AKP, melody makes these ideas

Figure 5.6 Musical notation

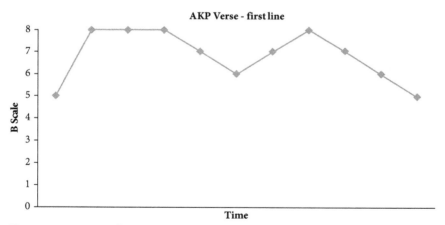

Figure 5.7 AKP verse line one

feel natural and easy to take in. In the second line of the verse (Figure 5.8), we see a change in melodic direction. Here the line starts on the seventh, a note associated with "thoughtfulness and longing" (Machin 2010: 219). Notes then descend gradually one note at a time. Van Leeuwen (1999) notes a descending melody has the meaning potential of sadness, thoughtfulness, inward looking. Here with lyrics of

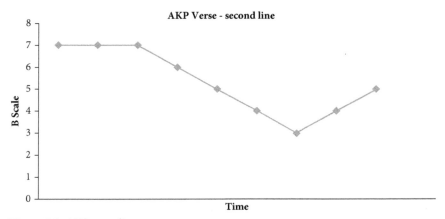

Figure 5.8 AKP verse line two

"same mountain," "same God," "our summer is one," and "roses of the same garden," thoughtfulness toward unity in the past and present is suggested in melodic choices. The two note upward melodic change at the end of the line offers hope and energy suggesting though there have been problems in the past, there is hope now and in the future (van Leeuwen 1999).

But it's not all a party

In the two choruses, the pitch drops and there is a lower male voice dominant in the hierarchy of sound (see Figure 5.9). The direction of the melody is also one which descends, again adding a sense of a dark past and seriousness to the song. So, although the verses are high pitched and offer hope, the choruses are there for listeners to reflect on the seriousness of the past and the seriousness of AKP's present. This combination adds a sense of gravity and seriousness to the song. The second note is related with promise of something to follow, where the seventh suggests a sense of missing something or being nostalgic (Machin 2010). The dominance of these notes harks back to a pious past but also to a promise of good things to come. The offer of hope is further suggested in the upward movement of the melody at the end of each phrase.

In the finale of the song, again not only melody but also rhythm plays a large role in suggesting the importance of voting for AKP. It is here in the lyrics where people are urged to vote for AKP "again, again, again" while participants in the visuals wave their hands for emphasis. It is also here where we see pauses in the music. Unlike the song up to this point which has flowed smoothly, here rhythm is broken with gaps between each line of lyrics and music. These add emphasis to the lyrics which are telling people to give their votes to AKP "again." This is a relatively energetic attack on the melodic phrase while AKP supporters vigorously wave their hands. Though pitch variation for the most part is minimal with every second line ascending in pitch, it is the disruptive

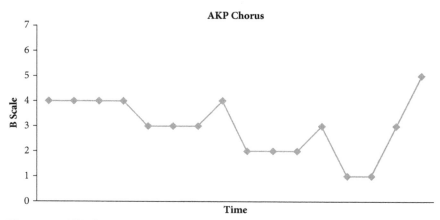

Figure 5.9 AKP chorus

nature of the melody here which draws listeners' attention. The melody moves from the third to the fourth, creating a sense of building (Machin 2010: 109), accompanying the line "sing it together." With the combination of the words, melody and rhythm, joy of coming together under AKP is connoted.

CHP's "Geliyor KILIÇDAROĞLU!/Kılıçdaroğlu is coming"

We now turn our attention to the main opposition, the People's Republic Party's (CHP), campaign video.[3] This was composed by the well-known musician Onur Akın. It was originally composed for the 2009 local elections when Kemal Kılıçdaroğlu ran for mayor of Istanbul. It was then revised for his 2011 national election campaign for prime minister. The two versions are slightly different from each other, with the original lyrics referring to Istanbul changed to Turkey such as in the line "My Istanbul you embrace him too" to "My Turkey you embrace him too." Pitch has also changed, with the new version being slightly higher. Here we look at the video from 2011 to reveal how the lyrics, visuals, and sounds articulate positive discourses about Kılıçdaroğlu, unity, and negative discourses about AKP and a society in danger.

Lyrics for CHP's musical advertisement

Here are the first few lines of lyrics of the song: [4]

1. Swords are drawn, this is a duel
2. Short stick and long stick will get it right
3. There will be sun after the darkness
4. Swordman Kılıçdaroğlu is coming

The lyrics tell a story of Turkey's people suffering due to unnamed forces and Kılıçdaroğlu as a hero who will save them. This story structure creates a set of binary opposites, a strategy seen in film where a basic structure shapes concerns and a lack of comprehension about social changes into simple oppositions, where individuals or groups represent each side (Wright 1975). This is a strategy which can represent wider issues and anxieties present in society at particular times. In these lyrics, this structure is actualized in the form of an unnamed elite who are opposed to Kılıçdaroğlu and the people. As such, this draws upon a discourse of populism, dividing Turkish society between those who support and oppose the present government (Laclau 2005). A close examination of the representation of social actors and their actions reveals how these discourses are articulated.

Kılıçdaroğlu is a hero

The most dominant social actor represented in terms of numbers and power is Kılıçdaroğlu. He is the only social actor named individually and named positively. In Turkish, Kılıçdaroğlu means "Son of the swordsman" and "Kılıçdar" means "swordsman." It is not only the numerous formal namings of "Kılıçdaroğlu," but also the honorific "swordsman" in "swordsman Kılıçdaroglu" which connotes hero-like authority. In fact, "swordsman Kılıçdaroglu" is repeated eleven times, being an overlexicalization used to emphasize his name and his hero-like qualities (Kress 1989). He is also named as a "Clean and honest person" ten times in the song, another overlexicalization. Ten times, he is represented as active in "Kılıçdaroğlu is coming." Though these represent no agency, in the context of the song, they suggest he is coming to rescue Turkey. Furthermore, a high level of certainty and a low level of modality is suggested in his "coming" by using the present continuous, connoting confidence and power in Kılıçdaroğlu's actions (van Leeuwen 1995).

Kılıçdaroğlu is also represented as powerful, though indirectly. Consider the first three lines of the song above. Here there is no agency represented. However, power is suggested in the actions of drawing swords, getting it right and bringing sun after darkness. Following these three lines of the verse, the chorus tells us "Kılıçdaroğlu is coming," suggesting it is he who is responsible for these powerful and positive actions. Though, like most lyrics in pop, details and context are withheld rendering these pronouncements obscure, it is nevertheless a discourse of power and positivity surrounding Kılıçdaroğlu which lines such as these articulate.

"The people," Kılıçdaroğlu, and populism

The only other social actor named in the lyrics is "the public." It is named once as "my Turkey" in "Swordman Kılıçdaroğlu asks, My Turkey you embrace him too." This representation works to represent Kılıçdaroğlu and the public together, in an "embrace." The word "too" presupposes he has already been embraced by some segments of the public, such as Istanbul and the CHP party where he was popular. By using the possessive "my" before Turkey, it is suggested that Kılıçdaroğlu has embraced Turkey as his own, connoting closeness and belonging.

Elsewhere, representations of the public draw upon populism, here meaning "the people" pitted against "an elite" other (Laclau 2005; De Cleen and Carpentier 2010). Consider this verse:

1. If they are robbed of their riches and drowned
2. Our public will speak again
3. Not one, ten, but millions

In these lines, a "people" are constructed through namings and numbers. First the people are named as "they," "our public," "millions," and elsewhere as "the public." These namings suggest a mass of people, not just a few. "They" are victimized in the first line, conditionally "robbed" and "drowned." Robbed of what and by who is not specified. Elsewhere, thievery is suggested in "Robbers are fed, not the public." Again victimization is represented, the people not being fed or benefitting, this being the reserve of "robbers." However, the conditional first two lines pit "our public" against the unnamed elite. The public are active "speak[ing] again." And it is a large public in the "millions" who are speaking. Though again, there is no context of what the people say. In the context of the song, this may be construed as voting against "robbers," those who "rob" and "drown." Elsewhere, the people are again constructed as powerful and against the elite in "Let's enlighten the darkness." Though who we are in let "us" and how we will enlighten the darkness are metaphorical and abstract. All the same, representations like these set up a populist discourse, one which divides the public between elites and their benefactors and non-elites and those who do not benefit from them.

Representations of the elite working against the interest of "the people" are another essential part of populism. Though never named, in the context of the song, we can assume the elite are the AKP government responsible for the political conditions at the time. This exclusion de-emphasizes the government and makes it easy to reduce sympathy toward it (van Leeuwen 1996). As seen above, passive sentence constructions and abstractions are used such as "robbers are fed." With no agency, context, passivations, and circumstances are all unclear, characteristic of abstractions used to delegitimize the government (van Leeuwen 1995: 99). Representations like these create a sense of injustice by those who feed robbers, without providing evidence of such crimes. Elsewhere, a negative present is represented in lines like "There will be sun after the darkness" and "The end of lies and theft is seen"; sandwiched between these lines is the chorus of "Kılıçdaroğlu is coming, Clean and honest person." These lines presuppose there are lies, theft, and darkness. As such, a despotic AKP is constructed pitted against the people. These representations work to not only suggest Kılıçdaroğlu is the answer to the people's problems; they also work to divide Turkey by representing AKP negatively.

Visuals in CHP's musical advertisement

Unlike AKP's fast-edited and professional-looking promotional video which used actors and computer animation, CHP's visuals consist of found materials, including TV coverage, taken from campaign rallies, meetings, and protests. As such, the visuals lack the slick professionalism of the other, though they suggest authenticity, further connoted through the use of television channels and news agencies' logos superimposed on images. The visuals articulate a discourse that CHP is important, the people are unhappy, and Kılıçdaroğlu is a popular, active, legitimate CHP politician who listens. In terms of salience and the sheer number of visuals, the CHP party is dominant, even more so than Kılıçdaroğlu. Unlike in the lyrics, he is not represented as a hero, but as a legitimate, active politician. His legitimacy comes from his actions and also peoples' responses to him. People are angry and protest and it is Kılıçdaroğlu who listens and gets their cheers. Together, these representations articulate discourses about CHP strength, Kılıçdaroğlu's legitimacy, and "the people's" anger. A closer look at how social actors, including the CHP party, are represented makes this clear.

The importance of CHP

Probably the most dominant discourse in the visuals is the strength and importance of CHP. This discourse is articulated through salience and visual overlexicalization. Like the AKP video, CHP uses colors associated with their party and their logo throughout the video. In fact, their logo and parts of it appear in a large number of the visuals. The party is represented as dynamic, suggested by the logo and parts of it not displayed as static, but moving with the music. Color also plays a role. The original colors of the party are red and white. However, in the video, colors are highly saturated, more so than CHP's standard logo. Rich, saturated colors have the meaning potential of emotional intensity, boldness, directness, and engagement which draw viewers' attention (Machin 2007: 49). Kress and van Leeuwen (1996) note that color saturation can make an image more than real. Here, saturation draws viewers' attentions to CHP; it is represented as exciting and more than just another political party or a party from the past.

CHP is also represented as important by the sheer number of shots depicting its logo, flag, and colors. Kress (1985) notes that overlexicalization occurs when a word appears more times than is expected and is used for emphasis. In the visuals, we see a visual overlexicalization used to emphasize CHP. The logo and parts of it make up the first twenty-one seconds of the video. It then appears as part of images throughout the video, as can be seen in Figure 5.10. Here, part of the logo (white arrows shooting outward on a red background) is superimposed on top of a large crowd, salient through foregrounding, thus indicating importance (Kress and van Leeuwen 1996). Furthermore, the crowd is shot through a red filter, red being one of the colors of CHP.

In fact, this image also reveals the importance of "the people" over the individual. Most shots in the video are of crowds, not individuals. Here group shots work to

Figure 5.10 CHP logo

collectivize social actors, so they are represented as a united group, not as individuals. Here and in other crowd shots, they are united in actions such as waving flags, chanting, protesting, clapping, and cheering. This constructs the people, united at times against the government, at other times cheering Kılıçdaroğlu.

Kılıçdaroğlu is a legitimate national politician, not a mayor

Another dominant discourse in the visuals is Kılıçdaroğlu is a legitimate politician. He is mostly shot in close-ups, suggesting social proximity and looking upon his people, never into the camera. These "unstaged" images suggest authenticity, though connote less power than a demand image (Kress and van Leeuwen 1996). Throughout the video, he is active doing things associated with being a politician, such as delivering speeches, waving at crowds, meeting voters, and holding babies. These actions legitimate Kılıçdaroğlu as a politician. In Figure 5.11, he is authenticated in a number of ways. First he dresses as his people in shirt sleeves, but no tie. He is in a close shot and, like AKP's image of Erdoğan, he does not look at the camera in a demand image, but over the heads of the crowd and into the distance. This same gaze position is used in war monuments, as noted above, to suggest power in deep inner thoughts. Machin (2007: 112) notes that a camera angle which points up suggests power and high status. Here, the camera looks up to Kılıçdaroğlu suggesting power and legitimacy. He is speaking and waving his arms, as politicians do. Kılıçdaroğlu is further legitimized with his image superimposed over a background of a large crowd of CHP supporters. Here leader and "the people" are one and the same sharing the same visual space, though he is more important being individualized and more salient than his faceless crowd of supporters (Kress and van Leeuwen 1996). The logo of Halk TV news, with the words "live" and "the latest news" written on the bottom of the screen, further legitimates his status as a national politician, not a candidate for mayor of Istanbul. He is important enough to warrant live news coverage and being part of the "latest" news.

Figure 5.11 Kılıçdaroğlu as legitimate politician

"The people" suffer under AKP

Throughout the visuals, as in the lyrics, there is a discourse of victimization of "the people" by the political elite. Unlike the lyrics, these problems are represented in more concrete terms, though again, there is a lack of context and agency. In order to articulate a wide sweeping anti-AKP discourse, protesters from different sectors in Turkey are represented. Visuals represent protests, though many lack any details of where, under what circumstances, and who. And most of these shots are group shots where anger is represented by a large group, but what that anger is and in what circumstances is not represented. Faces of those in the images are collectivized, represented as groups or faces obscured, crying, sitting, and protesting (Machin 2007: 118). Furthermore, most of these victims do not face the camera in offer images. As such, weakness is suggested and it is the "social order" which is powerful and oppressing the people (Kress and van Leeuwen 1996: 124). The gritty "realism" of images suggests the viewer is being shown the real condition of "the people," where the many are unhappy with the current administration and situation. This would be very different if the images were staged using actors, makeup, and proper lighting, as we saw with the AKP video.

Accompanying words superimposed on some of these images support ideas represented in the images. One sentence reads, "People who are oppressed are always the same in this social order" and another reads, "People who cry are always the same in this social order." Again, no particulars are given as to who the "people" are and how they are oppressed and why they cry. However, lexical choices like "people" and "the same" suggest unity, while negativity of "oppressed" and "crying" is in the co-text of "in this social order," suggesting it is AKP's social order which is responsible for the people's misery, further drawing on populist discourses.

Some shots give viewers clues as to which groups in society are victims of AKP. Protesters in bandages suggest health protests, women protesting holding bread indicate a protest about the cost of living, police violently arresting people suggest police brutality while a protest outside a union building offers some circumstantial context. Slogans superimposed on images of protesters such as "stop injustice," "stop hunger," "stop sorrows, tears," "stop unemployment," "stop moral exploitation," "stop immoral politics," and "stop lies, theft, corruption" again give some context, though this is minimal. All the same, the lack of context grants the images more generability, being usable in a greater variety of contexts, connoting protests and discontent are widespread affecting a wide spectrum of the people.

Figure 5.12 is one which represents victimization. A man looks off camera. His blackened face and hat suggest he is a coal miner. This image is both unique and at the same time typical of images of victims. It is unique in that it is one of the few images of an individual other than Kılıçdaroğlu. Here we are given a visual point of identification making it easy to sympathize with him and his unhappiness (Kress and van Leeuwen 1996). The image is also a lot like other victimization photographs. It is gritty connoting the real. "The people" are unhappy, notable in his facial expression. "The people" are powerless, suggested in the offer image chosen. Considering Turkey's abysmal record on coal mining safety blamed partly on lax government inspections and corruption, the image reminds viewers of the perils of manual labor, such as coal mining, as a result of AKP's neoliberal economic policies. As such, these images articulate a discourse of victimization of "the people" at the hands of the AKP elite.

The importance of exclusions

By drawing heavily on a populist discourse, the images are divisive. CHP and Kılıçdaroğlu are represented as powerful and legitimate, the power that listens to "the people." The people are constructed as those who are suffering under AKP and those who support CHP. Machin (2007: 121) underlines the importance of considering who is not represented in images. In these images, many are excluded. There are no obvious examples of minorities such as Kurds represented in the visuals. Though CHP has

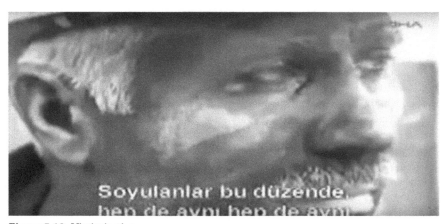

Figure 5.12 Victimization

a tenuous relationship with the Kurds (Way and Kaya 2015), their absence excludes them from CHP's Turkey. Another group missing is upper- and middle-class religious Muslims, a large part of the Turkish population. Lower-class religious Muslims are included in the visuals, represented by women who have their heads covered. But these images are used to articulate discourses of the people suffering or legitimating Kılıçdaroğlu. Some of these images show lower-class covered women protesting or picking from rubbish bins. In other images, veiled and hijab-wearing women greet Kılıçdaroğlu, shaking his hand and holding CHP flags. However, missing are those who have benefited from AKP policies such as religious middle- and upper-class Turks. By excluding minorities and many religious Muslims, the images do little to bring together a polarized society.

Musical sounds

An emphasis on legitimacy

Musical sounds are used in this video to suggest legitimacy, unity, modernity, and strength. The song was written and sung by Turkish composer Onur Akın, a prolific songwriter and soloist in the Özgün or protest folk music tradition. Like the AKP song, genre plays a crucial role in defining this song's politics. Protest folk music in Turkey has associations with the Left and is perceived as being supportive of the secular state (Stokes 2010; Way 2015). Choosing a well-known protest folk performer to write and perform their campaign song suggests sympathies and associations with this musical and political tradition.

This song's sounds draw upon both Özgün music and Anadolu rock. Though Özgün music is renowned for its politics, its sounds are heterogenous, amalgamating arabesk, taverna, folk music, and Western mainstream popular music. Anadolu rock, popularized in the 1980s, is a Turkish subgenre of rock, its sounds borrowing from the West and Turkey. Though it is far less political today, Gedik (2010) notes its leftist sympathies before Turkey's 1980 coup d'état. In this song, we hear distorted electric guitar sounds alongside more traditional instruments like a Turkish fiddle, paying homage to these music traditions. For CHP to choose to use these genres and instrumentation, left-of-center legitimacy is suggested, in contrast to AKP and its rightwing political agenda.

Positivity around CHP and Kılıçdaroğlu

The rhythm of the song suggests confidence, strength, and unity, but also divisiveness. This is not a Fantazi song like that of AKP. This is a march. The rhythm is heavy and made obvious by instruments and vocals rhythmically tied to each other. The rhythm is somewhat labored, though there is bounce to it and a sense of joyful energy especially during the choruses. Here we have a strong, obvious uncomplicated beat, inviting listeners to stamp their feet or march to the song in unison. This suggests strength, unity, and confidence, similar to the feeling one gets when one sings together.

It is also similar to a military march sung in unison as in "left, left, left, right left." This takes on political significance in Turkey. CHP has had close military links and a strong military is a part of its political platform. In the past, Turkey has had two military coups and two military interventions which targeted Islamic religious groups and leftists, among others, in their subsequent purges. Many people are wary of this threat and many have suffered due to the strength of the military and its coups. In this way, though confidence, legitimacy, and strength are suggested, the song's rhythm also alienates many.

Voice, melody, and loudness are used in the choruses to articulate a discourse of legitimacy, confidence, and unity surrounding CHP. The vocalist sings with an open throat and a relaxed voice throughout the song, connoting confidence as opposed to tension, confidence, and trust in regard to Kılıçdaroğlu and CHP (van Leeuwen 1999: 131). In the choruses, the male vocalist is joined by a number of other male voices. It is here in the song that loudness of instruments and vocals are highest, with the meaning potential of weight and power (Machin 2010: 340). The vocalists sing the same high-pitched notes in unison carrying the meaning potential of belonging to a group, of being a part of a positive joint experience (van Leeuwen 1999: 79). Here, it is a group united around CHP. It is while lyrics repeat "swordsman Kılıçdaroğlu is coming, Clean and honest person" we hear these united voices, suggesting unity in praise for Kılıçdaroğlu as leader of CHP. Melody in the chorus also signifies confidence. The melody moves from the first to its second, where it remains for three notes, before descending in pitch. A second is related with the promise of something to follow. In this case, it is the promise of Kılıçdaroğlu leading Turkey into positive times. Together, in the chorus, we see vocal arrangement, loadness, melody, and lyrics working together to connote positivity when voters unite around CHP and Kılıçdaroğlu.

Melody also plays a role in connoting confidence and unity surrounding Kılıçdaroğlu in the verses. In fact, there are only eight notes played in the song, a small number of notes giving a sense of confidence (Machin 2010: 109). In the verses, we see three slightly different melody lines which correspond to the three lines of lyrics in the verse (see Figure 5.13). At the beginning of the third line, the song's melody moves from E to a high B note (number 12 in the graph), which is the highest note sung in the song. Machin (2010: 101) suggests higher pitches are related with outward expressions of emotions. It is at these points in the melody where lyrics and images articulate discourses of "unity" surrounding Kılıçdaroğlu and CHP. It is the role of the melody here to add positive emotions to such discourses. High-pitched male vocals can also carry the sense of domination (van Leeuwen 1999: 134). For example, lyrics such as "the sun will rise after the darkness," "Let's enlighten the darkness," "not one, not tens but millions," "you are Anatolia, grow in its ashes," and "My Turkey you embrace him too" are sung during these high peaks. And it is these lines, both metaphorical and highly symbolic, which carry with them emotional attachment, suggested by the melody. The pitch then descends with the meaning potential of a lack of energy or sadness (van Leeuwen 1999). Here we drop from the high fifth down to the lower seventh. The seventh has the meaning potential of pain and sadness, thoughtfulness, and longing (Machin 2010: 219). Sympathy and sadness are suggested alongside

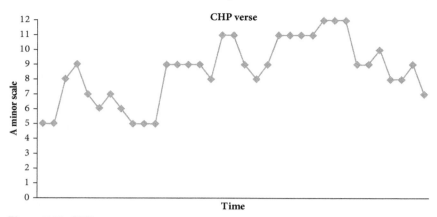

Figure 5.13 CHP verse

images of victimization. However, this sadness is answered in the choruses which follow immediately. These proclaim Kılıçdaroğlu a hero, the answer to problems and victories alluded to in the verses.

The dangers of AKP

Though there is confidence and unity suggested in musical choices, there is also danger and evil. A narrow pitch range has the experiential meaning potential of constraining strong feelings. This constraining heightens uncertainty, caution, and danger. In the lead-in to each verse, there is a two-note pattern of the fifth to sixth (E and F). This melody signifies danger, being reminiscent of the two-note leitmotif used in the *Jaws* films which also alternates between two notes. In these films, the leitmotif is used to represent danger, evil, and menace and has been used extensively ever since with similar connotations (Wingstead, Brandström, Berg 2010: 199). Here, danger and uncertainty due to AKP rule are connoted. The danger suggested in the musical sounds is made clear by lyrics which describe dangers in AKP's Turkey such as being "robbed" and "drowned." However, the sense of danger is short-lived as immediately after this riff, the pitch rises to the first (A) as the verse begins, offering hope and praise for Kılıçdaroğlu.

Conclusion

National elections in 2011 were important for both AKP and CHP. AKP wanted to gain enough seats in parliament in order to change the constitution from a parliamentary democracy to a presidential system. In this way, many of AKP's elites, including Erdoğan, could continue to dominate Turkish politics. For CHP, it was also an important election. This was Kılıçdaroğlu's first foray into national politics as a candidate for prime minister.

Both political parties harnessed the power of music to promote their candidates and agendas. This is done across the three modes of lyrics, visuals, and musical sounds in the two musical advertisements I have just analyzed. Each video articulates discourses similar to those articulated by each party in regard to religion, social conservatism, and the importance of each party and their leaders. However, both also articulate discourses which are highly divisive.

AKP's video articulates discourses which exclude those in Turkey who do not subscribe to their religious and social conservatism, in the past and in the present. It excludes those who may not prioritize being a practicing Sunni Muslim. It excludes those who value secularism over political Islam. It represents the past in ways which suggest suffering of the people who are now happy due to AKP governance, again excluding those who do not think the same. Likewise, CHP's offering excludes minorities, such as Kurds. It excludes those who do not look favorably upon the military. It excludes upper- and middle-class religious Muslims.

In these ways, both videos are divisive. Neither reaches out and tries to embrace the whole of Turkish society. Instead both represent their visions of how they see Turkey, in ways which are to their own benefit, while ignoring Turks and Turkey in all its diversity and depth. In a country which is highly polarized, these music videos do nothing to unite. In fact, if anything, they build metaphoric walls in a place which needs bridges and understanding.

6

Concerts as Multimodal Communication

Grup Yorum is renowned in Turkey for being a radical left-wing political Özgün music group. Their concerts are pretty much guaranteed to be an edgy affair with both good music and a large measure of politics which upset the authorities. On January 30, 2016, Grup Yorum was booked to play at the Atatürk Theatre in Izmir. Myself and a few friends went to see them. When we arrived outside the venue, we were greeted by bus loads of police in helmets, riot gear, and shields blocking the path to the concert hall. Police buses, water cannons, pepper-spraying guns, and plainclothes officers ran street battles with about fifty young (mostly) men. One by one the protesters were separated from the running groups and dragged on to waiting police vans. The authorities had canceled the concert at the last moment and arrested the group members. There was no news about the concert cancellation or the arrests in mainstream media. Later, on Group Yorum's WhatsApp account, the group announced members had been arrested on charges of "spreading propaganda" before even plugging in an instrument. My friends and I left disappointed and went to a local bar which hosted a band that played covers of Red Hot Chili Peppers and the likes.

In this chapter, I examine concerts by bands which represent themselves as political to uncover what discourses their performances articulate and how this is done. Here, concerts are considered as a multimodal experience, employing a wide range of semiotic resources with an array of meaning potentials. It is not only the performance of music, but other resources such as gestures, audiovisual presentations, posters, banners, discussions between songs, movement and even choices of events, venues, and songs which have meaning potential. I have been to a large number of concerts as a fan in Turkey seeing Hayko Cepkin, Duman, One Against All, Social Threat, Grup Kızılırmak, Grup Yorum, REDD, Mor ve Ötesi, ManGa, The Ringo Jets, Balina, Palmiyeler, Moğallar, and countless other local rock and punk bands. I have even had the pleasure of playing in warm-up bands for some of these concerts.

The groups listed above and their concerts are very different in terms of genre, instrumentation, and even politics. Some are far more politically engaged than others. Political issues tackled in concerts include neoliberal economics, police brutality, Kurdish rights, democracy, specific government policies, AKP, and social and religious conservatism. Responses by the authorities to these concerts also vary. Most concerts proceed with no noticeable interventions by the authorities. Others, such as Grup

Yorum, are not so lucky. Though politics articulated vary between groups and concerts, common among these acts are discourses of community, subversion, and authenticity. It is here we turn to after a short examination of the institutional context of concerts.

Concerts, authenticity, and the music industry

I once interviewed the band Nomeansno for a radio station I was working at. Other than witnessing and remembering a great show, I also recall one of the band members telling me in the interview: "We make no money from playing—it just about pays for the van and the petrol. Do you know where we make money? On T-shirts. We should stop playing and just sell T-shirts." Though I understand the band's frustration at their economic woes, their experiences on the road are not unusual. Concerts are performed to promote the sales of CDs, downloads, and vinyl. Recordings are the primary medium for rock and pop. Corporations make more money selling multiple copies of identical consumable goods like CDs, vinyl, and even T-shirts than individual live performances (Auslander 2015).

Despite a lack of financial rewards for concerts, live performances aid in sales and also in authentication. Auslander (2015: 359) notes, "The function of live performance is to authenticate the sound on the recording. In rock culture, live performance is a secondary experience of the music but is nevertheless indispensable, since the primary experience can not be validated without it" (ibid.: 359). So, the recording is the standard to which live performance is judged (Gracyk 1996: 74–75; Auslander 2015: 358). Concerts authenticate popular music in two ways. First, being authentic, "a musician must have a history as a live performer, as someone who has paid those dues and whose current visibility is the result of earlier popularity with a local following" (Auslander 1999: 76). Second, "it is only in live performance that the listener can ascertain that a group that looks authentic in photographs, and sounds authentic on records, really *is* authentic in terms of rock ideology" (ibid.: 78). That is, listeners can ascertain visually whether sounds heard on recordings can be made live. This authenticity and liveness is genre bound. For example, in jazz and classical music, recorded and live performances are considered different art forms. In pop, some musicians pride themselves on not being able to perform live. In many forms of popular music, including rock, folk, Özgün music and others, being able to play live is essential for authenticity, as is political commitment and being anti-corporate. These are partially determined by the use of semiotic resources by music makers in concerts and recordings.

A sense of community in concerts

As I noted in the introduction, concerts multimodally articulate discourses of authenticity as well as community. The building of a sense of community in performance has been noted by a number of scholars who study popular music as well as classical music. A concert community may be defined as "a group of people joining together publicly over a shared passion, in the same geographical setting, who are united by a social matrix" (Dearn and Price 2016: 3). This is seen across a whole range of music genres.

The quality and longevity of a sense of community is open to some debate. Some scholars see this sense of community through musical performance as fleeting, dispersing as fans leave musical venues (Shank 2014), such that "the communal bond unifying such an audience is most likely to be little more than the common consumption of a particular performance commodity" (Auslander 2008: 64). Other scholars believe there is more to a performance than simply consuming. Concerts give fans a chance to interact with others creating a sense of community. This allows "the individual listener … the opportunity to commune with fellow fans and to experience an illusory bond with the performer" (Gracyk 1996: 78).

Some scholars take an even more optimistic perspective, claiming "audience members socialize with companions, interact with other audience members, and can eventually become part of a listening community," creating a more long-term sense of community (Dearn and Price 2016: 2). In this sense of the word, listeners share and value "a particular cultural experience and develop a collective feeling of responsibility towards the future of their organization" (ibid.: 9–10). Though here, Dearn and Price are referring to an organization, such as a classical music concert hall, I believe this can also apply to fans of a particular band. Fans can also feel responsible for a band's future, as is the case with many Grup Yorum fans, this band being the focus of this chapter.

Live popular music such as rock and folk music has been credited with community making and identity building. In regard to live popular music, Hesmondhalgh (2013: 86) sees community in terms of "publicness," which can mean both the "sociability among people who do not know each other" and "a notion of political community grounded in citizenship." This definition of community includes the fun, social, and political aspects of concerts which allow people who are "co-present" to join in "sociable publicness." It is this act of publicness which gives listeners a sense of belonging, contributing to a person's self-identity. In live folk music performance, a similar sense of community can be observed. Eyerman and Jamison (1998: 121) claim, "Folk clubs and, eventually, major festivals, particularly Newport, Rhode Island, provided a new social space for experiencing a sense of community and collective identity, a new organizational form for cultural expression." It is going to these events, feeling part of a crowd with a common sense of purpose, musical, or otherwise, which aids in a sense of community. This happens in a number of ways, including singing together. This common experience is credited with "consciousness-raising" and creating a sense of collective identity (ibid.: 123). Collective singing "can also capture, in a brief, transient moment, a glimpse of, and a feeling for, a spiritual bonding which is both rational and emotive at one and the same time" (ibid.: 36).

Collective singing is only one strategy I note in this chapter. Through a close reading of a concert I reveal how Grup Yorum uses semiotic resources in their concert to not only entertain, but also express authenticity, a sense of community, and intertwined with these are discourses of political protest.

Grup Yorum's twenty-fifth-anniversary concert

On June 12, 2010, Grup Yorum performed an almost three-hour concert to honor its twenty-fifth anniversary in İnönü Stadyumu in Istanbul. Unlike most Group Yorum concerts, this one was not canceled or curtailed. There was no notable police harassment. Instead, it was an elaborate concert, a spectacle which attracted 55,000 people. Not only fans of the band came, but a variety of social and political groups attended. The concert employed a large variety of semiotic resources to entertain and articulate discourses of authenticity, community, and subversion, discourses common throughout many live music events by politically active groups. It used not only live music, but streamed and recorded music, images on large screens, dancers, and a host of guests. This makes it a great case to examine in detail. Also, on a practical note, it was recorded and can be found on the internet, making the job of analysis much easier than doing it all by memory and notes.[1]

Though I will on occasion make reference to other concerts, this performance is the focus of this chapter. Grup Yorum is an (in)famous Özgün music group renowned for its Marxist politics. I chose a concert by Grup Yorum because they are uncompromising in their politics which they foreground in all their activities, reminiscent of The Red Skins and Billy Bragg. Unlike the aforementioned, many band members have been and are serving time in jail for their concerts and political beliefs. Most recently, all members of the band were arrested and spent time in prison after a number of confrontations with police and authorities after Turkey's 2016 military coup attempt. Membership of the band is constantly changing partly due to it being a "collective" and partly due to arrests and police intimidation.

Grup Yorum fits into the genre of Özgün music which mixes Western rock and jazz with Turkish folk sounds. This is noticeable in instrumentation, melodies, song choices, and topics. Özgün music has its roots in Turkish folk music, emerging with democracy after Turkey's three-year 1980 military coup. Though music which may be considered subversive is incorporated into a variety of musical genres, Özgün music is renowned for its politics of protest.

Grup Yorum represents itself as a Marxist group with deep sympathies for The Revolutionary People's Liberation Party/Front (Devrimci Halk Kurtuluş Partisi-Cephesi—DHKP-C). The DHKP-C is a Marxist-Leninist party founded in 1978. It has carried out a number of assassinations and suicide bombings, and is classified as a terrorist organization by Turkey, the United States, and the European Union. The group is anti-American and anti-NATO. It believes the Turkish government is under the control of Western imperialism. The DHKP-C aims to destroy this control by violent and democratic means. Grup Yorum's sympathies for the DHKP-C can be seen, for example, in the selection of song titles on their *Bora Fırtınası* album. Song titles refer to DHKP-C members who died in 1996 in prison hunger strikes over their living conditions, known as the "1996 death fest." On the *Geliyoruz* album, there is a song named "Sibel Yalçın" who was a DHKP-C militant killed by police. In 2012, İbrahim Çuhadar led a DHKP-C attack on a police station. He died in the attack and Grup Yorum members attended his funeral. I argue in the following analysis that Grup Yorum articulates many of DHKP-C discourses multimodally in their concert.

It is these political discourses which are enmeshed with ideas of community and authenticity which are emphasized in the concert. How this is done is now examined in detail.

As is the case with all concerts, we can assume the aim of the concert was for fans to have fun, while the band promotes its music and other consumables. In this sense, Grup Yorum's concert was a success, it being an elaborate spectacle of sights and sounds which attracted 55,000 fans. Here, we look beyond these successes and examine how Grup Yorum uses a multitude of resources to articulate a number of related discourses. Grup Yorum creates a sense of community by articulating discourses of unity. But the unity it articulates is exclusive to the political Left, and only a particular type of Left politics. A range of icons, issues, and figures from national and international leftist politics are used to articulate discourses in line with those of the DHKP-C. That is, egalitarianism, anti-capitalism, anti-imperialism, sympathy for workers, pro-Kurdish rights, pro-unions, and the legitimacy of armed struggle. And it is a legitimate and authentic Grup Yorum which leads this community. The following analysis details how this is done in this concert. Though I discuss lyrics and musical sounds, the focus of this chapter is on how dominant discourses in the concert are articulated using semiotic resources both common to and distinct from recorded songs and music videos. The concert lasted just under three hours. Obviously, I do not have the space here to analyze in detail the whole concert. Instead, I select moments in the concert where a range of resources are used to articulate these discourses across various media and modes.

A selective sense of community

A sense of community is a common discourse articulated in concerts across genres which can be expressed in a variety of ways. Recently, I watched a concert by One Against All and Social Threat, two hardcore punk bands from Izmir. They create a sense of community through referring to their audiences as "Izmir Core United," "the crew," and name events as "Izmir Core Unity," lexical choices emphasizing unity among fans and bands. In concerts, there is a blurring of lines between "the crew" and band members. Fans know most of the lyrics and sing along with the band during performances, the feeling of community enhanced by sharing the same activity of singing. Band members share their microphones with fans as they sing (see Figure 6.1 and Way 2016c for more details). Another hardcore punk band, Confront, creates a sense of community in other ways. Most band members stand firm, legs apart looking down at their instruments in a sincere "into the music" pose. Occasionally they look up and glare at the audience. In stark contrast, the lead singer represents himself as "one in a community" of hardcore punks with a political engagement. He wears the same clothes as his audience—a long T-shirt, jeans, and a baseball cap around the wrong way. He sports a very short haircut and earrings. He spends the whole set not facing the crowd and singing to them, but in the crowd, facing the band and singing while crowd members "in the know" sing along with him. They lean into the microphone and sway in unison along with the singer. The discourse articulated here is one of not

Figure 6.1 Sharing microphones with "the crew"

being a performer singing to a crowd, but a singer being one of the crowd, singing with his crowd, being united as one in a group of rage.

Grup Yorum uses a range of semiotic resources to articulate a sense of community between itself and its audience members. One way this is done is through spoken word. On stage, there is the band, two choirs, an orchestra, and a male and a female lead singer (see Figure 6.7). After their first two opening songs, the two lead singers speak to the audience for the first time. The talk begins with:

> Hello friends, brothers, hello to those of you who have a place in your heart for 25 years of these "fair fight and hope" songs.

Here a community is articulated. Closeness is connoted in naming the audience "friends" and "brothers." What the community has in common is a love for Grup Yorum music, represented metaphorically in "a place in your hearts." Grup Yorum's credibility is also suggested in its longevity (twenty-five years) and its political credentials represented in "these fair fight and hope songs." In this same introductory spoken word segment, the community is further defined as workers who are exploited and "make everything," civil servants credited with "your actions, and your disobedience, your protests," poor farm laborers who "put in a big effort for cotton, tobacco and hazelnut farms," and fighting students and jobless youth, who all make up "our big family." The speech ends with:

> Endless thanks to you, our public, we are proud of being a student of you, our public. Hello to everyone who is a member of all nations and beliefs of Anatolia and friends who share our dream of a free and equal world of non-exploitation and non-oppression.

Here, two groups are represented, though part of a community. "You, our public" is defined as something different from "we" the band, connoted in the use of "our" twice. On the one hand, the use of the possessive pronoun "our" suggests a relationship of ownership, the band owning the public. However, the relationship is then turned on its head, with the band naming itself "a student of you." This connotes egalitarianism, the band using the possessive, yet being a student of "our public." The second sentence again is on the one hand inclusive, but on the other exclusive. Lexical choices such as "everyone" and "a member of all nations and beliefs" suggest inclusiveness. However, there is also exclusiveness. It is members of "Anatolia," the land in which most of modern-day Turkey occupies which is included. Also included are those who share the same hope for "a free and equal world of non-exploitation and non-oppression." This is an honorable goal, but one with Marxist connotations, lexical choices such as "free," "equal," "exploitation," and "oppression" suggesting a leftist critique of Western free market economics.

In this opening speech, we find more exclusion from Grup Yorum's unity through the use of pronouns. Capitalists and job owners are named as "they" and activated negatively in "they work you like a slave," "they fired you with out question," and "they steal your children's bread." Further negative representations see "they" in agentless actions such as "our friends whose arms are broken off, burning bodies, and people who died in ship yards and mines when they work." Civil servant bosses are also excluded, though presupposed and represented negatively in "We know you [civil servants] for being against being a servant, even though this is deemed proper." Here, it is presupposed that bosses treat civil servants in a demeaning manner as servants, presupposition a powerful tool in articulating discourses. This same strategy is used in representing rich landowners who again are presupposed in "farm labourers who curse the land and have received a sentence for being poor." It is landowners who are presupposed giving a sentence of being poor.

This introductory spoken word segment also includes Grup Yorum's role in this represented community in:

> We take the road for telling the joy of living, hope, and living like humans and making the public's art. We started 25 years ago... We turned our face to be Anatolia's public voice which started thousands of years before us. We learnt from them what is art. Art should be a collective work and the voice of the public who make oneself understood and telling everything from bread to love. We give value to collective productions creative power and pleasure as our best value, when they impose selfishness and individualism.

Grup Yorum is represented here as storytellers "making the public's art." The public, as defined earlier, is an exclusive public. The group is active in "We turned our face to be Anatolia's public voice." Here Grup Yorum represents itself as Turkey's public voice, a grand role indeed. A sense of history and continuity legitimizes its claim to this role. It "started 25 years ago," and is continuing a voice for Turkey's public "which started thousands of years before us." These historic claims legitimize the group, just as historic claims legitimize nations (Billig 1995). However, "the voice" and "public's art" are exclusive. It is not all art, but art with leftist connections, seen here in leftist lexical choices such as "collective work" and "collective productions." The collective idea is seen throughout the concert. For instance, near the end of the concert, the drummer thanks not just the choirs and orchestra, but also "cameramen, editors, guests, people who sell tickets, technical staff, poster makers, organising company, music company. This is a collective work." Again, its brand of Marxism is drawn upon. The last sentence creates an "us" and "them." Instead of values of "collective productions, creative power and pleasure" which are "our best value," those who do not adhere to Grup Yorum's Marxist principles are represented in "they impose selfishness and individualism." This is an oversimplification of a far broader and intricate cultural and political landscape. However, the vague action of "impose" and the abstract naming of "they" serve the purpose of representing those who do not share the group's values negatively in contrast to the positive representation of the group and its ideas.

Speeches between songs are not the only way a sense of community is achieved. Eyerman and Jamison (1998) note singing together creates a sense of community. This is a common strategy used in concerts I have witnessed globally from Rage Against the Machine at Brixton Academy to The Who in Detroit Michigan to Duman in Cyprus and throughout this Grup Yorum concert. Most of the songs chosen for the concert are well known by fans of Grup Yorum, many of them written and performed by Marxist folk or Özgün groups. For example, lyrics from "Uğurlama/Farewell" are taken from a well-known poem by Ibrahim Karaca, a left-wing activist. Many in the audience have heard this performed and sing along in unison with the group. This is encouraged by the male lead singer who shouts "to you," encouraging the audience to sing while he listens. This act connotes egalitarianism, because unlike most instances of crowd sing-alongs, this is not a call and response activity. Instead, the audience are metaphorically given the microphone before the singer, singing lines the singer does not sing. When he starts singing again, a backup woman vocalist sings along with him and the audience. Everyone sings the same notes and lyrics, suggesting all are equal parts of a community.

Body movement also plays a role in creating a sense of community. During the chorus of "Haziranda Ölmek zor/It's hard to die in June," choir members, band members, and the audience all sing along with the lead singer. Here, seen in Figure 6.2, the woman lead vocalist raises her right arm and sways it back and forth encouraging the audience to do the same body movement and sing along. During "Hasta Siempre/ Until forever," the lead singers lead the audience in synchronized clapping, with the drummer keeping the beat while band members, choir members, orchestra members, and the audience all sing the chorus of "Che Guevara," sharing in one revolutionary voice. Here it is not only the singing of a song together, but also the same body movements which bind the community.

Lighting also plays a role in creating a sense of community. The song "Büyü/Grow up" is sung by Nejat Yavaşoğlu, the singer of another politically active leftist group named Bulutsuzluk Özlemi. He is one of a number of "guests" who perform, connoting commonality between these leftist-leaning performers. During this song, lights and spotlights are aimed at different groups on the stage—choirs, orchestra, Grup Yorum—

Figure 6.2 Community through body motion and sounds

suggesting their importance in the music making. The lights also take turns aimed at pockets of the audience as they sing, dance, or just listen. This action connotes everyone is important and a part of Grup Yorum's community.

Community dimensions: Unity of an international Left

As fans dance and sing along to songs in the concert, there is a real sense of a community. It is fun and at the same time dangerous. I remember feeling this way when I used to go to hardcore punk shows as a teenager, knowing the music would be exciting, as was the omnipresent threat that the show was going to break out into a mass brawl (it rarely happened). As a fan of Grup Yorum, you feel a similar sense of danger, this time knowing you are part of an event which is under the close eye of the authorities and an event which can erupt in violence (involving the authorities) at any moment. Part of the fun and danger is also in the politics being expressed. Fans know and like the idea of being party to Grup Yorum's radical politics. Included in its politics is Marxism and armed struggle. As part of its community, Grup Yorum articulates unity between itself, its fans, and left-wing politics globally. Again, this is done in a variety of ways. The most common way is through visual representations of Marxist icons, imagery, issues, and figures from Turkey and abroad. Though many of these figures have very different ideas and values, here in the concert they are represented as united, a part of Grup Yorum's community.

Throughout the concert, images of Turkish Marxist poets, musicians, and political figures are displayed on two large screens bookending the large stage. Again, these serve to indicate who is a part of Grup Yorum's community. In one case, the anti-imperialism lyrics of "Haziranda Ölmek zor/It's hard to die in June" were written about the death of Nazım Hikmet, a left-wing poet who died on June 3, 1963, in Moscow. Displayed on the large screens are photos of Hikmet and other left-wing poets including Sabahattin Ali and Aziz Nesin. Many of these are close-up shots, some legitimate the poets posing with a pen while others create sympathy by showing these men in police custody. Imagery also includes a full screen shot of the Grup Yorum logo, live shots of band members playing, and audience members singing. This montage of images creates an integration of images, suggesting commonality (Kress and van Leeuwen 1996). It is this commonality of passion for music and Marxist politics articulated through a variety of modes which creates a sense of community in Grup Yorum's concert.

In another case, unity of Turkish Marxist music performers can be seen during the song "Çeşmi Siyahım/My black-eyed beauty." While the band plays their rendition of the song, and fans sing and sway to the music, the screens display black and white pictures of the song's originator Mahzuni Şerif, a Turkish Alevi protest folk singer, poet, and author. He is in different poses, some with Turkish landscapes in the background, some in close-ups, him wearing a basic suit, and people paying tribute to his death. All these offer a point of identification, suggesting closeness and sympathy respectively (Figure 6.3). Şerif's importance and unity with other leftist performers is connoted in a series of stills which depict those who have played his music. Displayed on the big screens are Selda Bağcan—a left-wing performer playing the bağlama, Edip Akbayram—an Özgün musician who suffered governmental harassment and sang this song in 1991, members of Moğollar, Cem Karaca, Ahmet Kaya—a Kurdish performer and Tülay German—another performer who was sentenced to fifteen years in prison for his political views before fleeing the country. All these artists are integrated into a video, connoting commonality with Şerif and Grup Yorum. This is followed by live shots on the screens of the crowd cheering, showing their unity and support for these performers. When the song ends, the singer finishes with "Thank-you to the artists before us who were anti-capitalists." What is represented here is continuity, a theme used a lot in this concert, but also a community united against capitalism.

Grup Yorum's community is not confined strictly to Turkish leftist figures, but includes unity with leftist figures outside of Turkey as well. In "Haklıyız Kazanacağız/ We are right, we will win," this is done through a number of modes, including the following lyrics:

1. Armed with our young rage
2. We have your rocks in our hands
3. The fight you taught us is ours
4. It's growing on our shoulders
5. Growing, the fight you taught us
6. Our fight is growing on our shoulders.

Here the idea that there is a progression in time in leftist politics is again connoted in representing two groups: those from the past and present. Here, those who struggled in the past are represented as "you" and "yours" activated in "The fight you taught us." "We" and "us" are protesters in the present who are "armed," have "young rage" in the

Figure 6.3 Unity with musicians

"fight [which] is growing on our shoulders." Lyrics do not make clear exactly who these figures from the past are or where these fights take place. Here visuals make these ideas more specific.

The visual montage on the screens during this song displays close ups and moving images of international leftist figures from the past such as Marx, Lenin, Stalin, Mao, Ho Chi Minh, Castro, and Che Guevara. In some shots they are speaking at rallies, saluting soldiers, flanked by fans, and relaxing in the shade. They are powerful, yet cool. Elsewhere in the concert, international Marxist icons such as a Soviet flag, a red flag with yellow star, and a sickle in a hand further suggest an international scope. Violent confrontations between Marxists and police are represented. Crowds look powerful being represented as large groups facing the cameras and throwing projectiles at the police. A group of Marxist protesters with their left fists in the air walk on the street in unison suggesting strength in numbers. Revolutionary violence is also signified with stills and footage of soldiers saluting, armies on horses, a soldier carrying a flag, Chinese propaganda footage of a soldier and dancer with a gun, soldiers walking in formation in front of a red background, peasants hugging soldiers, soldiers shooting, and soldiers on tanks. Here, visuals connote a community of a united international Left, a type of leftism involving armed struggle and revolution.

Between songs, the group's bağlama player delivered this speech, linking some of Latin America's leftist musicians with Grup Yorum:

> Latin American musicians are joined with the socialist movement. They create a new way. We learn from them, we watch them, we are inspired by them. We don't forget Victor Jara, Mercedes Sosa ... they broke Jaras's guitar, but all over the World, we listen to his songs, and we now sing his song. That day, we were 5000 listening in Santiago Stadium, today we are 50,000 people listening. Again, one voice and one breath.

Here, Latin American musicians are "joined with the socialist movement" while Grup Yorum is active "learning," "watching," and "being inspired," linking Latin American musicians with Grup Yorum. Global unity is also suggested in the claim that their songs are heard and sung "all over the world." And the strength of this unity is signified in numbers, a discourse of legitimation (van Leeuwen 1999). In the 1960s Victor Jara played to crowds in Santiago, represented here as "5,000 listening." However, the present leftist musical community's strength and continuity are connoted in "we are 50,000." Furthermore, unity both historically and between band and audience is suggested in "one voice and one breath," metaphorically linking Latin American Marxist musicians from the past with Grup Yorum in the present.

The community Grup Yorum represents also includes present-day leftist figures. Between songs, Venezuela's Communist Party General Secretary Jorenimo Carrerasi delivers a prerecorded audiovisual message. His speech includes an overlexicalization of the word "unite" appearing three times in his first three sentences. Furthermore, a protest musician from Venezuela performs Victor Jara's "El Aparecido." The singer, who is not named, shows unity with Grup Yorum by wearing a white open-necked shirt like the band and all of its guests. The singer, along with both lead singers of Grup

Yorum, sings together in Spanish, a gesture suggesting unity with Latin America. All three take turns leading the vocals connoting equality. The two singers, the band, and the choirs sing the chorus with the guest as one voice in unison again signifying unity.

Dimension of community: Marxist concerns

Grup Yorum expresses concerns for issues which are of concern to Marxists worldwide. How this is done connotes a community of fans, performers, and others united in concerns for issues such as workers' rights and sympathy for the poor. Again these are expressed through a variety of modes. The song title "1 Mayıs/1 May" is also the day of International Workers' Day. Before the song begins, Erol Ekici, the General Work Secretary for Turkey's DİSK union, thereby a representative of workers, comes on stage to join Grup Yorum flanked on either side by the two lead singers. The fans appreciate the gesture while this pose suggests they are one and the same. Musical sounds contribute to this sense of unity. During the song, singers and the choir sing together in unison. The rhythm of the song is a march, typical of songs associated with the military, militants, police, or other highly disciplined organizations. This connotes strength and discipline. In fact, this same marching sound is also notable in other songs, such as "Gündoğdu." In this song, we see both the lead singers along with the two choirs on stage all sing the same notes and the same words at the same time, further suggesting unity. Lyrics include:

1. Our way is the revolutionary way
2. We are workers, villagers
3. Against the fascist order
4. We are fighting a public war against imperialism.

These lines make clear Grup Yorum's political commitments which are in line with those of revolutionary Marxism. These include "workers" and "villagers" as part of "our" community, while positioning "the fascist order" and "imperialism" against "our revolutionary ways." In "Umudun Zeybeği/Zeybek hope" the line "When we are arm in arm, sprouts turn to fruit" represents being in a union metaphorically as "arm in arm." This simplification of unionism smooths over all the politics and power grabs involved in unions, like most other large organizations. However, this simplification represents unions positively, as part of our community, as does the second part of the sentence which again uses metaphor to represent the advantages of unionization in "sprouts turn to fruit." Again, a vast simplification is used to represent unionization positively.

Support for workers is also connoted through visuals displayed on the big screens. One group of workers represented sympathetically is miners during the song "Madenciden/Miners." This is relevant in Turkey as it has one of the poorest records of mining safety globally (Kotsev 2014). Before the song begins, a video dramatization on the screens begins with a black screen and a bass and echo enhanced sound of water dripping. Next, a wet, dark, close-up of a coal mine interior is shown. A pick axe hits a wall in slow motion with a loud, bass-enhanced sound effect of the hit while the sound of dripping water continues. Next is a close-up of the face of a dirty miner wiping his eyes in slow motion. This creates a point of identification and sympathy for the miner in his dark and dank surroundings. The song begins.

Lyrics represent miners sympathetically in lines such as "We work hard for everyone but nobody is happy in our home." Here miners are active working hard. "Everyone" and "nobody" play off each other enhancing a message of sympathy. This poetic reference implies the danger, stress, and poor wages miners face in Turkey. The musical sounds and the appearance of the lead singers can be described as downbeat and serious. They do not dance and clap and raise victory signs. Instead, they stand with serious facial expressions and sing "the truth." These expressions are projected onto the screens in close-ups. Images on the screens show the band, the orchestra, the lead singer, and famous leftist politicians edited together. The song ends with a chant started from the group and then throughout the crowd of "Miner labourers are our honour." This communal chant makes clear Grup Yorum and the audience's symbolic solidarity with miners. Though this multimodal package does raise the issue of miners' poor conditions, it does not address the issue of privatization being blamed for miners' poor conditions, a discourse taken up by opposition groups. Instead vague politics and catchy phrases take precedence over clear and obvious policy debates.

The poor are another group included in Grup Yorum's community, a group associated with international Marxist concerns. In today's Turkey, poverty is synonymous with "Gecekondu" or shantytowns. The performance of "Gecekondu ile Gökdelen/Shanty town versus skyscraper" is a statement against the common AKP policy of clearing shanty towns and replacing them with overpriced, high-rise TOKI dwellings (see Chapter 4 for a detailed description). This song's support for shantytown dwellers is centered around an entertaining choreographed piece. Stage right is a group of dancers. They are dressed very colorfully, though they look shambolic, due to a lack of uniformity in each dancer's costume. Stage left is a dancer dressed in a very tall white costume which looks like a high-rise building and two bodyguards, a metaphor for big business, the government, and TOKI (Figure 6.4). His head protrudes above the building costume and he wears a witch's hat. Though he wears a big polka-dot bow tie which may be worn for ridicule, seriousness is connoted through facial expressions. He never smiles and leers at the "dwellers." The dwellers try to "invade" the white building together in their dance. The body guards shoo them away. Individually, they do not have enough power and are dispersed.

As a group, they get organized and push down the high rise. Such actions suggest dwellers have power in numbers. The high rise is dragged away by the bodyguards and the brightly colored dancers skip happily. The narrative is aided by musical sounds and lyrics. The drummer is the lead vocalist. He has a whining, tense voice and drags out word lengths, sounding like a rotten businessman. He sings from the perspective of the businessman telling dwellers to "Gather everything. Enough is enough. Bit of a joke." Here elongated words add emotions to his demands to leave the shantytown while his nasal voice adds irritation and tension to what he says (van Leeuwen 1999). Though this performance multimodally points to inequalities in modern-day Turkey and the importance of collective organization, very few details of how to organize and how to succeed are given. Furthermore, in today's Turkey, organizing physical aggression as suggested here in the performance is very likely to leave one in jail, as was witnessed

Figure 6.4 Strength in physical unity dance

in Gezi Park protests and thereafter. All the same, the discourse of organized physical resistance and protest is articulated, drawing upon Marxist discourses again while including sympathy for the poor, a group which is part of Grup Yorum's community.

Community dimensions: Kurds and the DHKP-C

Elements of Kurdish culture make up a large part of Grup Yorum's concert and reflect their support for Kurdish rights, a concern shared with the DHKP-C. This support is much appreciated by the crowd, many of whom are Kurds and Kurdish sympathizers. Kurds are represented as part of Grup Yorum's community through choices in songs, lyrics, spoken word, languages used, personnel in the band, dance, and costumes. Though support for the DHKP-C cannot be explicitly expressed due to legal repercussions, how Grup Yorum represents Kurdish issues makes the DHKP-C an essential part of its sense of community.

Within a Turkish context, the Kurdish movement is closely associated with some brands of left-wing politics. For example, the HDP, which is Turkey's Kurdish rights–oriented political party and the third-largest political party at the time of writing, considers itself against capitalism which "exploits and alienates the masses" ("Who are we" 2016). As discussed earlier, the DHKP-C, a group closely affiliated with Grup Yorum, is Marxist and sympathetic toward Kurds. Song selection, language, and dance suggest such sympathies. "Munzur Dağı/Munzur Mountain" is the name of a song and a mountain near Tunceli (or Dersim in Kurdish). It is home to a large Kurdish population. "Keçe kurdan/Kurdish girl" is written by Kurdish singer Şivan Perwer and

Grup Yorum perform the song in the Kurdish language, a semiotic resource which until recently was illegal. This is repeated in the song "Caney caney." During "Reşo," the Grup Yorum choir express unity with Kurds in another way, by dancing the Halay, a dance associated with Kurdish tradition and celebration.

But it is sympathy for armed struggle, including Kurdish armed struggle, which links Grup Yorum with the DHKP-C. "Dağlara gel/Come to the hills" is an overtly political song. In most cases, Grup Yorum concerts are canceled if they play this song due to perceived implications the song promotes joining the PKK. In this concert however, it is allowed. Here, a number of resources are used to suggest Kurdish armed struggle. Firstly, armed struggle is connoted by the line "come to the hills," especially as it is sung by a band with Kurdish sympathies. It is in the hills and mountains of South-East Turkey where the PKK have fought with the Turkish authorities (see Chapter 7's analysis of Grup Kızılırmak for more details). This area is further suggested in musical sounds. By foregrounding the zurna, a traditional wind instrument, Eastern Kurdish Turkey and tradition are connoted. This same "instrumental" strategy can be heard in other songs such as "Umudun Zeybeği/Zeybek hope." Furthermore, the lead singer and some of the women singers from the choir sing a "zılgıt." This sound, which is something like a bird call, is associated with weddings, parties, and celebrations, again heard extensively in the southeast of Turkey and associated with the East more than the West.

Body movement also plays a role in connoting Kurdish armed resistance. According to the government, "Cemo/A woman's story" expresses support for the DHKP-C and has thus been prohibited from being performed in the past. It was performed on this evening. Lyrics poetically tell the story of a young person who goes to Dersim mountain, a place synonymous with Kurdish fighters. He wears a "cap with a star," indicating his affiliation with communism. He carries a rifle, a metonym for armed resistance. During this song, body movement communicates resistance as well. The male lead vocalist, along with the Grup Yorum band and many audience members, sings the song together. The male singer, members of the band, and choirs wave their arms aggressively with one finger protruding above their heads in the air (Figure 6.5). This is a symbol for victory used by Kurds in Turkey. Originally, it was two fingers, but performers know that the police would shut down the concert if this is displayed. But everyone knows what it means and the audience join the singer. The drums are upfront in the mix, keeping everyone chanting and waving their arms in unison. Here we have a symbolic visual and musical message of community support for Kurdish fighters.

The performance of the song "Kızıldere" is another instance where sympathy for armed conflict is suggested. Kızıldere is the name of a place in Turkey with deep political connotations. It is here on March 30, 1972, where Mahir Çayan, a political activist, took up arms. Çayan admired Guevarist guerila groups in Latin America, and he created a strategy which was called the people's revolution and democratic revolution. He and ten friends took two NATO technicians hostage in an old village house in Kızıldere in order to secure the release of Marxist activists Deniz Gezmiş and his friends. But soldiers did not accept their demands and bombed the old house leaving only one person alive. This has become a political cause by some who claim the army acted wrongly. Playing songs which retell these highly political acts sympathetically aligns Grup Yorum and its community with such ideology.

Figure 6.5 Hand gestures of resistance

Sympathy is shown toward these activists in a number of other ways, visuals playing a key role. On the screens beside the stage, a montage of footage is shown. There is old footage, grainy and in long shots of the place of the massacre. Soldiers appear in long shots jumping out of trucks with guns and uniforms. These long shots connote a large social distance between viewer and soldiers, emphasized by a still of the aftermath, the destruction of the house. There is new color footage of the annual commemorative parade for the incident. People carry red banners and pictures of Mahir Çayan. A close up of a banner reads, "We have not come here to turn back. We came to die." Representations of protesters suggest inclusiveness, such as young activists, a man in a wheelchair, older people, women, and men, some in close-ups connoting sympathy and closeness. There are extreme close-ups of Mahir Çayan, signifying sympathy and his importance to backers of his cause. Group Yorum is shown at the parade in a close cropped group shot playing music (Figure 6.6). The camera angle looks up to the group, connoting power and legitimating their political credentials. The montage ends with slow motion of red flags flapping in the breeze. This montage suggests not only sympathy for Mahir, his cause, and DHKP-C, but also the importance of Grup Yorum and its Marxist credentials.

Armed resistance is a part of DHKP-C's ideology. The lead singer again suggests this in a spoken word break near the end of the concert. He says:

Alright, my friends. We shared lots of emotions together this evening. We refreshed our hopes with this concert. Songs in this concert enlarge our longing for an independent land and it strengthens our resolution for reaching our goal

Figure 6.6 Grup Yorum play at Kızıldere

these days. If we exist, we have hope. If we exist, we can fight. We will see each other again when we achieve our goal... Good-bye

Pronouns again play a role in defining a community, though this time it is a community longing for an independent Kurdistan. "We" and "our" are used throughout this speech. Lexical choices such as "shared" and "together" suggest unity. "Our hopes," "our longing," "our resolution," and "our goal" all suggest unity in a desire for "an independent land." These are typical of many Kurdish rights groups. However, also expressed here is "If we exist, we can fight." Here it is not just through democratic and diplomatic avenues which are suggested, but also violent methods, connoted in the lexical choice "fight," something more extreme groups believe is a legitimate avenue. This being spoken in the midst of songs which show support for armed struggle and DHKP-C makes clear the political alliances connoted by Grup Yorum for its community.

The DHKP-C, and the revolutionary movement in general, are anti-imperialists and especially anti-American. Grup Yorum expresses this same sentiment, excluding America from its sense of community. This is articulated in a number of segments throughout the concert. One such time is during the reading of the poem "Geçit yok/ No pass" by Tuncel Kurtiz. He reads the following with a gritty voice, suggesting the truth, authenticity, and "telling it as it is" (van Leeuwen 1999; Moore 2002):

1. Yankie give no pass, imperialism
2. They will be accountable for the bombs
3. Murder America
4. We are Kurds, Turks, Arabs
5. We are the public
6. We know we know
7. Imperialists fault
8. We are as cruel as them.

Here an "us" and "them" is created with "us" being a united "public" who "knows." America is represented as "them," named informally as "Yankie," "murder America," "imperialists," "them," and "cruel." They are collocated with "imperialism," "bombs," and "fault" and activated in "give no pass." With revolutionary spirit, though in vague terms, "we" will hold them "accountable" and "we are as cruel as them." Typical of lyrics, this poem again creates "us" and "them" groups based around popular notions and in this case Marxist notions, but offer little in the way of concrete criticism and firm solutions.

Elsewhere, anti-Americanism is witnessed in the song "Defol America/Go to hell America," where a large group of well-known Turkish politically active performers including Haluk Levent, Nejat Yavaşoğulları, Ibrahim Karaca, Gup Marsis, Suavi Murat Kekilli, Ruhi Su Dostlar Chorus, Hakan Yeşilyurt, Sevcan Orhan, and Sevinç Eratalay fill the stage. They line up alongside the lead singers of Grup Yorum, represented in unity by standing "shoulder to shoulder." Some share microphones, some put arms around each other, pressed very close to each other suggesting closeness in their unity. While the drummer keeps the beat, they encourage the whole stadium to chant "America Katil/America the murderer." After the song, the lead singer leads the audience in a chant of "America the murderer. America the murderer. Go to hell." Lights go on the audience, connoting they too are part of a community which hates America.

Community dimensions: A community led by Grup Yorum

As is the case in many concerts, the band leads the evening's entertainment through song, dance, and visuals. The band succeeds at entertaining while also articulating discourses of an (selective) egalitarian community united around Marxist ideas. However, there is also a dominant discourse of legitimacy of Grup Yorum. That is, although Grup Yorum articulates Marxist beliefs including egalitarianism, the concert suggests it is led by Grup Yorum. This discourse can be seen in a number of ways, including the positioning of performers on the stage and clothing (Figure 6.7). On stage, there are four distinguishable groups, identifiable by clothing and position. At center front stage and to stage left are members of Group Yorum. Choosing to place themselves at the front of the stage gives them salience, suggesting importance. The two singers for the band—a man and a woman—stand slightly in front of the band (in Figure 6.7, only the woman is visible). They all wear open-necked white shirts with rolled up sleeves and khaki colored trousers, except for the woman singer, who wears a simple, open-necked long dress. She wears no makeup and flat shoes. This is not glamorous pop star attire, but very "normal" everyday clothes. For the rest of Grup Yorum, wearing the same clothes points to anonymity, sameness, equality, part of a group, like soldiers or police (Machin and van Leeuwen 2005). The choice of khaki-colored trousers again suggests the military or militants, khaki the color of soldiers. The white-colored shirts suggest a sense of formality, the concert being a special occasion, as opposed to colorful shirts which suggest flashy showmanship. Choosing to wear open-necked shirts with sleeves rolled up suggests casualness, but also "rolling up your sleeves" to get to work, a metaphor for unity with workers and the seriousness of the "work" at hand.

Stage right and slightly behind Grup Yorum's two vocalists is the "Grup Yorum Choir." The choir is Grup Yorum's "students," a feeder source for the band. They too are dressed in white open-necked shirts. Red scarves around the necks of women singers

Figure 6.7 Stage position

suggest leftist political alliances, as is the color of the backdrop stage curtains. Behind both these groups, suggesting less importance and dressed in black, is the "Istanbul Symphony Project," a full orchestra including but not limited to violins, cello, French horns, trombones, trumpets, and clarinets. At the rear of the stage also dressed in black is the "Ladies and Gentlemen" choir. Stage placing and indistinguishable outfits suggest sameness but also less salience and importance than Grup Yorum.

Sounds and poses also suggest that Gup Yorum leads the community. Though there is an orchestra and two choirs, it is the sounds of Grup Yorum; drums, electric guitar, acoustic guitar, bağlama, bongos, and electric bass which are salient in the mix of instrumentation. The lead singers are most salient in both visuals and sounds, suggesting their importance. Grup Yorum is arranged on stage throughout the concert striking a pose similar to their posters (Figure 6.8). The bağlama and bongo players are seated and the guitar and bass players stand all in the same order as their posters. By striking the same pose in concert, an intertextual visual authentication occurs. Similar to Auslander's (2015: 359) authenticating process where band authenticity is determined by whether or not it sounds like the recording, here it is a visual authentication process where the band indeed looks like the poster.

A community led by Grup Yorum is connoted more explicitly through spoken word. Consider this short speech by the bass player at the end of "Umudun Zeybeği/ Zeybek hope":

> Our children die early. We play these songs in the hope children will not die of hunger and a lack of medicine and they live happy in a free world.

Here, the pronouns "our" and "we" suggest unity between the families of children who die and the group. "Our" group is represented as victims of death, "hunger," and a "lack of medicine." Deleted from this representation is who is responsible for such victimization. In the context of the song, it is presupposed that those opposed to unionization are responsible (see above), presupposing it is right-wing governments like AKP and large corporations. Grup Yorum is represented positively, in a role of

Figure 6.8 Grup Yorum poster pose

playing in the hope of a better world, acting positively by "play[ing] the songs in the hope," yet not really solving problems. It is small reminders like this which indicate the importance Grup Yorum gives itself in its constructed community.

For Grup Yorum to be seen as leading a community, the band has to present itself as authentic/legitimate protest musicians. One way to do this is through references to prison. This is not to deny that many of its members have ended up in prison. However, in some genres, being associated with prison authenticates a band. For example, being from the streets and having run-ins with the police are part of hip hop's authentication. Songs and videos are plenty with references to prison and being anti-police, such as Body Count's "Cop Killer" or Public Enemy's "Fuck the police." We saw this in Dev's "Dans Et," where the band positions itself against the police (also see Way 2015b). This is also something I have seen in Özgün music. For instance, on the evening of September 6, 2013, I saw a performance by İlkay Akkaya, the lead singer from Grup Kızılırmak. Between songs she shared jokes with the crowd to get them to laugh with her about injustices she has endured as a protest singer. During one of these talks, she described how one of her concerts had been canceled and she had been arrested. "Isn't that a surprise," she said giggling, her hand on her chest, a sign of deep feelings of sincerity in Turkish culture. The crowd joined in her laughter. She described her ordeal while in police custody and her confrontational style of banter between herself and the police. "Why are you here?" asked the police. "I don't know. You tell me." She replied. "You are a communist," replied the police. "Is this a crime?" she asked and giggled. The audience took her cue and we laughed along with her. Stories like these create a bond between herself and the audience. These also legitimate her as a subversive musician who gets arrested and in the face of harassment maintains her subversiveness. These anti-establishment qualities are essential for folk and Özgün music in the West and in Turkey.

This same sense of subversive authentication is articulated in the Grup Yorum concert in a number of ways. Between songs, the woman lead singer says:

> Hello to our friends in prison, the 12 September 1980 military coup prisoners. Even now they are still putting people in prison—even though the coup is finished, they imprisoned people who share ideas of the left. The free prisoners are an active voice. The Yorum collective with its production of ideas are critical and wonderfully oppositional against prison, isolation, cruelty, and all pressures. Grup Yorum members are jailed. There is always a part of us in prison, in spite of F type prisons, they share their poems, melodies, and their conversations with us for 25 years. Endless thanks to these free prisoners.

Turkey's 1980 coup targeted many left-wing political activists who were arrested and are still in prison. These are named as "our friends in prison," "free prisoners," "people who share ideas of the Left." These namings make clear it is prisoners of the Left who are "our friends," not others who have also been unjustly arrested and imprisoned in Turkey. It is Grup Yorum members, those who "share their poems, melodies, and their conversations with us for 25 years." A bond is articulated, legitimizing both those performing on the night and those imprisoned through "There is always a part of us in prison." These connote authenticity to Grup Yorum as a politically active and subversive group.

Jailed members of Grup Yorum are also a part of the performance, further authenticating Grup Yorum's anti-establishment credentials. Between songs, recorded telephone and video messages from present and former jailed Grup Yorum members such as guitarist Muharrem Cengiz are played. The messages express support for Grup Yorum, while the videos show unity with Grup Yorum through dress, wearing white open-necked shirts like those worn by Grup Yorum. Song titles such as "Bir Görüş Kabininde/A prison's visiting room" are played while lyrics represent hope for prisoners, as in "Death collects the flowers, but the flower seeds never end." Through poetic metaphor, lyrics suggest that despite arrests and police harassment, the leftist project of Grup Yorum continues, though as per normal, no details are offered.

Conclusion

This chapter has examined how concerts articulate discourses of community by examining in detail moments from Grup Yorum's twenty-fifth-anniversary concert. Though this is only one concert, the construction of a sense of community is a common feature in concerts. This has been noted in classical concert going (Dearn and Price 2016), rock concerts (Auslander 1999), and folk (Eyerman and Jamison 1998). Like other concerts, I have demonstrated how musicians employ a wide variety of semiotic resources to create this sense of community. In this case, these connote a community of resistance. It is here we see my three broad modes of lyrics, visuals, and musical sounds, "stretched" to also include body movement, dance, lighting, stage position, spoken word, recorded messages, and video playback. These and others can all be used to create a multimodal subversive sense of community.

Grup Yorum also exploits these semiotic resources to subvert dominant notions of capitalism. It exposes the unfairness of capitalist projects such as globalization (by critiquing imperialism), greed, social injustice, false imprisonment, and government and big business exploitation. It also articulates positive discourses of unity, egalitarianism, the rights of Kurds, the poor, and workers. These are represented as both international and Turkish issues which bind together its community.

However, we should also be wary of the limitations of concerts such as this. Concerts inevitably articulate discourses of authentication. Even in a concert such as this by Grup Yorum, discourses of egalitarianism are tainted with contradictory discourses of the power of Grup Yorum. Furthermore, though unity and equality are articulated, so are discourses which are divisive, creating groups of "us" and "them," othering America, the IMF, capitalists, managers, and the likes. Though many of the actions by these people and organizations can be seen as being motivated by self-interest, there are also many exceptions. No doubt there are many positive actions America is responsible for. The same can be said for all others not represented in Grup Yorum's constructed community. However, Grup Yorum is guilty of simplifying social actors, issues, events, and conflicts into simple representations. For example, who is "America"? Is it the military, big business, the government, or poor minorities who live in the United States working day to day to make ends meet? Representations such as those in the concert offer little in the way of details and almost nothing in terms of realistic practical solutions.

What the concert offers is a vague critique of society through the prism of a community built on a very specific brand of Marxism, that of the DHKP-C. This organization's perspective offers opinions and solutions which may be seen by many as very narrow. By Grup Yorum vaguely articulating such discourses, along with all the others mentioned above, this concert successfully creates a community of subversion, but what exactly is this subversion is confusing at best.

7

Music Videos against Government Policies

From 2006 until 2010, I was the manager of a radio station which we claimed played music not heard on the multitude of Turkish radio stations. This was a great chance for me to be exposed to a huge variety of Turkish music. A year after I left the station, I was in Izmir talking with a friend about music and politics. We were comparing Turkish and Anglo-American music which we thought were politically progressive. I claimed in the West this music was usually associated with various forms of rock, hip hop, and folk, while he claimed it was mostly linked to Özgün music. Both of us played a few videos from YouTube which we thought typified our claims. I was surprised he did not play any rock or hip hop and said so. My friend rose to the challenge and played the video for Duman's "İyi de bana ne." Here was a video which not only sounded great, but was blatantly criticizing the AKP government. Though the sounds were aggressive and emotive, it was the images which criticized a whole list of AKP policies in the video which drew me into the song and made me want to listen and watch the video over and over again.

Popular music which criticizes government policies is not unique to Turkey. Pop stars do this the world over. For example, Malaysian singer Namewee has questioned Malaysia's national energy provider over blackouts, the Specials AKA's "Free Nelson Mandella" was part of a global campaign against South Africa's Apartheid policies which included the incarceration of Nelson Mandela. John Lennon sang "Imagine" as part of a critique of US war policies. Gil Scott-Heron's "The revolution will not be televised" criticized the Nixon years. Elvis Costello's "Ship building" criticized the United Kingdom's war policies in the Falkland Islands and Public Enemy's "Fight the power" was a tirade against the abuse of power by white authorities in the United States toward blacks. The list is long, inexhaustible, and well documented on internet websites and in books such as 33 *Revolutions per Minute: A History of Protest Songs*.

A scan of scholarly work on music's role in criticizing governments reveals this is a contentious area in terms of how the two fit together. In Chapter 3, I noted how views range from the highly optimistic to views which are far more limited. Even the most optimistic reading acknowledges limits to music's critique of government policies such as it rarely deals with other country's politics and it does not necessarily express conventional politics well, but is more compatible with political ideas (Frith 1988; Street 1988, 2013; Terkourafi 2010). What also seems certain is political, social, and historical contexts not only shape the political perspective of musicians (Street 1988), but also define the potential meanings of songs and videos. This is evident in Eyerman and Jamison's (1998) observation that even after the policies which are criticized are long forgotten, new policies and new events make some songs relevant again.

In this chapter, we look at music videos which criticize Turkish government policies. In Turkey, these videos take on particular significance, seeing as the Turkish media and its government are intertwined to the extent where subversive discourses are all but silenced. Despite this context, some popular music videos criticize AKP's neoliberal economics, social and religious conservatism, relations with Kurds, corruption, and its foreign policies. Though videos criticize in different ways using various semiotic resources, in this chapter I focus on the role of visuals. I do this to illustrate their importance in videos, such as the Duman video I mentioned above. I do not examine visuals in isolation, but analyze them within the context of musical sounds and lyrics which together communicate criticism in these music videos.

This chapter is divided into sections based on government policies which are critiqued by musicians. First I briefly examine how two music groups criticize the government's socially conservative policies, though in very different ways. This is followed by an in-depth analysis of one video which critiques the government's policies toward its Alevi and Kurdish populations. Lastly, I examine a video which critiques a specific government policy, that is, the decision to go to war in Iraq. The aim of this chapter is to critically examine how musicians from a range of genres criticize both general policy ideas and specific government policies. Here, I am interested in how pop music videos "do" political criticism.

Videos which attack AKP's social and religious conservatism

Part of AKP's political program has focused on Islamic and social conservatism (see Chapter 4). Their policies have resulted in both legal and symbolic changes. Public statements by Erdoğan and other members of AKP, such as "women are not equal to men," "women should stay at home and not go to work to bring down unemployment," "women should have a minimum of three children," and "women should not laugh in public," are part of AKP's socially conservative public discourse which is widely reported and discussed in the media. These ideas are legitimized through AKP's interpretation of Islam. Socially and religiously conservative government statements and actions are criticized by a number of bands, including Hayko Cepkin and Duman. Here we take a brief look at how these musicians do this in different ways.

Social conservatism under attack by Hayko Cepkin

Hayko Cepkin is an alternative metal musician whose videos, for the most part, are not politically contentious (Figure 7.1). However, he has performed for the Halkevleri, one of the biggest radical Left movements in Turkey against AKP. Furthermore, he has also

Figure 7.1 Hayko Cepkin

spoken out publicly against AKP on a number of occasions including a video in which he invites people to join Halkevi and "struggle for democracy and freedom."[1]

Hayko Cepkin's 2005 "Fırtınam" ("My storm") is a pleasant musical mixture of traditional Turkish-Armenian sounds, rock guitars, and Cepkin's wailing voice. It is his most successful single in terms of airplay on radio and television. At the time of writing, the video had in excess of three million "hits" on YouTube.[2] Drawing on folk, rock, pop, and arabesk traditions, lyrics describe a turbulent love affair. As such, these lyrics have no obvious political reading. However, it is the visuals and music which subtly, but clearly, critique. The visuals tell a story of a struggle to break from the social conformity advocated as part of AKP's conservative ideology. The only participants represented are Cepkin and his band. The visual narrative may be read in three parts: Cepkin walks through dark woods, soon everything he touches brightens up, and finally, he turns into a rocker and lightens up his dark surroundings. This narrative works on a metaphoric level, with the aid of music, to articulate both the negative aspects of social conservatism and the positivity of social subversion.

The visuals use a variety of strategies to criticize social conservatism. At the beginning of the video, Cepkin is represented powerless as unseen forces dress him into conservative clothing: a white shirt, a black jacket, and trousers. Though agency is not represented, choices in clothes suggest the party who is dressing Cepkin is conservative, the likes AKP promotes and represents. The environment is dark connoting negativity while lighting on Cepkin is overexposed (Figure 7.2), connoting truth, clarity, almost other-worldliness and hope (Machin 2007: 70). He trudges through an ever-darker forest, a metaphor for social conservatism evident by his dress. During this walk, Cepkin's actions are without consequence or agency, suggesting a

Figure 7.2 Overexposure of lighting, dark setting, and conservative clothes

lack of power (van Leeuwen 1995, 1996). He walks aimlessly, searching, gesturing. He climbs a hill, a metaphor for Cepkin's "uphill battle" against conservatism and his struggle to free himself from it.

Traditional sounds with connotations of conservatism are "up-front" in the mix emphasizing their importance during this forest walk (van Leeuwen 1999: 14). But there are also electric guitar sounds present. By juxtaposing the traditional melody from "Magic Duduk" by the Armenian group Givan Gasparyan with Western-influenced rock guitar sounds, there is the suggestion of difference and subversion to conservatism and tradition. These sounds act as a counterpoint to AKP claims that "We Turks are all conservative" and other statements intended to homogenize Turkey's heterogeneous population.

At one minute into the video, Cepkin's actions start revealing agency connoting power, such as his touch brightens the darkness and turns earth into bright gold (Fairclough 2003: 150). He also starts lip-synching. These actions suggest Cepkin is gaining some control over his otherwise bleak situation. The dark forest then opens up into a dark field, a metaphor for more freedom. At 2:18 into the video, Cepkin gestures with his hands, reaches inside himself, there is a bright flash and he is transformed into a rock singer, indicated by his unconventional red outfit, tattoos, an accompanying band all dressed in black and him performing "live" in the field (Figure 7.3). He also now throws light from within himself into the air and the whole landscape temporarily lights up. Here, there is agency, connoting great power and positivity once he has metaphorically broken free from the constraints of conservative society and transformed himself into one who challenges such ideas (van Leeuwen 1996).

Figure 7.3 Rock transformation

There is also a change in music with Cepkin's visual transformation. Here, the electric guitar starts playing rock power chords, a genre with connotations of subversion and rebelliousness (Frith 1981; Street 1988; Machin 2010). Cepkin's voice quality and timbre also change. Cepkin's voice opens up, singing more aggressively. There is less emotional control and restraint, symbolizing an emotional outburst. Vocal harmonies are brought up in the mix, producing a more "up-front" vocal presence. This allows Cepkin to be heard over the louder more aggressive instrumental soundscape. The gritty quality of Cepkin's voice contributes to a realistic modality (van Leeuwen 1999: 175), connoting Cepkin's "real" struggle with real AKP social issues (ibid.: 131). Furthermore, during the first chorus, which coincides with Cepkin gaining agency in his actions and then his transformation into a rocker, vocal pitch range is increased with much higher notes sung. Tagg (1990: 112) observes how high notes carry with them connotations of effort, assertiveness, and urgency. Together, these vocal aspects with visuals of Cepkin becoming a rocker connote a heightening of emotions as he breaks free of restraints, including AKP social conservatism.

AKP's religious conservatism under attack by Duman

The previous examination reveals that Cepkin uses visual metaphor and musical sounds to criticize. Duman's 2009 "Iyı de bana ne" criticizes more directly (Figure 7.4). Though there is no official music video for this song, there are a number of unofficial

Figure 7.4 Duman

videos. The fan-made video I chose attacks many aspects of AKP from a Kemalist perspective.[3]

Visuals are a series of stills depicting AKP politicians, issues, and symbols which criticize Erdoğan and AKP. Lyrics describe a nameless person or institution responsible for many negative actions. Written lyrics are superimposed on the visuals connoting their importance and making a direct connection between anti-AKP visuals and lyrics. These two modes focus the song's grunge-style aggressive musical elements resulting in all three modes complementing each other in producing a critique of AKP and a number of its policies, including Erdoğan is a poor leader, AKP relations with the United States are too close, and political corruption is rife.

Here, I examine one aspect of Duman's critique, that is, how this video articulates a discourse that AKP's Islamic religious conservatism is "backward." This can be seen in the visuals throughout the video including a screen grab of a television news headline which reads "Turkey's secular nature is broken under AKP, sourced from the EU." In another visual, Turkey's president of the time, Ahmed Gül, holds hands with a Saudi politician connoting closeness between Turkey and religiously conservative Saudi Arabia. In another, Erdoğan kneels subserviently in front of a bearded and robed Islamic cleric. An image of a mosque's minaret flanked by AKP flags coincides with the lyrics "We have a problem." All of these point to AKP's affinity to Islam and its perceived threat to secularism.

Aydınlığımızı kestiler.

Figure 7.5 Religious conservatism

In another image (Figure 7.5), we see a black and white still of a light bulb cloaked in an Islamic headscarf. "AK" in AKP stands for "true," "pure," or "light." The party's symbol is a bright yellow light bulb. Here, light is removed and replaced with a dark bulb, darkness connoting evil, lies, and obscurity. By cloaking the dark bulb in an Islamic headscarf, religion and "backward"/"not enlightened" is suggested. Superimposed on the image are the lyrics "They cut off our light." Here, an "us" and "them" group is constructed with AKP named as "they" distinct from "our" group of non-supporters. They are represented negatively with agency and metaphorically by "cutting off" light. Using the metaphor of casting "us" into darkness to represent the rise of religious Islamic conservatism frames AKP's religious views very negatively. This line and the whole chorus are performed at double speed with an aggressive yelling style of singing. This loud gritty style of singing emphasizes Duman's anger (van Leeuwen 1999: 131). Visuals and lyrics clarify the anger is directed at AKP and its emphasis on socially conservative interpretations of Islam.

AKP's treatment of minorities under attack by Grup Kızılırmak

Grup Kızılırmak's "Çeşmi Siyahim/My black eyed beauty" is one of many musical contributions which highlight the plight of Turkey's religious and ethnic minorities, Alevi and Kurds being the largest of these groups respectively (Figure 7.6). Musicians

Figure 7.6 Grup Kızılırmak

include Ahmet Kaya, Şivan Perwer, Grup Yorum, Aynur Doğan, Agire Jiyan, Ciwan Haco, and Ferhat Tunç. Grup Kızılırmak's video highlights the injustices of government policies toward both these groups. Alevi is the second most popular religion in Turkey behind Sunni Islam. Though a branch of Islam, traditionally they have been "branded as heretics by the Sunnis" (Zeidan 1999: 75). Even today "the Alevis still carry the stigma of being sectarian 'others' " (ibid.). This status of an internal "other" has resulted in "centuries of persecution, prejudice and misconceptions at the hands of the majority Sunnis" (ibid.). Kurds, regardless of being Alevi or Sunni, have also faced persecution and endure "the Kurdish question," which is their struggle for recognition and the right to live as equals in Turkey. It is judged by many as the most important and destructive problem in Turkey today (Barkey and Fuller 1998). AKP has had mixed success with resolving it, though this seems to be motivated more by gaining votes than actually finding a solution. Furthermore, relations between AKP and Kurds have taken a turn for the worst since 2015, again related to wider political events (see Chapter 4). "Çeşmi Siyahim" criticizes government policies affecting this "double defect" of being both religiously Alevi and ethnically Kurdish.

Why Grup Kızılırmak's "Çeşmi Siyahim"?

Grup Kızılırmak has produced thirteen albums since forming in 1990. Its Marxist political orientation is well known, choosing to perform at Cuban benefits and Marxist conferences, with its music highlighting the plight of minorities and offering solidarity ("Grup Kızılırmak" 2013). With such a political outlook, group members have been arrested and concerts banned or canceled. Even the band's name suggests bonds with Kurds: The Kızılırmak River is a part of Turkey with deep Kurdish roots. Naming bands after local names such as Ladysmith Black Mambaso and Cypress Hill is "evocative of place, and often history and rurality" (Connell and Gibson 2003: 43). Here, the band is named after a river in eastern Turkey which in the past was the historic boundary between Kurds to the East and Greeks to the West. Today, it is a very poor area populated by many Kurds and Alevi. For many in Turkey, the name evokes Kurdish and Alevi people and their struggles from the past and present.

The song "Çeşmi Siyahim" is in the style of Özgün (authentic protest) music, a cultural hybrid of Anatolian musical traditions alongside Western musical styles and perceived as being politically Left of center. "Çeşmi Siyahim" is a cover of a folk song originally performed by Mahsuni Şerif in the 1960s. However, Grup Kızılırmak did not record it until 2002, with its accompanying video first uploaded onto video-sharing website İzlesene.com in 2007 and YouTube in 2008.[4]

The style of protest in "Çeşmi Siyahim" is not one of direct references, but more suggestive. However, key to this video's criticism of government policies toward Kurds and Alevis is the representation of places and people in places. These articulate discourses of sympathy, commonality with past protesters and criticism toward AKP cultural policies. The visual narrative represents a voyage by the band which travels to a poor village where band members witness the working and living conditions of villagers. Then, they travel back to perform in front of a large crowd. Likewise, the lyrics also describe a journey. This time somebody is leaving a place to go to the mountains. A close examination of visuals in the video reveals how these play a role in criticizing AKP policies toward Kurds and Alevis.

Video representations of the plight of minorities

As part of criticizing AKP policies toward minorities, this video creates sympathy toward Kurds and Alevis. Most of the video is set in a poor working village. Dress on both men and women villagers indicate this is an Alevi and Kurdish village. Band members appear in a number of long shots walking through its streets. The village is typical of those which have suffered due to Turkey's mass migration from rural to urban centers over the past eighty years. Migration has "had a marked effect on development where provision of basic services in rural areas continues to be hindered," resulting in "a much lower standard of living and access to basic services for the smaller rural population" ("UNICEF in Turkey" 2010). Alevi villages are also known to suffer more than Sunni ones (Zeidan 1999: 75). In the video, band members walk past and observe villagers who stare at the cameras, look elsewhere, or watch others work. These representations of actions do not affect anyone or anything, suggesting a lack of power (Fairclough 2003). Men and boys engage in poorly paid manual work such as grinding and molding metal, separating wheat, working fields, and constructing buildings (Figure 7.7). The settings of decrepit buildings, dark interiors, poor houses, and working environments signify poverty. The abundance of close-up shots of villagers grants viewers a point of identification, drawing viewers close and humanizing them,

Figure 7.7 Alevi and Kurds' working conditions

making it easy to sympathize with their plight (Machin 2007: 118–119). By creating sympathy for Kurds and Alevi, Grup Kızılırmak indirectly criticizes government policies which have resulted in less than ideal circumstances for a large number of Kurds and Alevi who live in Turkey.

Lyrics complement visuals which evoke sympathy, as does the choice of the song being played in a minor key. The lines "My wealth (capital) is my pain/concern my friend, my wealth is my curse/frustration" is repeated twice. Collocating wealth and capital with the nouns "pain," "curse," "concern," and "frustration" four times expresses a negative attitude to wealth. Though circumstances are unclear, a common trait in music (Machin 2010: 92), one can speculate that like the Kurds and Alevi represented in the visuals, wealth is not something they have the luxury to enjoy. Here, visuals focus the vague notions of poverty into sympathy for the economic plight of Kurdish and Alevi villagers.

Relations between the band and minorities

Villager shots are montaged together with shots of the band. However, unlike the villagers, the band is always shot as a group. These group shots signify anonymity, less importance, and homogeneity (Machin and van Leeuwen 2005: 132). As such, the plight of the villagers is connoted as important while the band is de-emphasized. Furthermore, how the band shares visual space suggests relations between the two groups. In all village shots, the band and villagers share common locations of narrow streets, dark spaces, and a small traditional café. However, they rarely share the same shot. By framing the band and villagers in a common location, a loose "integration" takes place between the two groups which suggests similarity, closeness, and

Figure 7.8 Worker and band social exchange

sympathy. However, by separating them in shots, difference is also articulated (van Leeuwen 2005: 112).

On the rare occasions when the band and villagers share the same shot, difference is again connoted by the groups not engaging with each other. Band members seem like ghosts, framed in the background of compositions, simply observing. This lack of engagement distinguishes those who are oppressed (workers and minorities) from those who fight oppression (the band). In fact, the band is further differentiated from villagers by having the luxury of going on road trips unlike the villagers. In one sequence, the group interacts with villagers symbolically and literally. Here, the band drinks Turkish coffee in a traditional coffee house (Figure 7.8). The colorful patterned cushions, off-white walls, and decor make it clear the place is a traditional workers' "kahvehane," not an upmarket café. A waiter interacts with the group by exchanging glances and pouring coffee into their cups. Interestingly, the coffee "cezve" (coffee making vessel) looks like the cezve the group observed being made previously. This sequence links the worker who makes the cezve with the waiter with the band, creating a bond of understanding about the plight of minorities and workers in rural Turkey.

Connections with protesters from the past

Not only do visuals suggest sympathy and unity with minorities, they also articulate support for protest and political subversion. In the lyrics, this is heard in the lines "You laughed at the poor condition of Mahzuni my friend, Even if he perished in the hands of strangers." Aşık Mahzuni Şerif was a Turkish Alevi protest folk singer, poet, and author who suffered intimidation by having his house burned down, being investigated, and accused by Turkey's State Security Court for protesting against the

Figure 7.9 Band and Yilmaz Güney

government including declaring "Hem Kızılbaş, hem Aleviyim/I am both Kızılbaş and Alevi," before fleeing to Germany in 2001 where he died. Until 2000, both Kızılbaş and Alevi sects of Shi'a Islam were not allowed to openly practice their religion. Here, "you" antagonize Mahzuni by laughing at him, just as the Turkish authorities antagonized him. Though this representation lacks detail, "you" are represented negatively and opposed to the group of "us" who are oppressed, protest, and subvert.

This same discourse can be seen in the kahvehane sequence described above. Here, band members share the same location with a picture of Yilmaz Güney (Figure 7.9). Güney was a Kurdish filmmaker, actor, communist, and protester who was imprisoned in 1961 for publishing a communist novel. From that time until his death in 1984, Güney struggled with the Turkish authorities resulting in imprisonment, then fleeing to France before having his citizenship revoked. While band members drink coffee, a picture of Güney hangs in the center of the background. It is salient, being in the center of a neutral colored wall. By the band sharing a space with the picture, the two visual elements (band and Güney) are linked, both critics of Turkey's treatment of Kurds and Alevi (van Leeuwen 2005). This shot is followed by a full screen close-up of the same picture. This close-up aids the viewer in identifying Güney and emphasizes his importance to the band (Machin 2007).

Protest here and now

The band is also symbolically represented as protesters themselves. Clothes, hair, and instruments are important semiotic resources for bands (Machin 2010). Band members do not dress traditionally like the villagers, but some have long hair, sideburns, wear jeans, denim, and leather jackets, while black and other dark colors are dominant. Here, these are used to connote rock, a genre with anti-establishment and rebellious associations (Frith 1981; Street 1988; Machin 2010). These same style choices can be seen in rock imagery from the Rolling Stones' *Black and Blue* album cover to most images of Motörhead, the Stranglers, and Muse. Electric guitars and a full rock drum kit are seen both in the village and in the concert scenes. In some cases, they are salient, dominating the foregrounds and connoting importance. Here, rock semiotic resources are used as symbols of subversion to those in Turkey who promote a more Eastern outlook, including the government.

But visuals which echo rock are not enough to suggest the band is against government policies opposed to minorities. Lyrics and musical choices make this clear. The narrator sings of journeys involving "mountains" with "vineyards." References to the outdoors draw upon folk aesthetics and authenticity, but they also express protest in the context of Özgün music. The narrator invites the listener to join her journey in "Come on, my friend let's go for a walk over the high mountains," similar to mountain lyrical references in the previous chapter. In Turkish literature and history, people who experience problems with authorities escape "to the mountains." Here, they become fugitives or bandits, taking up guns, some stealing and some fighting oppressive authority figures. Some of these characters have been romanticized, represented as heroes similar to Robin Hood (see "Yalnız Efe" by Ömer Seyfettin). There are also present-day connotations associated with the mountains of southeast Turkey, where Kurdish fighters battle with the Turkish military. By the narrator "walking" to the "mountains," alongside visuals of Alevi and Kurdish villagers, opposition to the government and its policies are suggested.

This opposition is represented positively through key changes in the song. Though the song is in a minor key, between each line of sung lyrics there is a short musical solo in Cmaj, the major key suggesting something positive, unlike a minor key. With accompanying lyrics which refer to mountains and the possibility of resistance, maybe even armed resistance, the video works multimodally to positively represent resistance for Kurdish and Alevi victims of AKP policies.

Grup Kızılırmak and political opposition are legitimate

Grup Kızılırmak's political message of protest against government policies about minorities is legitimized in the video's concert sequences. Rock's authenticity is closely related to live performance and "It is live rock which binds audience to musician" (Frith 1981: 80). Though Grup Kızılırmak is not a rock act, a similar criterion of being authentic through live performance is used in folk music, including Özgün music. Furthermore, choosing these images suggests a degree of respect in terms of the band being functionally identified as professional musicians (van Leeuwen 1996: 59). This legitimacy is emphasized by shots of a large enthusiastic crowd who reacts to the band and their political messages by clapping, cheering, and dancing. It also signifies the band's power, being able to produce such reactions. Perspective and camera angles are used to connote the band's legitimacy and power. Band members are shot both individually in close perspective and as a group. The close-ups connote intimacy and support for the band, while group shots suggest team spirit (Machin and van Leeuwen 2005). In most shots, the camera is tilted up signifying power and legitimacy.

Alternatively, audience shots are taken from above connoting less power (Machin 2007: 114). Also, there are no individual shots, the audience is always represented as a large homogenous group unified in their approval of Grup Kızılırmak (ibid.: 118). Like the villagers, the audience have limited power (in this case, responding to the band), share the same space as the band, and sometimes are in the same shots. However, unlike the villagers, the audience is represented positively as happy, enthusiastic, and energetic, not oppressed. In this visual hierarchy of audience and band, the audience may symbolize hope of subverting oppression through protest which is articulated and led by legitimate protesters like Grup Kızılırmak.

This analysis reveals how Grup Kızılırmak's attack on government policies is not direct and obvious, but poetic and subtle. This is done largely through metaphor and in very abstract ways. This may be a survival mechanism for the band, a radical band which is still performing today (mostly under the name of its singer İlkay Akkaya). Members of bands who are more obviously political, such as Grup Yorum, end up in prison in today's Turkey. As such, though subtle, the visuals together with musical sounds and lyrics play a role in articulating criticism.

Musical attack on AKP's foreign policy by Bariş Akarsu

Critiquing governmental war policy is something we see in many pop songs such as Green Day's "21 guns," Elvis Costello's "Shipbuilding," and Edwin Starr's "War." Here I examine a pop music star's foray into similar politics through a music video. In this case study, I examine how Bariş Akarsu, a musician firmly in the pop music mainstream, did a "political" song and video, as was seen internationally with Beyoncé's "Formation." Beyoncé's video and Superbowl 2016 performance were said to be about Black rights in America. Akarsu's video is a critique of American and Turkish involvement in the 2003 Iraq War, a theme also seen in "No need for War" by a group of Turkish musicians (Mor ve Ötesi, Aylin Aslım, Bülent Ortaçgil, Athena, Feridun Düzağaç, Koray Candemir, Nejat Yavaşoğulları, and Vega).[5]

Akarsu rocketed to fame in late 2004 and in 2007 suddenly died. He released a total of three albums, in 2004, 2006, and 2007. "Kimdir O" is the second video from his first album, described as an anti-Iraq War video by his website, Wikipedia, and fans. Turkey's mainstream media played the video sparingly, possibly due to AKP's close relations with Turkey's media and its leadership's support for the war. All the same, it has received some Turkish radio and video channel airplay as well as over 753,000 "hits" on YouTube at the time of writing.

So what was Akarsu protesting against?

The invasion of Iraq by American and British troops in March 2003 caused a split between Turkish public opinion and AKP. Despite efforts by AKP to find a negotiated solution, American pressure, threats, and promises convinced AKP's leadership to cooperate with the United States (Aydin and Aras 2005; Artunişik 2006; Yeşiltaş 2009). The agreement reached between the United States and Turkey was "highly beneficial to Turkey" with aid, loan guarantees, and Turkish deployment of troops in exchange for 62,000 US troops and more than 250 planes in Turkey (Altunişik 2006: 189). However, AKP's leadership were defeated in a parliamentary vote. It had failed to persuade the public or even the parliament to support the war despite Turkish media's lack of opposition (Özgüneş and Terzis 2000; Jenkins 2012) and there being a long history of political and military cooperation between Turkey and the United States. AKP's leadership chose to support the US war based on practical politics despite public opinion which was set against it (Altunişik 2006; Yeşiltaş 2009). Despite this initial setback, on March 20, overflight rights were permitted and Washington named Turkey as one of the "coalition of the willing." AKP also allowed American use of its airbase in Adana and Turkish territory for humanitarian purposes, including the transportation of equipment. For this, a $1 billion aid package for Turkey was budgeted as well as the continuation of Turkish troops in Iraq (Altunişik 2006: 190). By October 7, 2003, AKP was further embroiled in the war, winning more concessions with the Turkish Parliament voting in favor of sending Turkish troops into Iraq, even though this did not happen during the war.

Presently, close US-Turkish relations persist, despite differences. Both countries share membership in organizations including NATO and the G-20, the United States actively supports Turkey's membership into the European Union, and both cooperate on peaceful uses for nuclear energy and missions into Syria and Iraq. This close historical relationship is likely to continue due to the belief by Turkey's political elite that its security depends on remaining a strategic ally of the United States, despite popular resistance.

How does Akarsu criticize foreign policy?

Akarsu's "Kimdir O" articulates a range of popular political discourses such as "all politicians are evil," "Turkey is subservient to America," and "all war is bad." It is how these ideas are communicated through lyrics, musical sounds, and especially visuals that allow this to become something heartfelt, sincere, and authentic. All three modes draw on indie rock aesthetics to connote Akarsu as an authentic musician who is concerned and angry with Turkey's war policies. Lyrics do not directly critique AKP's Iraqi war policies, but more through abstract, internalized poetics which point to anger. In fact, "war" is excluded from the lyrics altogether. The visuals are more concrete, where Akarsu is depicted playing the role of a news speaker emotionally singing in a newsroom in front of a large TV screen which plays a montage of mostly Iraqi war footage. Foremost in the visuals of this video is Akarsu. And it is here I look first.

"I'm a politically engaged indie rocker"

Akarsu and a newsreel which represents a host of victims and antagonists make up the participants in the visuals. The vast majority represent Akarsu as a passionate, thoughtful, and sometimes overwhelmed and even angry newsreader. Situating Akarsu in a newsroom setting with archive news footage as a backdrop draws on a naturalistic modality, where such a context offers authenticity to his popular political stances.

Visuals personalize Akarsu and take the viewer close to his emotional intensity. He is always shot in a close-up: face, head, or detail shots. These personal perspectives which highlight his indie credentials through dress, ornamentation, and hairstyle give viewers a point of identification and connote intimacy with him and his views (Machin and van Leeuwen 2005: 132). By addressing the camera in about half of the shots, images suggest power and demand a response (Kress and van Leeuwen 1996: 127–128). Anger is expressed through facial expressions, sneering, falling forward, and hand gestures such as aggressively slapping the news desk.[6] Anger is also connoted in vocal style. During many of these shots, especially in the chorus, Akarsu almost yells lyrics. He sounds like a speaker at a political rally trying to be heard over AKP and arouse anger. Sometimes, his voice "breaks" with emotion suggesting sincerity in his anti-war views. Phrasing is staccato with aggressive bursts of energy suggesting sincerity, certainty, weight, and authority (van Leeuwen 1999; Machin 2010: 112). Van Leeuwen and Wodak (1999: 98) note that recontextualizing social practice can include reactions which "represent the private feelings of participants, their secret worries and fears, hopes and desires, joys and griefs." These shots and vocal style choices show Akarsu reacting to the war angrily, but not violently, allowing viewers to witness his sincere personal feelings, key to authenticity.

In other shots, he is in offer images, gazing off camera (Kress and van Leeuwen 1996: 124). In these shots, Akarsu's facial expressions connote concern and thoughtfulness, encouraging viewers to think of what he is saying. In some of these offer images he reacts to the "newsreel" montage, placing his hands on the screen and lowering his head in sympathy with images of destruction and injury.[7] Here, he is represented morally evaluating images, another addition in this recontextualization (van Leeuwen and Wodak 1999). During these moments, we witness his inner feelings of tender despair. These actions not only connote Akarsu as a caring indie rocker, but also draw viewers' attention to his feelings about the war by breaking newsreader codes of remaining composed and cool in order to connote neutrality and objectivity. Feelings are further suggested by his singing style. During the verses, Akarsu's voice is relaxed, at times breathy and in control singing over a bed of gentle, light guitar sounds connoting a close social distance and intimacy (van Leeuwen 1999: 25). While the guitar sound whines under the second and fourth lines of each verse, Akarsu reacts by singing in a breathy manner, suggesting listeners are privy to him revealing his inner self. Phrasing during the verses can be characterized as gentle outbursts such as by jazz singers like Julie London. This suggests musing and introspection, complementing visuals which also connote thoughtfulness.

The notes Akarsu sings also suggest his thoughtfulness and toiling (see Figures 7.10–7.12). During the verse, the first sequence is grounded with the fifth connoting stability, the third minor connoting sadness or pain while the fourth is a building note giving a sense that something is about to happen, such as rising anger. The second sequence in the verse is grounded in the fourth, again anticipating action, while the painful third minor and second suggest unfinished business or a linking note to the chorus.

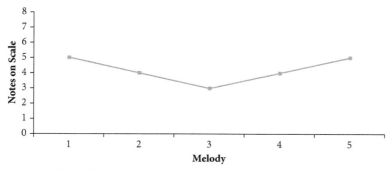

Figure 7.10 Melody of first two lines of each verse

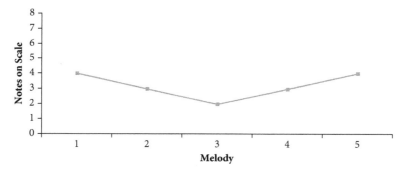

Figure 7.11 Melody of second two lines of each verse

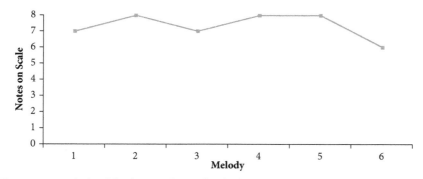

Figure 7.12 Melody of the first two lines of each chorus

The chorus also connotes much pain and wistfulness, notable in the abundance of sevenths. Many of these notes add to the sense of toil, unfinished business combining with the emotional entrapment communicated through the restricted pitch range. Of course the musical sounds do not tell the listener what is unfinished or where one is trapped, these ideas and attitudes are loaded onto the lyrics and visuals.

Subversion in the newsreel

Though indeed, Akarsu being represented as an authentic indie rocker dominates the visuals, there is also a discourse which articulates popular anti-war sentiments. Characters in the "newsreel" are key to this. For the most part, these images are less salient than Akarsu, acting as a backdrop to Akarsu who is in the foreground and in focus. Sometimes they are salient when Akarsu is absent from shots, though this is in a minority of shots. In the newsreel, victims of war suffer, Africans run, American soldiers attack, wildlife struggles, anti-war protesters protest, bound prisoners scuffle, 9/11 victims run and cry while formally dressed politicians speak, clap, and smile. These images are presented in a fast cutting montage where there is no clear agency, specific goals, context, or connections between elements and participants. However, by choosing a naturalistic modality, authenticity is connoted while drawing upon discourses of American aggression, innocent victimization, privilege of the elite, and "war for oil." These criticize Bush and AKP despite both parties being excluded from visuals, perhaps an ideological choice to discourage sympathy and a point of identification with both parties (van Leeuwen 1996: 48).

American soldiers and the US military in the newsreel clearly articulate an anti-war discourse. Images of individual soldiers are excluded, discouraging sympathy toward them (Machin 2007: 118–119). They are either not included or in blurred shots taken from a distance.[8] This is very different to the way the same footage of US soldiers would be seen in American news. They are represented acting negatively with agency shooting, bombing, attacking, and running in a pastiche of archive footage. No clear goal is represented and context is mostly absent.

Unlike the impersonal representation of American soldiers, victims are represented in ways which demand sympathy, drawing again on anti-war discourses. Victims do not engage viewers for the most part, being "documents" of war offered for scrutiny and sympathy. Some victim shots, however, evoke sympathy through demand images, victimized by absent perpetrators (Fairclough 2003: 150). These include extreme close ups of middle-eastern children crying or lying down injured. They directly at viewers—wanting a response of sympathy or help in stopping the war.[9]

A popular sentiment at the time was the idea that the United States and its allies went into Iraq to gain control of Iraq's vast oil reserves, their supply being uncertain due to the West's failing relations with Iraqi leader Saddam Hussein. This "oil war" discourse is drawn upon in a shot of a newspaper headline which reads "The real reason for our war: Petrol." Another newspaper headline, "The ice caps are melting," is a reference to global warming, a direct result of oil consumption. There is a sequence of shots of oil-covered birds, some attempting to walk and fly, showing the result of oil spills, again drawing on an anti-oil discourse. One of the images in this sequence is of a dead, oil-covered bird foregrounding an unfocused background of gray, oily water and ships.[10] These compositional choices link the three elements together: ships spill oil into water which kills wildlife. In front of these images, Akarsu sits behind a news desk and names Bush "a clown" and asks "who is [his] next" bad news victim. By representing environmental disasters due to oil and lyrically attacking Bush, it links Bush to oil disasters, drawing upon an "oil war" discourse.

Bush and his collaborators are criticized visually, though never seen. This is seen in a sequence which connotes elites as self-interested and out of touch, symbolized through luxury and ceremony. Guests wear formal attire in a clean bright hall which hosts a nondescript yet glamorous conference or ceremony shot in a naturalistic news-like modality. Setting and participants connote wealth and power. Guests smile, hold hands, clap, and look off camera. These shots connote distance from the real consequences and horrors of war depicted in the gritty scenes of victims throughout the newsreel. Here, elite society is represented in stark contrast to the realities of war faced by those "on the ground." But relations between this group of elites and the destruction which makes up most of the images are unclear. All the same, these usefully connote a sense of connection between the work of the elite, political power, and war. Here, a discourse which is anti-establishment is connoted, further legitimizing Akarsu's authenticity.

Politicians are also criticized in the lyrics where unnamed politicians are criticized in terms of being self-serving and despotic through namings, collocations, metaphors, and actions. Only Bush and his collaborators are represented but never directly. Bush is named mostly in the third person "he," and his collaborators, such as AKP, as "you" and "loyal servants." "He" can easily be identified as Bush in: "A white palace on the hill, A clown in a palace." These two lines establish through word play that the setting is "the White House on Capitol Hill." Elsewhere, "Loyal servants kiss his robe" makes two things clear. Firstly, "he" is represented as a despotic leader in the White House, the word "robe" connoting a leader with regal powers such as a king. "Servants" who "kiss his robe" connotes his power exceeds democratic accountability, his relations with others being undemocratic and unbalanced. In fact, this is a criticism of AKP's relations with Bush. Here the AKP leadership is named "loyal servants," connoting Turkish leaders' subservience. This is in contrast to using the lexica "leaders of our nation." Furthermore, their action of wanting to aid America is represented as "kissing his robe." The decision by AKP to support America was far more complicated than merely acting on America's wishes, it being based on practical politics as noted earlier. But lines such as these articulate populist anti-establishment sentiments, crucial in indie rock authentication.

Conclusion

This chapter has examined four music videos which criticize government policies. These examples come from different genres, different political orientations and criticize in a variety of styles. Hayko Cepkin criticizes, not one specific policy, but a spectrum of policies which promote social conservatism. He does this metaphorically through visual and musical sounds which do not directly attack AKP, but offer a poetic critique. This may be part of a strategy to represent himself as an "artist" and/or to prevent suffering the wrath of the Turkish authorities. Duman criticizes a number of government policies such as AKP's close relations with America and political corruption, though here we examine its critique of AKP's emphasis on Islamic religious conservatism. Its attack is far more direct than Cepkin's, though still abstract and metaphorical. It also offers solutions, some based on Kemalism. Despite being the most politically radical group examined in this chapter, Grup Kızılırmak uses a poetic style and metaphor to critique the government's policies concerning Kurds and Alevis. Here, a sense of sympathy is created, as well as radical solutions including protest and (armed) struggle. This is done through the representation of places and people in places. These representations not only articulate subversion to Turkish authorities but also authenticate the band as an Özgün protest band. Finally, I have examined pop star Barış Akarsu's political song. Here, he attacks a very specific government policy to go to war. Closer examination reveals there is a montage of discourses, though most inevitably articulate Akarsu's authenticity as a thoughtful, sincere, angry indie rocker. Indie rock musical sounds and visuals sit alongside emotional performance, gritty visuals, and lyrics that abstractly articulate anti-war discourses. Anger, thoughtfulness, and frustration are clearly articulated, though clear politics are far less obvious. Musical sounds connote sincerity in the discourses articulated in lyrics and visuals.

Despite these very different videos, common traits emerge. All the videos employ visuals to articulate discourses of authenticity. In some cases, such as Barış Akarsu's "Kimdir O," this is a dominant discourse, taking precedence over all others. In the case of Grup Kızılırmak, this discourse is articulated, but not as obviously as in the case of Akarsu. Another common trait revealed in these close readings is these videos all articulate subversion to government policies, though this subversion is done in vague terms representing ideas, issues, social actors, and their actions in abstract ways. This observation is in line with those of scholars who claim popular music is less compatible with specific politics and political parties and more compatible with political ideas (Street 1988, 2013; Frith 1988). Many of the discourses articulated lean on popular discourses at the time instead of concrete criticisms of concrete policies. That is, representations do not deal in specifics with detailed circumstances, victims, or even perpetrators. As such, issues are blurred at the expense of more coherent arguments. By relying on popular discourses and abstraction, these offer a very limited political role in terms of fans understanding of issues raised.

However, as indicated in Chapter 4, such criticisms of government policies take on critical importance where opposition is discouraged and even punished, notable in the large number of students, activists, academics, journalists, and musicians languishing in Turkish jails, exiled, and harassed. These are real options for musicians who criticize too obviously. In this context, this chapter demonstrates what sort of criticism is being articulated in videos which subvert government policies and exposes how this is done.

8

Online Music in Social Movements

Right was the tyrant king who once said, "Beware of a movement that sings" ...
Whenever and wherever the opposed challenge the old order, songs are on their lips.
(Industrial Workers of the World [Wobblies] in Fowke and Glazer 1973: 9)

In June 2013, a friend of mine rang me up and asked if I wanted to join him and some friends in a musical protest march in support of the Gezi Park protests. A few hours later, a group of about seventy musicians, students, academics, and others followed our "band leader" through the streets of Alsancak in central Izmir singing, strumming, blowing, banging, and clapping. People enjoying the great weather sitting outside restaurants and bars cheered their support as we paraded through the narrow streets. Though I felt our musical message was heartfelt and people we walked past understood our musical support for Gezi protesters, I suspect that any deeper political message or sense of community between us was very limited. After about an hour, we disbanded. Some went back to their protest camp on the seafront, while others went to the pubs we had just past, while still others went home.

Ours was only one of literally thousands of musical events associated with Turkey's Gezi Park protests. Established bands and performers like Duman, university orchestras, and choirs took to a stage in Gezi Park and performed. A joint performance by the German musician Davide Martello and the Turkish musician Yiğit Özatalay saw a grand piano brought into the park for an evening performance (see Figure 8.1). One-off and spontaneous performances by individuals and groups could be heard across the protest camps. At times, hundreds of people would join together for a communal dance while the crowd sang "Jump! Jump! Who doesn't jump is Tayyip." Like other social movements, from black rights, to women's rights to the Occupy movement, music played a part in Gezi.

Gezi Park was a social movement, which can be defined as "central moments in the reconstitution of culture. In the creative turmoil that is unleashed within social movements, modes of cultural action are redefined and given new meaning as sources of collective identity" (Eyerman and Jamison 1998: 6). In Gezi, for a very short time, dominant conservative Turkish culture promoted by AKP was reconstituted by those who protested, creating a new collective sense of identity (Şenesen and Kırık 2016: 84). Cultural activities included dance, street art, live music, and literally hundreds

Figure 8.1 Davide Martello and Yiğit Özatalay perform at Gezi Park protests

of songs and music videos which appeared on YouTube during the first month of the protests in support of protesters. After the peak of the protests, more songs and videos were posted, visually and musically referencing the protests. This chapter examines two of these: one a song accompanied by cut-and-paste visuals uploaded during the height of the protest and the other a professional promotional video released after the protests. These serve as a case study to examine how music, including everything from musical protests on the street to slick professional promotional videos, articulates politics associated with a social movement as well as how these authenticate musicians, protesters, and fans alike.

A short history of Gezi Park protests

Turkey's 2013 protests started in Istanbul's Gezi Park on May 28, as a demonstration by a few city planners and environmentalists to save a public green space. By May 31, approximately 3.5 million people were protesting in over eighty cities. Protests attracted diverse groups who were against aspects of the ruling AKP such as perceived infringements on democracy, freedom, repressive police tactics, and government policies (Işik 2013: 25–27). Police with the clear backing of the government responded with live ammunition, tear gas, water cannons, plastic bullets, and beatings which resulted in over 3,000 arrests, 8,000 injuries, and 6 deaths. Amnesty believes "police officers were instructed and encouraged to use force unsparingly" and "Turkish authorities committed human rights violations on a massive scale" using the tactics of "force, threats, insults and prosecution" ("Gezi Park Protests" 2013). Since the protests,

Figure 8.2 Gezi Park Protests

Amnesty International notes how there has been a systematic failure to bring police and authorities to justice with a corresponding prosecution and harassment of protesters and sympathizers. In the meantime, the park's fate has been left to the courts, stacked with AKP supporters (Figure 8.2).

The protests can be seen as a manifestation of a split in Turkish politics and society between secularists and Turkey's ruling AKP (de Bellaigue 2013). Part of AKP's economic liberalism has been the privatization of most public/state institutions including the areas of communication, transportation, industry, and energy (Uzgel and Duru 2010: 24). Gezi Park was seen by AKP as part of this privatization project. It planned to transform Gezi Park from central Istanbul's last public green space into a private shopping mall and a mosque, the contract awarded to private interests closely associated with the government (see Chapter 4 for a description of relations between AKP and the Kalyon Group). Government actions, including these, have alienated many who find it increasingly difficult to express their views.

Songs and videos posted online during the protests

During the month of June, over 100 videos which supported Turkish protesters were uploaded onto YouTube. For the most part, these "videos" are not professionally edited productions, but a song which is accompanied by visuals that are hurriedly cut and pasted from a limited pool of visuals of the Gezi Park protests. Some of these disappeared as quickly as they were posted, some have since disappeared while others remain. Some of these videos adapted well-known songs and changed the words, such as Çağlayan Yıldız who changed "Every Breath You Take" by Sting, Erdi Uçar sang "Chapulling in peace," taken from John Lennon's "Imagine," and Rebel K changed Depeche Mode's song "Enjoy the Silence" to "Enjoy the Teargas." Other songs and videos are original compositions, some by one-off bands such as the Chapullers' "Chapullers Master Song," some bands are well known such as Duman and Grup Yorum, while others are musicians from outside Turkey such as Elena Faidra Vasiliadi and Periklis Tsoukalas's "Resistanbul—Musical support message to Turkish Freedom."

While there was almost complete compliance with state authority over mainstream media, these videos became a symbolic rallying point for the protests. These were widely shared and some were sung by those against the government in public places and during clashes with the police. Despite government efforts to control the internet, these songs and videos appeared as oppositional while the mainstream media, for the most part controlled by the government, either ignored or glossed over the protests.

Marsis "Oy Oy Recebum"

Though I analyze two videos in depth in this chapter, all the songs and videos are considered throughout (Figure 8.3). None of the songs or videos were shown on conventional media, most were "unofficial," but all appeared on the internet, an integral part of music fans' pop experiences (Railton and Watson 2011). This first analysis is taken from a sample of the 140 "during protest" songs and videos I collected during the first month of protests by performing a daily scan of the internet and by the help of protesters' recommendations. I believe Marsis's "Oy Oy Recebum" is typical of these.

Formed in Istanbul in 2005, Marsis has released two albums, in 2009 and 2012 on independent labels. It has produced two official videos alongside a large number of unofficial videos which appear on YouTube. A typical rock lineup of vocalist, electric

Figure 8.3 Marsis promotional photograph

guitar, bass, and drums alongside a Karadeniz (Turkey's Black Sea region) fiddle and occasionally a Tulum (Turkish bagpipe with links to the Black Sea region) gives it a distinct sound. It claims to have a "significant political attitude," naming nuclear power plants and Black Sea languages and cultures among its concerns. The chosen video was the first of four associated with the song, first released on YouTube on June 6, 2013.[1] The link has been changed on numerous occasions, for reasons one can only assume, such as government manipulations or the group's fear of reprisals. It boasted over 186,000 viewings at the time of writing, though again this has changed due to the original link changing quite recently. Although this video is "unofficial," it appears on Marsis's Facebook page, suggesting the band's involvement or at least its approval. The title, chorus, and melody are a remake of the song "Oy Oy Eminem" made popular by Mustafa Topaloğlu. The original is a love song about a woman named "Emine," ironically the name of the wife of Recep Tayyip Erdoğan. Turkey's mainstream media did not play the song, it relying solely on internet distribution.

The role of authenticity and populism in social movement's music

My analysis reveals how music associated with the Gezi Park social protests fulfill roles typical of music associated with social movements (see Chapter 3). That is, these songs and videos positively publicize the protests and create a sense of unity between protesters and musicians while negatively representing society's elites. This analysis also reveals how these videos authenticate not only musicians (first person authenticity) but also fans and protesters (second person authenticity). I find it useful here to analyze the videos in terms of populism. As discussed in detail in Chapter 3, the central idea in populism is "the people" are represented positively pitted against "an elite" other (Storey 2001; Laclau 2005; De Cleen and Carpentier 2010). I argue here that videos and songs such as Marsis's draw upon a simplified version of populism when recontextualizing the Gezi Park social movement. For this reason, I examine lyrics, visuals, and musical sounds under headings which highlight populism, emphasizing how Marsis draws on populist discourses, typical of counter cultural and social movement songs (Eyerman and Jamison 1998).

"Dear Mr. President"

Marsis's lyrics are in the style of an open letter to Erdoğan, using vague and ironic references. The lyrics can be summarized as "There is a cruel despot. He is vain and does not listen. The people will be heard and noticed." At this level we see lyrics suggest a pair of simple binary opposites, a strategy noted by Wright (1975) and a strategy we saw in CHP's campaign video. Here, there is an elite which is represented negatively opposing the people, a cornerstone of populism. In the visuals, we see a similar discourse in Marsis's use of the same found images seen across the whole sample. Here, the elite are represented as the police and politicians and the "people" as protesters. The visuals represent a brutal society where the leaders are vain, pompous, and removed while the people rise up. Both lyrics and visuals draw on populist discourses, typical of social movement music.

The "people" are non-violent, but against the elite

Visual representations of protesters' actions articulate positive discourses, though with limited power. Most actions are non-transactive such as protesters walk, chant, wave arms, run, march, wave flags, clap, and hold hands. Protesters also throw stones and smoking tear gas canisters, build barricades, run and mill around the street. Police representations include their negative effects such as victimization and smoke-filled skies (see below). However, here protesters' actions do not include negative consequences such as injured policemen and property. They are empowered as legitimate, authentic protesters without negativity. The limited number of actions which are transactive represent protesters as non-violent. They read and offer food to police and bang metal objects together (a sonic symbol of Turkish protest). Together, these actions draw upon positive popular and populist discourses of the people, as opposed to the elite.

A united people

In the lyrics, participants are named in ways which pit a united people against Turkish politicians. The use of pronouns plays a role. Protesters and the band are named as "us" and "we," defining a group or community different from Erdoğan's "you." Lines such as "Check us out" and "Count how many of us" presuppose the "us" group is numerous and powerful, large enough to boast about. The line "You kept calling us 'çapulcu' " makes clear that "we/us" are "çapulcu" [street person], a name Erdoğan gave to protesters. The name "Çapulcu" later became a badge of honor to those who protested or sympathized with them. Other namings such as "the voice of Gezi" suggest unity, the protesters being united as "a voice." Though represented as one, this naming ignores the diversity of protesters including Radical Muslims, gay rights activists, environmentalists, students, and professionals. But this is part of a strategy of collectivization, connoting protesters as a united people. In fact, there is word slippage between protesters and "the public" in "Did you think the public are sheep?" connoting they are one and the same, suggesting a united people opposed to the government, a key concept in populism and also music associated with social movements.

A sense of unity and the scale of protests are also seen in the visuals. This is seen in images throughout the sample and in this video. Ariel shots, crowded streets, bridges, parks, and tunnels all show a large number of protesters. Unity, along with scale and inclusiveness, adds legitimacy to protesters' demands and actions. In Figure 8.4, protester unity is articulated. This is a group shot where individuals are less important than the team (Machin 2007: 118–119). Protesters are in a line facing

Figure 8.4 Unity

the camera, though not looking at the camera. Their faces are discernible, granting a limited point of identification. They are active lifting, passing, grabbing bags thereby positively affecting the park by collecting and disposing of rubbish. Like a production line, they work together to move the bags away from the camera and out of the park. It is representations such as this which articulate discourses of protester unity, despite actual political unity being far less obvious.

Vocals also articulate protester unity. Throughout the song, the vocalist is up front in the mix. However, in the final fifty seconds of the song, the lead singer's voice shares the foreground with a chorus of vocals, a common trait across the whole sample. By having all voices singing the same words and the same notes with no one voice foregrounded, this comes "to mean solidarity, consensus, a positive sense of joint experience and belonging to a group" (van Leeuwen 1999: 79). Here it is the unity of protesters which is connoted, accentuated by lyrics and images. The simple repetitive lyrics of "Jump, jump, who doesn't jump is . . . " is conducive to a fun sing-along. Vocal style further connotes a party by the occasional "whoopa" and "yip," adding to the party atmosphere. These musical choices alongside visuals which show protesters engaged in fun activities like drawing peace signs and holding hands articulate a discourse of the fun of a united protest.

The people "know"

Here, in the lyrics, we find the people "know" but what they know is never explained while Erdoğan doesn't listen and he is a doer of abstraction. These representations draw upon populist discourses and are typical of countercultural and social movement lyrics (Eyerman and Jamison 1998). For example, Bob Marley sings "Get up, stand up" rallying the people, asking questions and suggesting knowing but never specifically saying about what. Turkish acts such as Bariş Akarsu, Mor ve Ötesi, Grup Kızılırmak, and Duman also follow this trend (Way 2012, 2013, 2015b, 2016b). Discourses of protester knowledge can be seen in:

1. You kept calling us "çapulcu"
2. One day you will be held to account

In the first line, protesters are passivated by Erdoğan's non-material action of name calling, articulating sympathy for protesters and negativity toward the government (van Leeuwen 1996). The tone changes in the second line, it being a warning. To be in a position to utter a warning suggests power. However, no details about agency or actions are offered. This is characteristic of a naturalized de-agentialization where an action is "represented as a natural process by means of abstract material processes" (van Leeuwen 1995: 76). Here, retribution is represented as a natural process with Erdoğan being "held to account" for his negative actions. Agency is withheld and the action is abstract. This points to the people with power, knowing retribution is on the way, but no details of actions or knowledge are forthcoming. This is symptomatic of other lines such as "Did you think the public were sheep." Here again, the people are knowledgeable, "we" are not sheep. But what "we" know, what "we" say, and how "we" act are all abstract. All the same, within the context of the lyrics, one presupposes that it is protesters and/or their sympathizers who will act against Erdoğan. This serves the purpose of articulating a discourse of protesters' power and authenticity without giving away details. It also represents them knowing that there will be revenge for Erdoğan's deeds.

"We are the real deal"

Gezi protests were the largest Turkey had seen for years and being seen as a legitimate, authentic protester was important for protesters and bands alike. It was a badge of honor to have gone to and be seen at the protests. Some images here represent protesters as authentic. Echoing hippy culture and peace demonstrations of the 1960s, protesters play guitars, flick and paint peace signs, spray graffiti, clap together, and hold hands, all actions which articulate second person authenticity. These are symbolic signs of resistance, recycled from popular culture, echoing Eyerman and Jamison's (1998) observations of movement's recycling music and culture. They do little to address the issues of Gezi, but represent protest as cool, legitimate, and peaceful among the chaos, authenticating "you" the protesting fan. Figure 8.5 articulates this clearly.

Figure 8.5 Party

Here a protester is in a close-up playing an accordion. He wears a Guy Fawkes mask, made popular in Turkey by 2005's *V for Vendetta* film where a masked hero takes on a corrupt dictatorial government. This mask was popular among protesters and is used here as a semiotic resource to articulate subversion. His pose signifies coolness as he leans away from the camera, moving to the music, playing his accordion as a fire burns in the background. This represents a party, being anti-establishment and an authentic part of the protests.

Musical choices also connote the fun and power of a protesting people. This is notable in melodic, tempo, and instrument choices made in the instrumental bridges played between verses and choruses. Figure 8.6 represents the first half of the bridge, the second following a similar pattern. Notes are not constrained but have a wide pitch range to connote the venting of strong feelings of excitement and chaos. The melody is dominated by the third and ends on the sixth, both notes with the meaning

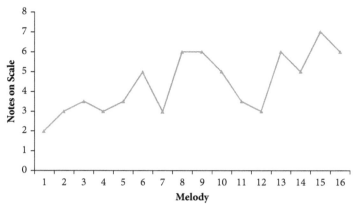

Figure 8.6 Instrumental bridge

potential of happiness, while the penultimate note is the seventh with connotations of thoughtfulness and longing (Machin 2010: 218). These note choices suggest the excitement of protesting alongside its dangers and associated sadness. Excitement is also connoted with an ascending pitch movement which "can energize, rally listeners together for the sake of some joint activity or cause" (van Leeuwen 1999: 103). The joint activity here is protesting against the AKP government. However, the second half of the bridge ends back down on the third, bringing the chaos to a more "grounded" footing, again reminding listeners of inherent dangers.

This sequence is played at breakneck speed with a fiddle in the foreground. Choosing to foreground the high-pitched fiddle symbolizes urgency, fun, and chaos unlike the low-pitched distorted guitar heard elsewhere (Tagg 1990: 112). Tempo also plays a role. Van Leeuwen (1999: 110) notes how fast note changes or "disjunctive sound production" can come to stand for a "lively and energetic approach, or a bold or forceful attack." In the context of images of police violence and protester actions, the melody suggests energetic, yet dangerous, fun.

A powerful and legitimate Marsis

As noted above, Marsis represents itself as part of the protests through pronouns. Imperatives define this role as the band being knowledgeable protest leaders. In the lyrics, Marsis commands Erdoğan to "Come hear the voice of Gezi," "Check us out," and "Count how many of us." These lines connote Marsis's power, being in a position to command. Furthermore, Marsis knows that their voices of protest ought to be heard through the authority of such imperatives. Marsis's power and authenticity is further articulated in the imperatives "Jump Jump, Who doesn't jump is...." These imperatives also authenticate fans and protesters alike. The chant "Jump Jump, Who doesn't jump is Tayyip" was part of Turkish protests where protesters would chant, jump, and sing together. By commanding protesters and fans to participate in an act of defiance, Marsis represents itself as being a powerful voice of protest, commanding, and leading. This, in turn, suggests the band is anti-establishment, a key component of rock authenticity. By altering a chant used in the protests, Marsis and fans are legitimated as being part of "those in the know," those who participated in the protests. This is a clear case of first and second person authenticity, Marsis conveying the impression that Marsis is a leader in the know and "that listener's experience of life [are] being validated, that the music is 'telling it like it is' for them" (Moore 2002: 220).

This part of the song also connotes protest is a party. This discourse is a common theme throughout rock history including The Clash's "White Riot," Placebo's "Rob the bank," Public Enemy's "Party for your right to fight," and the Beastie Boys "(You gotta) fight for your right to party." Here, the Black Sea folk sounds and distorted rock guitar are replaced with a ska-inspired melody and dance rhythm. Gone are the connoted dangers of protesting. Instead, ska-style dance party music accompanies vocals which instruct listeners to "jump." Throughout this part of the song, the tempo increases suggesting fun and energy (Tagg 1984: 22) like "The chicken dance" at weddings. Though the chant sequence starts on a Cminor, suggesting sadness, it changes to and finishes on a Gmajor, with more positive connotations.

Images and lyrics complement this musical party while clearly identifying who is invited and who is not. A series of three visuals correspond to the lyrics "Jump, jump, who doesn't jump is . . . ." Cut to the rhythm of the first two words are visuals of those who Marsis commands to jump and who they consider are legitimate, authentic protesters. Included are football supporters, home owners, conservatively and Western dressed young and old Turks, and foreigners. These images signify the all-inclusiveness of protesters, them being the people. Cut to correspond to the line "who doesn't jump is . . . " are images of police, the media, and governing AKP politicians. This sequence not only works multimodally to make clear who are outside Marsis's group of protesters, but also articulates the all-inclusiveness of the people.

. . . Pitted against an elite

In populism, the elite are represented against the interests of the people. The elite in the lyrics are politicians while the visuals represent them as both police and politicians. Lyrics identify the government as Erdoğan, him serving as its metonymy. He is mostly named "you," distinct from "us." He is also named informally as "my Recep" connoting a lack of power (van Leeuwen 1996). In the context of a love song, such as "my Emine" (which this song parodies), "my" connotes closeness and possessiveness. However, here in the context of many negative actions, "my Recep" connotes irony, belittling, and wrongdoing as when a parent says, "oh my Recep, what have you done?" articulating opposition.

Representations of action also suggest a despotic elite. Lines such as "You kept hitting even when we said 'stop' " connote Erdoğan is a despot. The first half of this line is a material process with material effect connoting negative power (van Leeuwen 1995: 90). However, agency, actions, passivations, and circumstances are all unclear. According to Amnesty International, though violence against protesters was condoned by Erdoğan and his government, it is well documented that police kicked, beat, shot tear gas, and pepper-sprayed protesters, not Erdoğan ("Gezi Park Protests" 2013). The action "hitting" is abstract, a generalization which dilutes specifics. However, it has the effect of delegitimating Erdoğan, a common trait in generalizations (van Leeuwen 1995: 99). Furthermore, the second half of the line emphasizes a despotic leader pitted against the people, one who hits out even when "we" the people say stop.

Visuals signify politicians as being vain, pompous, and removed from the people. Images include "in situ" shots and posed ones. Non-posed shots see Erdoğan fall off a horse and eating with his hands. Neither image connotes power or positivity. Posed images include Ankara's AKP Mayor Melih Gökçek posing with Mickey Mouse dolls in an opulent office while the Minister for the European Union Egemen Boğış is photographed from above as he looks up with his hands clasped in prayer, suggesting weakness (Machin 2007). AKP politicians look ridiculous and far removed from the people, mixed into a montage of chaos, protesters, and police violence.

Though we have images of politicians, it is police violence which dominates the visuals, represented in ways which emphasize police brutality. The most common strategy represents police actions as material and transactive connoting great power (van Leeuwen 1995: 90). Police, as part of the elite, spray pepper, tear gas, and water cannons at unarmed protesters. Groups of police hold, beat, hit, and kick individual protesters and dismantle camps. These are powerfully negative, articulating police abuse of power, a popular discourse at the time. Figure 8.7 exemplifies this type of representation. It originates from Reuters photographer Alexandra Hudson, appearing in newspapers across Europe and many of the sample's videos. The image became a "leitmotif for female protesters" during the protests (Hudson 2013).

The image's leitmotif status may be due to the photograph employing a number of strategies which articulate popular discourses including police violence and protester

Figure 8.7 Leitmotif

sympathy. Positioning of participants within the image emphasizes difference between these groups. The foreground features a masked policeman on the left spraying pepper at an unarmed woman on the right. In the background, again on the left, a wall of masked and helmeted policemen look right symbolically dividing authority from protester in a type of "separation" within the composition (van Leeuwen 2005: 13). Throughout the sample, most photographs see protesters separate from police, dividing the elite from the people. Separation is even more pronounced between AKP politicians and protesters who never share the same shots emphasizing difference (Kress and van Leeuwen 1996).

Viewer position in relation to social actors, representations of actions, and type of shots signify where sympathies lie. There is no symbolic interaction with the police, their gazes are elsewhere, and faces concealed with helmets and masks (Kress and van Leeuwen 1996: 127–128). They are shot in a group, accentuated by identical uniforms and shields, further increasing anonymity and symbolic distance between viewer and police (Machin and van Leeuwen 2005). As mentioned above, one policeman sprays an unarmed woman. She is photographed individually, looking down and toward the camera. Viewers see her discomfort expressed in facial expressions while closeness is symbolized through her proximity to the camera, connoting sympathy (Machin 2007: 118–119). Her dress and handbag signify her ordinariness, "respectability" being one of the people, accentuating sympathy unlike shots of masked youths hurling petrol bombs. It is images like this which make clear the elite are against the people.

Musically, a dangerous elite is connoted in melody, tempo, and instrumental choices. This is exemplified in the opening guitar riff which is repeated throughout the song. The melody (see Figure 8.8) is characterized by both low pitch and a very narrow pitch range. The low pitch suggests power in a way a higher pitch does not (van Leeuwen 2005). The pitch range is restricted to the song's key note, its second and third. Though the first and third connote stability, the second suggests "something in between, the promise of something else," articulating the uncertainty of protest.

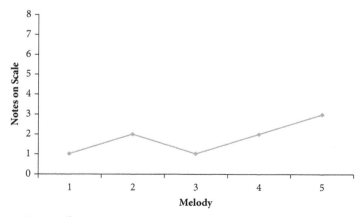

Figure 8.8 Guitar riff

The narrow pitch range also has the experiential meaning potential of constraining strong feelings. This constraining heightens uncertainty, caution, and danger. The melody connotes danger, being strikingly reminiscent of the two-note leitmotif used in the *Jaws* films which also alternates between the key note and its second minor. In these films, the leitmotif is used to represent danger, evil, and menace (Wingsted, Brandström, Berg 2010: 199). We saw this same melody choice used in the CHP election campaign video analyzed in Chapter 5. As danger becomes more eminent, the tempo of the leitmotif increases. In Marsis's song, this riff is played fast, suggesting imminent danger like the film. During this riff, a distorted guitar is up front in the hierarchy of sound. This is unlike the rest of the song where the traditional Karadeniz fiddle is foregrounded. Distorted guitar sounds are associated with heavy metal, a genre with its own connotations of danger and menace. Together, melody, tempo, and instrumentation connote danger and menace while visuals and lyrics make clear its source is the government and police.

"I can't hear you"

Among the negativity surrounding the government suggested in the lyrics, it not listening is dominant, this being a popular notion among oppositional voices (Traynor and Letsch 2013). A variety of strategies are used in representing action which connotes this. Consider the line "Were your eyes blind." Here, the action of Erdoğan not listening is recontextualized into him being blind. This is typical of descriptivations where actions are deactivated into permanent qualities of social actors (van Leeuwen 1995: 95). This is common throughout the sample, other songs naming Erdoğan "the blind Sultan." As such, a dynamic process becomes the permanent negative quality of an arrogant non-listening government.

The line "Come hear the voice of Gezi" also articulates a discourse of non-listening through objectivation where a process becomes a nominalization. This de-emphasizes actions while adding "purposes and/or legitimations" (van Leeuwen 1995: 94). In this line, protesting is de-emphasized, becoming the nominalization "the voice" while "come" and "hear" are prioritized as a command at the beginning of the line. This construction serves the purpose of emphasizing Erdoğan is not listening because he has to be commanded to do so. It also serves to represent the people as "the voice." Though represented united as a voice, what the people have to say is left out, just like the lines "come check us out," and "look how many we are."

A non-listening elite can be seen in the visuals as well, such as in Figure 8.9. Here Erdoğan is speaking and not listening. His formal dress, microphones, and background indicate he is at a press conference. Formal dress and setting connote his distance from the people, who protest in Gezi Park and on the streets. He leans forward aggressively. His eyes, mouth, and face suggest anger. Erdoğan looks off to the left, not engaging the viewer (Kress and van Leeuwen 1996: 124). The background is a blurred Turkish flag and black. The blurring and darkness suggest far less certainty than a clear image of a flag. The result is a negative representation of a non-listening, aggressive politician, not a sympathetic ear.

Figure 8.9 Erdoğan

Post-protest music videos

Despite the violent end to most protesting by the middle of the summer of 2013, some musicians have made lyrical and visual references to the protests. These appear in their official promotional music videos, a far cry from the cut-and-paste offerings during the protests. This use of Gezi symbols confirms two of Eyerman and Jamison's (1998) assertions that symbols from past struggles are recycled and used in other ways and also that music lives on far after a social movement has finished. Not surprisingly, references are notable in videos by Turkish bands such as Beyoğlu Kumpanya's "Bu Daha Başlangıç," Dev's "Dans Et," and Ozbi's "Asi," but also international group Placebo's "Rob the bank." Common among these post-protest promotional videos are visual and sonic re-enactments, dramatizations, actuality, and other representations of the Gezi Park protests. One of these videos—The Ringo Jets' "Spring of War"—is analyzed here.

The Ringo Jets

The Ringo Jets are a rock trio formed in Istanbul in 2012 (Figure 8.10). They have performed and recorded throughout Europe and have one officially released CD from 2014, of which this song appears. According to an interview I did with them, they are a rock band, not a "political" band, though "Spring of War" is touted by the band as "saluting" the Gezi Park protests. In fact, the song was recorded six months before the protests. It was only after the protests were finished that the band's producer decided it would be a good idea to use Gezi visuals to "salute" the protest. Nevertheless, fans' comments (analyzed in Chapter 9) demonstrate how many fans interpret the song in political ways. This video received 177,350 views on YouTube at the time of writing.[2]

Figure 8.10 The Ringo Jets

The song's genre is blues-inspired indie rock, with lyrics that comprise three repeated lines. This lyrical simplicity echoes Eyerman and Jamison's (1998) assertion that lyrics of songs associated with social movements are easy to remember and sing along to. The video, like others released at the time, uses the limited amount of footage of the protests from mainstream television and that found online. The following analysis considers how the three modes of lyrics, visuals, and musical sounds work together to articulate popular and populist discourses associated with the Gezi Park social movement.

"Us" versus "them"

As is the case with songs and videos recorded during the protests, these post-Gezi videos also draw upon populist discourses to show support for this social movement. There are only three distinct lines sung throughout the song, the second and fourth repeated. These are:

1. Well they are isolating, manipulating, toxicating and its suffocating us.

2. Well you can smell in the air, The Spring of War is here
3. And it is complicated, tolerated, formulated and it humiliated us.
4. Well you can smell in the air, The Spring of War is here

In the lyrics we find no individual social actor's names, only the use of the collective pronouns "us" and "they." This lack of specific social actors has been noted as one characteristic of popular music lyrics. In CDA it has been shown that pronouns are one of the best grammatical categories for the expression and manipulation of social relations, status, and power (van Dijk 1998: 203). This song's lyrics are far too vague to be about a simple people against the government and its forces. It is the visuals which make clear "they" are police and the government, while "us" are "the people." All the same, the pronoun "us" hides all sense of difference at any level in this representation of protesters as regards issues of poverty, political orientation, and unequal access to resources and opportunity that cut across Turkish society irrespective of religious/secular affiliations. It is this use of pronouns which draws upon the populist dichotomy of "us pitted against them."

A despotic elite against "our" interests

How actions are recontextualized further draws upon populist discourses. The authorities, or "they," are represented with power in the lyrics in line one above. These four actions of "isolating," "manipulating," "toxicating," and "suffocating" are material processes with material effects connoting great negative power (van Leeuwen 1995: 90). However, "isolating" and "manipulating" are abstractions, void of any context and detail. The lexical choices of "toxicating" and "suffocating" may be a reference to the toxic spray from water cannons used by the police or the heavy-handed use of tear gas. Or these may be metaphors for the government's toxic divisive discourses and its socially conservative policies which many critics claim are suffocating. Both of these ideas are suggested in the visuals. But the lyrics do not make clear what exactly the government and police are doing. Here we see recontextualizations lacking any detail, common devices in generalizations (van Leeuwen 1995: 99), and here play their role in a populist discourse where leaders are represented as extreme despots who victimize "the people."

Setting, context, and causalities also become abstracted in "And it is complicated, tolerated, formulated and it humiliated us." The pronoun "it" obscures agency. Considering the visuals, we can assume "it" represents "the present situation in Turkey caused by the government and police." But what is "complicated, tolerated, formulated" and what "humiliates" is not articulated. This list is a criticism of the elite. But it is not specified what exactly they have done nor if they are responsible for all of these things. What is represented here is not simply a government with an ideology or set of policies which the band opposes. Instead, a despotic government is represented which acts against the people who tolerate the situation. And these populist discourses, such as unemployment which is common across much of Europe at the time of writing, are rooted in broader shifts in the global economy, and here become fused together.

Figure 8.11 Police brutality

Unlike the lyrics where there is no individualization, the visuals represent participants who are collectivized and individualized, contributing to populist discourses. Police are collectivized throughout the video, denying any close symbolic social proximity. In Figure 8.11, police are foregrounded and given salience (van Leeuwen 2005). There is no symbolic interaction between viewer and police, their backs are facing the camera. Alternatively, we see a single generic (van Leeuwen 1996) protester being beaten behind the police. Sympathy is connoted by this image of a single protester passivated by the negative actions of the police. Sympathy is articulated differently than if we could see a close-up of the victim. As such, it is the brutality of the police that is prioritized here through salience and actions rather than the suffering of their victim. Elsewhere, police hit out at a protester and shoot water cannons, again suggesting violence and brutality.

We also find the police named in captions as seen in Figure 8.11's "Minister of state denies police brutality" and Figure 8.13's "Police forbid citizens to access Gezi Park." In the first case, the caption is ironic, juxtaposed over an image of police brutality, thereby criticizing not only police actions but the credibility of government authorities and the mainstream media. In the caption for Figure 8.13, again we see a collectivized "police," denying fans a point of identification, making it easier to treat the police as the enemy, as part of a despotic elite against "our" interests (van Leeuwen 1996).

We do get individualization with politicians. The Prime Minister, the Minister of State, and the Minister of Finance are all represented individually in photographs. In Figure 8.12, Erdoğan is shown in a still to the right of the screen. We also find members of the government represented through honorifics, such as the "Minister of State" and the "Minister of Finance" and the "Prime Minister," though never named. Honorifics grant viewers a point of identification, though social proximity is denied through a lack of naming. Furthermore, the point of identification in the context of this negativity identifies who are at fault, a part of a discourse about a wider criticism of the elite.

Figure 8.12 Individualization and poses

Machin and Mayr (2012) point to the way that poses are one important way that participants can be represented. In Figure 8.12 we see Erdoğan looking upward with arms uplifted in a pose of prayer. This both reminds viewers of the government's anti-secular stance and also connotes self-grandeur, suggesting a despotic non-listening politician. We also find the caption "I gave the order" and "Our police wrote an epic legend," pointing to his arrogance in the face of the violence seen in the video, while lyrics keep reminding fans that this is about "them" and "us."

Musical choices in rhythm, melody, and instrumentation play a role in connoting a despotic elite. The rhythm of the song drags and feels somewhat labored due to the time signature of 9:8. This is a traditional Turkish time signature, unusual in Western pop music but commonly heard in "Roman" or "Gypsy" music in Turkey. Traditionally it is played in fast tempo songs using a clarinet darbuka, violin, and a drum at weddings and other celebrations. But here, there is no bounce or lightness or sense of joyful energy. The time signature firmly grounds the song in Turkey, while distorted guitar and a slower tempo give the song its dragging feel. With lyrics and visuals which identify police and the government as a despotic elite pitted against "the people," the multimodal meaning-making package makes clear who are responsible for this "feeling."

Furthermore, the melody emphasizes low-pitched notes which suggest sadness and gravity (van Leeuwen 1999), unlike higher notes which tend to be associated with optimism and higher levels of energy (Machin 2010). The sounds are also rough with distorted guitar sounds which suggest dirt and grittiness, rather than smooth and rounded. Such sounds are associated with certain kinds of truthfulness through a lack of polish or restraint. In both the choruses and the verses, the singer ends each line on a note lower than the beginning of each line. For example, in the last line of the chorus the melody starts on a G, goes up to a high B before dropping down to an E. A descending vocal melody suggests inward thinking and a lack of energy and enthusiasm, unlike an ascending melody (van Leeuwen 1999). Again, visuals and lyrics point to the cause of these negative feelings.

Protesters, fans, and the band are "the people"

The lyrics to the chorus are "You can smell in the air, the spring of war is here," repeated seven times in the song. This is a case of overlexicalization, where a word or phrase is uttered more than would be expected used to signify importance. Here, we find the only case of personalized verbal communication as "you" is addressed. This personal appeal is used to draw the listener into the narrative and sympathize with the narrator's idea that a "spring of war" is imminent. It also suggests fans are part of the "war," thereby authenticating fans' anti-government ideas, a case of second person authenticity. Again, this line is abstract, the metaphor "smell in the air" used to represent imminency and "spring of war" which lacks any context such as details about the kind of conflict (physical, mental, within Turkey or external) and who is involved. The passive clause where "the spring of war is here" includes no agent and no indication as to who is starting the war. What we get, however, is a sense that this is just a beginning.

The visuals also connote protester and fan authenticity. Protesters, for the most part, are not individualized but represented in large groups, as seen in Figure 8.11. This treatment suggests the importance of "the team" over the individual (Machin and van Leeuwen 2005). Within the group we see a range of ages, genders, and even children. It has been observed that in news footage of people's uprisings in Arab countries children were represented as a strategy to suggest this really is "the people," including families, where children represent an innocent truth (Bouvier 2014). Here, unity, scale, and authenticity of the protests are connoted, drawing upon an all-inclusive "the people" pitted against the elite. Protesters are active moving in the same direction, waving their hands in unison, again suggesting unity. Strength is further suggested by the representation of a large group of protesters acting against police orders which are written in the caption. They are moving on to Gezi Park by energetically walking, shouting, and waving their arms. We also see scenes where protesters throw objects, push back at the police, bang a wall in protest, and defiantly walk in tear gas–filled streets and celebrate around a fire. There is a sense, visually, that while the police and authorities are ruthless and cruel, the people are strong, defiant, and united by fighting back. These images act as second person authentication for fans and protesters. Facial expressions and movement authenticate the feelings and frustrations of fans and protesters, the video "telling it like it is" (Moore 2002: 220) (Figure 8.13).

Musical sounds also play a role in suggesting protester power, strength, and legitimacy. This can be heard in the guitar solo. Here, the melody changes from the distorted grungy blues sounds in E major for the first time in the song. Guitar notes leap three octaves to a high A which is pulled up to a B. Later in the solo the guitar hits a high E stretched to an F, a full three octaves higher than the rest of the song. High-frequency notes connote being uplifted while large note changes suggest energy (ibid.).

Figure 8.13 Protesters as "the people"

Mixed with images of protesters' power and negative police actions, this melody has the meaning potential of a break from the sadness and danger of protest connoted in the rest of the song's melody choices. Here, hope and a rallying cry for change are suggested.

"We" are one with The Ringo Jets

The most individualized participants represented in the visuals are the band members, who comment on the events as they sing in the fashion of a newsreader, reporter, and weatherman (Figure 8.12). They are shown in close shots and allowed to engage directly in a "demand relationship" with the viewer creating a sense of social intimacy (Kress and van Leeuwen 2001). All are in relative close-up and directly address the viewer creating a point of identification with viewers. Their actions as news workers, formal dress, sincere looks, and news settings all suggest a low degree of modality. All these choices connote the band is authentic and part of the people who are knowing and against the despotic elite.

Musical choices further connote authenticity of the band. The genre of music is blues-inspired indie rock. The song is based on a twelve-bar blues pattern in E major. With the exception of the guitar solo, the instrumental melody is E, A7, E (twice during the verses) and then B7, A7, and E (for the choruses). Choosing to follow a blues melody not only suggests authenticity unlike classical music (Moore 2002), but also has the meaning potential of melancholic sentiments (Frith 1996). Indie rock elements are also part of the music. In the hierarchy of sound it is a distorted guitar which is up front in the mix almost competing with distorted vocals. These dominant sounds are associated with grunge indie rock bands such as Nirvana and Mudhoney, another genre closely linked with ideas of authenticity and subversion. What the band is subverting and how it is authentic are made clear in the other modes.

Conclusion

Characteristic of music in social movements, both Marsis's "Oy Oy Recebum" and The Ringo Jets' "Spring of War" recycle previous cultural artifacts to articulate subversion. Marsis uses images of peace signs and the wearing of Guy Fawkes masks from past social movements (real or otherwise) to connote the authenticity and coolness of Gezi Park protests. The Ringo Jets "salute Gezi" in their video by reusing recent images from the protests to connote an alliance with the Gezi Park protests and the band's subversiveness. Another characteristic common among these videos and social movements' music is their ease of singing along to and their simplicity. "Oy Oy Recebum" parodies a well-known popular song, with an easy "Oy, oy Recebum" chorus that fans and protesters can sing along to. "Spring of War" uses three repeated lines throughout the whole song with the catchy "Smell it in the air, spring of war is here" repeated every second line. More importantly for this chapter is what we have unearthed through our analysis in terms of music's political role in the Gezi Park social movement and how this was done.

Echoing previous research, these videos fulfill roles identified with music in social movements. They both publicize a movement and they both create a sense of unity (Eyerman and Jamison 1998). Upon closer inspection using MCDS, I have revealed unity is articulated through a simplified populist interpretation of events. The analysis of Marsis's "Oy Oy Recebum" details how recontextualizations articulate popular and populist politics seen throughout the sample of Gezi Park protest songs and videos. Populist politics are articulated by constructing "the people" made up of protesters, the band, and sympathizers who are positive, authentic, powerful, united in knowing, and having fun. Though "the people" are active, this is usually without agency. This can be seen throughout the sample where the people "imagine" (Erdi Uçar), "dream" (Grup Yorum), "scream" (Bülent Şimşek), "talk wisely" (Cehlan Ertem), and "say" (Marsis). These actions are of little consequence to others, though they serve the purpose of authenticating protesters and musicians as being anti-establishment. In fact, groups authenticating themselves is common throughout the sample, not only lyrically, but visually by representing themselves as protesters (Dev, Osbi) and musically by harnessing subversive style potential (Osbi and underground hip hop, Marsis, and indie rock). Protesters, music fans, and groups are represented as "the people" pitted against the authorities made up of the police and politicians. Police are represented as violent, articulating the popular notion that police abuse their powers. Politicians' actions connote they are despotic, are out of touch, and do not listen, again popular discourses concerning Erdoğan's government.

Similarly, The Ringo Jets' "Spring of War" also represent "us" the people (band, fans, and protesters) in lyrics who have tolerated and are put up on by a unnamed "they" who are ruthless, although what "they" have done is not specified and is represented only through abstractions while we are told this is the spring of a war. Titles on the screen using the genre of news use the honorifics "Minister" and "Prime Minister" to attribute acknowledged guilt by the elite. Visually, police are represented as part of a brutal elite, while politicians are non-listening. Protesters crowd the streets often moving together and fighting back. Members of the band communicate with us personally and sincerely. The music adds ideas of sadness and graveness. Overall there is a sense of a brutal regime and people who will tolerate it no longer. It is a situation that must be changed. But no specifics are given in any of the modes. Again, this is a case of populist notions of the people being pitted against authorities.

The close readings of music by Marsis and The Ringo Jets reveal that authenticity is a dominant discourse. What also is revealed is the ideas of a movement which started out expressing concerns for the environment and the government's privatization program are not articulated in either, or across, the whole sample of songs and videos. In almost all of these, there is no real articulation of the politics behind the movement. Though protesters want to be heard, what they are saying is absent. Articulations of political concerns and the offering of political alternatives are missing. Typical of the whole sample, these videos do not articulate the shortcomings of the AKP government's neoliberal economic policies and their repercussions, such as public green spaces being sold off to private corporations for huge profits. There are no references to the many AKP policies which have seen a rise in social and religious conservatism, a common complaint among those protesting. Environmental concerns are absent, despite this being the original reason for the protests. In fact, these videos add little to political discussions surrounding the issues the Gezi Park social movement raised. Though they offer the chance for fans to be authenticated as "anti-establishment," it ought to be recognized that this has only so much political potential, maybe less potential than other modes of communication which in Turkey, at least for the moment, do not exist. All the same, while the mainstream media ignored or backgrounded Gezi, these songs and videos were one of the few spaces where political issues rooted in populism became popularized and may have contributed in a limited capacity to public dialogue or even the scale of the protests.

9

Politics, Music, and Social Media Posts

In 1996, I saw Rage Against the Machine at Brixton Academy with a friend of mine (Figure 9.1). I was a big fan at the time and my friend was less so, but to her credit she came along. Throughout the concert the two of us moved to the music, I singing out the lyrics I knew, like most of the other "real" fans. At the end of the concert, I was full of energy after just witnessing what I thought was a good mix of great music and progressive politics. I said as much and then asked my friend what she thought, to which she replied, "I thought they were good to dance to, but I really didn't pay attention to what they were saying. Were they being political?"

The point of recalling this story is to highlight how fans listen to music and how they use music is a big determining factor in music's "politics." The importance of fans in making sense of music has been examined by scholars from Raymond Williams

Figure 9.1 Rage against the machine

(1963) up to the present (Street 2013; Zbikowski 2015), as we looked at in Chapter 3. Many scholars agree that the political intentions of musicians are only part of how we make sense of music's meaning, seeing as fans interpret songs and videos in different ways. What I do in this chapter is analyze in depth how fans indeed interpret the meanings in "political" songs and videos through a close reading of comments about music posted on social media.

Some of the music analyzed throughout this book attracts a vast amount of posted comments on sites such as YouTube. From the songs and videos analyzed in the previous three chapters, I have chosen to analyze comments following one musical recording from each chapter in the light of scholarly concerns about the role of social media in public debate and protest. I have not chosen to analyze comments from the political parties' videos analyzed in Chapter 5 as these generate little in the way of political debate, posts mostly being from the party faithful being full of praise. I could not select Grup Kızılırmak's "Çeşmi Siyahım/My black-eyed beauty" or Marsis's "Oy oy Recebum" as the comments were blocked from view, one can only guess for political reasons. I have selected comments which follow on from the YouTube recording of the Grup Yorum concert examined in Chapter 6, Barış Akarsu's "Kimdir O" which criticized the US and AKP's war policy and The Ringo Jets' "Spring of War," a video associated with the Gezi Park social movement.

There is a considerable amount of scholarly investigation into the potential of social media to facilitate civic debate and its role in protest movements (de Zuniga 2012). However, there is little work in multimedia analysis on social media sites, on how posted images and film clips, themselves carrying discourses, become focal points for discussions, comments, and online interactions (Geogakopoulou 2014). In this chapter I am interested in how the discourses communicated in popular songs and videos are discussed and related to in posted comments. It is through a close reading of these comments that I unearth how fans use and interpret political meanings in songs, concerts, and videos shared on social media.

Social media: Slacktivism or a real tool for democracy?

Scholarly debate on the role of social media and the internet in relation to the idea of democracy has produced a number of positions which I place into two camps. On the one hand, the internet is seen by some commentators as a place which has opened the public sphere, making it more democratic. Networked media are seen to challenge centralized control of media production and distribution by traditional organizations, reconfiguring communicative power relations (Von Hippel 2005; Jenkins 2006). In some cases, internet users are described as citizen-reporters, who contribute "to the setting of the agenda and performing a watchdog role . . . enhancing political participation" (Vatikiotis 2014: 297). In social movements, social media are seen by some scholars as being instrumental in successful protest movements (Howard and Hussain 2011).

On the other hand, numerous approaches have acknowledged the dubious democratic affordances of social media practice. There are various reasons for skepticism regarding democracy and social media. At a fundamental level, these include the lack of access to technology and inequalities of technological literacy (Hargittai 2008); the degradation of economy, culture, and values due to the demarcation between professionals and amateurs (Keen 2007); the limited analytical and critical value of alternative forms of journalism (Scott 2007); lazy online forms of activism ("slacktivism") that have no political impact (Morozov 2009); and weak social ties of movements initiated by social media (Andrejevic 2013). Many online forums tend to be characterized by hard language and insults (Coffey and Woolworth 2004). Dean (2010) points to the way that forums tend to find people more oriented not to attending to new and fresh points of view but to falling back on what is known and comfortable. YouTube comments tend to not focus on analysis of situations but rather to frame them in terms of preexisting personal and social interests or prejudices (Lindgren 2010). Following the work of Lindgren (2010), I want to analyze how the discourses articulated in a set of music videos are recontextualized in associated comments. This sheds light on how audiences use the politics articulated in musical commodities.

In line with the above observations about social media, I have found that the comments which accompany songs and videos examined in this book can be divided into four loose categories. Some support bands and their videos saying simply "well done," or repeat words or lines from the song. In some cases, such as Saian's "Feleğin Çemberine 40 Kurşun—Kinetik Tipografi" and Bariş Akarsu's "Kimdir O," this makes up the vast majority of comments. Another category repeats slogans and key phrases associated with either politics associated with the song/group such as "Kurdish rights," "freedom," and "the spirit of Gezi." The third category sees posters simply abusing and insulting each other. In fact it is this category that is most in the form of a dialogue with interactions between posters. Other comments link to themes but not in a sense of an obvious interchange. Of course these form an important part of the stream of comments and I will address these later in the analysis. But the last category, which is of most interest for the analysis here, is more fully developed comments about the politics associated with the musical recording which allows us to access the kinds of discourses that are used by viewers. Posters who write these fall into two groups throughout the sample: those who are against the perceived politics articulated in the video and those who support them. In the analysis that follows I examine comments to reveal discourses being articulated by posters both for and against the perceived politics of the musical recording. I also focus on sequences of comments which take the form of a more developed interchange, to look at the way that these discourses interact.

Changes in Grup Yorum's unity and community

The recording of the Grup Yorum concert captures an extraordinary musical event where musical sounds, an array of visuals, and spoken word entertained and informed literally thousands during the live event and millions afterward on the internet. There are over 1,400 posts accompanying the video which has been viewed 3,588,614 times since it was posted on March 14, 2012.[1] As is the case with the whole sample, all four types of comments are present. There are comments which praise the band as in "Grup Yorum are the people," praise the concert "this is great, thanks," and insult the band "You're all part of the PKK." There are key phrases and slogans such as "Fuck off America" and "Protest now." There are a large number of posts which insult other posters and their ideas, such as "I don't see any workers in the crowd. Well done white Turks" and "They're all the PKK." And there is a substantial amount of posts which are for and against the perceived politics articulated in the concert. It is this category that we look at here.

Not surprisingly, there are a disproportionate amount of comments which are political, far greater than comments associated with Hayko Cepkin's "Fırtınım" or Duman's "İyi de bana ne." Some posts deal with party politics, naming AKP, the main opposition CHP, Kurdish rights–oriented HDP, nationalist MHP, and leftist SOL Party. There are also posts commenting on Kemalism and Mustafa Kemal Atatürk, Left politics in general, socialism, racism, Kurdish rights, America, and Israel. Some posts comment on recent events in Turkey with political repercussions, such as the spate of bombings Turkey endured in 2016.

In Chapter 6, we examined this concert in detail and found that there were an array of progressive politics articulated including unity around the Left. Though Grup Yorum's unity is confusing, for the most part it is international, suggested through representations of international leftist musicians and figures. A theme of unity is also noticeable in the comments. However, unity is redefined by posters, shaped by their own interests. Consider:

> P1. The children of this country who got together under the Turkish flag in this concert after years of fighting in Turkey, people separated by being a piece of red, non-believer, communist, and right-wing fascist, it was very meaningful and the only thing we needed was to start the fight again and we have succeeded.

Here, we find unity of fans connoted in "the children of this country" suggesting a familial bond between fans more so than using the word "friends." Unlike Grup Yorum's unity, the fan limits unity to those "under the Turkish flag." This is a change in political groupings from an international unity theme of the Left and leftist causes.

There are more differences between the two visions of unity. The fan represents the concert as a meeting among fans who are named as disparate politically marginalized groups. Namings are sometimes informal and metaphoric, such as "a piece of red" to represent communists and "non-believer" to represent nonreligious secularists. These are presented alongside "right-wing fascists" in a list which connotes commonality (Fairclough 2003). The commonality being connoted here is politically marginalized groups in today's AKP-led Turkey who "got together . . . after years of fighting." Here, it is presupposed that indeed these groups have been fighting and the concert has stopped such action. Unlike Grup Yorum's unity which most certainly excludes the Right and capitalists, here they are included.

As seen throughout the sample, posts manipulate the politics articulated in music videos to those of personal politics. This personalized politics can be traced throughout Grup Yorum posts. For example, the above post produced a number of replies by three posters. Here we see how politics are manipulated by each poster. Though the above comment in this train of posts promotes unity, consider how this changes in the following exchange:

A.S.:   Congratulations. Let's become a suicide bomber and kill innocent people.

FT: You are the ones who become suicide bombers. We are the ones who die.

A.S.:   Fuck off you Mofo. Half of the suicide bombers are from DHKP-C and the other half is from the PKK and Armenian bastards. You cannot say this is the act of sacrifice, you SOB.

A.M.:   If you look at the suicide bomber case statistics, you can see that over 90% of them are because of the İslamic organizations. I wonder have you ever heard any words from a headscarf wearing girl or a Hacı wearing about love and life? There are no better people than you who cut onions in people's joy of being alive. I leave the comment to the readers, while support of ISIS is in its maximum in Imam Hatip High schools.

A.S.:   Who are the ones who exploded themselves in Kızılay square . . . in Güvenpark, Bursa, Istanbul, Ulus, who exploded themselves, son of a bitch . . . PYD, PKK, DHKP-C, we will put those letters to your mother's vagina you enemy of humanity.

A.M.:   In Kızılay, who exploded themselves is ISIS, who got treatment in AKP's hospitals and get educated in their camps. You're misrepresenting the facts here and write lies. Go and read, do some research, but don't do it from the "pool" media (all news is the same—pooled). By the way, don't be a digital man. Give me your phone from the messages and I'll stop by you and who fucks who.

As is obvious here, Grup Yorum's discourse of unity of the Left and leftist causes is omitted. Instead, the interaction between these three posters reflects hardened political positions in the spectrum of Turkish politics. This is a far cry from a dialogue between political positions, and more like a screaming match of insults. FT's position is quite vague in isolation. This was his one and only contribution to this train. He represents a "you" group of "suicide bombers" and a "we" group who "die." Considering it follows directly from A.S.'s comments, we can assume he is opposed to A.M. and much closer to the far more articulated position of A.M., the secularist (more on this below).

A.S.'s position is one which typifies a Turkish nationalist who has little sympathy for Kurdish and Armenian causes. A.S.'s first comment follows directly after P1's praise for Grup Yorum in which he or she describes the concert as the successful beginning of "the fight." However, this call for action is recontextualized as inspiration for "suicide bombers" who "kill innocent people." A.S.'s following comments squarely put the blame for terrorism on suspects who are usually blamed in some forms of Turkish nationalism: the PKK, PYD, DHKP-C, and "Armenian bastards." Though Armenians and Armenia are considered "the enemy" by some Turkish nationalists, no Armenian group has claimed responsibility or been proven to be responsible for the bombings Turkey has experienced in recent years. However, A.S. makes these claims with authority, as in "Half of the suicide bombers are from DHKP-C and the other half are from the PKK and Armenian bastards." Here we see two strategies used to connote authority: modality and statistics. Modality is related to the degree of "truth" we assign to a representation (van Leeuwen 1996) while the use of numbers, statistics, and percentages connotes a "scientific discourse" and is used as a way to legitimize claims in texts (Wodak and van Leeuwen 1999).This sentence is in the simple present with no modal auxiliary verbs, granting a high degree of certainty. Furthermore, the poster's views are backed up with statistics "half" and "the other half," aiding in legitimizing his dubious claims.

A.M. is a secularist who is opposed to AKP and also A.S. He counters A.S.'s claims using statistics again in "If you look at the suicide bomber case statistics, you can see that over 90 percent of them are because of the Islamic organizations." The poster even uses the lexical choice "statistics" and then actual numbers as in "90 percent." Here, A.M. leans on a scientific discourse to legitimize a stance which blames "Islamic organizations" for bombings, a lexical choice which groups together Islamic charities and mosque with ISIS. But this is done to attack AKP as seen in ISIS "got treatment in AKP's hospitals and get educated in their camps." Here, AKP is represented as possessing hospitals and camps where ISIS members get treated and educated. Again some of this is misinformation, as bombings in Turkey were blamed on not just ISIS, but also TAK (Kurdish Hawks) and the PKK. However, by linking Islam, AKP, and ISIS, an anti-AKP secular discourse is articulated, a far cry from the discourses articulated in the concert.

This interchange between the four posters illustrates how hardened positions are expressed, but little information is exchanged. FT, A.S., and A.M. share a common topic of "suicide bombers" throughout these comments. Though the original comment which started this train off was about unity, the train is really about expressing hardened political positions around a national concern at the time of bomb attacks. A.M., through statistics and low modality, corrects A.S.'s "facts" with "statistics." Insults are also a part of the exchange, where they take on more and more of the content of the posts as the train proceeds. FT insults A.S. by blaming "you" for becoming suicide bombers. This is replied with insults bookending "facts." These are then corrected by A.M. with statistics and insults about religious Muslims and AKP. A.S. again communicates "facts" and insults and A.M. finishes the train with more insults and threats. Far from a civilized discussion of facts, we get misinformation and insults framed within a discourse of polarized personal visions of what it is to be Turkish and what it is to be outside of this grouping based on personal politics.

Who is the clown in which palace? Bariş Akarsu's "Kimdir O"

This song and video, released in 2007, is a highly professional production which for the most part focuses on Akarsu.[2] He is represented as a legitimate politically engaged indie rock star concerned with Turkey's and AKP's involvement in the Iraqi war. There are a number discourses articulated including elites of the day (George W. Bush and AKP) are despotic leaders who do not listen. What is of interest here is how politics in a song are recontextualized by viewers nine years after its release. Comments show not only politics becoming personalized but applied to recent events. Here the despotic leaders, originally meant as George W. Bush and AKP elites, become an empty signifier, filled in with more modern "despotic" signified.

The year 2016 saw a number of significant political events in Turkey which are recontexualized here in the comments. Erdoğan's drive for an executive presidential system intensified, including the sacking of his Prime Minister Ahmet Davutoğlu who was seen as less than enthusiastic about Erdoğan's presidential desires. He was replaced by Binali Yıldırım, who supported the idea. Another event referred to in the comments is the July 15, 2016, attempted coup. These events are part of recontextualizations of the politics articulated in the music video. Here we see how politics in music products are recontextualized and used by individuals to fit in with their personal politics of the day.

One discourse seen in the comments is the excesses of Erdoğan. Back in my analysis in Chapter 7, we noted how AKP is represented as despotic and the US president of the time George W. Bush as the "joker king." Here, these same lyrics are used in posts describing Turkish President Erdoğan as a despot. For example, a comment taken from June 2016 reads:

"There is a White palace on a hill with a joker-king." Lyrics fit with Tayyip perfectly.

Lyrics used to describe George W. Bush now "fit perfectly" with Erdoğan. Not only is he named a "joker-king," he is named informally by the poster as "Tayyip," withholding respect and legitimacy (van Leeuwen 1996). A string of replies follow this posting. Many of these are in agreement with the original post such as "I agree with you."

But more interestingly, the despotic leader discourse is drawn upon further in some of these replies. Like the original post, G.B. quotes the lyrics "Black news, who is next" and claims "The lyrics perfectly fit." Here, Erdoğan is excluded, but within the context of posts which express anti-Erdoğan sentiments, the reader is left to assume that indeed it is Erdoğan who now is responsible for "Black news," while asking who his next victim will be. These comments lack any context and details, but offer insults. G.B. also vaguely critiques Erdoğan's record of filing legal complaints against those who insult him in "Anyway, let's not go to jail for no reason." This may be connected to omitting Erdoğan's name, yet clearly the poster articulates a discourse that Erdoğan is abusing the legal system by jailing and fining those who insult him. G.B. then makes clear he is not an AKP supporter by drawing on secular nationalist discourses, changing the conversation away from lyrics and to his own personal take on Turkish politics. He writes:

We are Turks, we support Turks, we support Atatürk, How happy I am to say I'm Turkish!

Here we see a grouping of "we" as Turks. "We" are active supporting Turks and Atatürk, the founder of modern secular Turkey. This grouping of "we" does not include all who live in Turkey, only Kemalists whose identity includes loving Atatürk. And even not all Kemalists are included, only strongly nationalistic Kemalists. This is evident by the last sentence which is a nationalist slogan attributed to Atatürk and can be seen in many public places throughout Turkey. As such, G.B. has taken a lyric, applied it vaguely to Erdoğan and his actions, but then changes the conversation to express the poster's vision of nationalism.

In this train of comments, opposition toward Kemalism is also expressed by comments which show support for AKP. Again, this is a far cry from the video which was critiquing George W. Bush and AKP for involvement in the Iraqi war. Y.Y. reminds a poster who criticized Erdoğan that the "man you refer to as a joker-leader" is "the head commander." Here we see respect and legitimacy connoted in this formal functional naming of Erdoğan, rebuking the previous viewer's comments. Though he claims, "There shouldn't be a Turkish supporter like you," assuming because he calls the president a "joker-leader," the politics then becomes very personal in the sentence "I don't support any political parties, cabinets come and go, but the important thing is the wellness of the state." Here, lyrics and the song have been used as a springboard to articulate personal politics. Though Y.Y. claims to not be a supporter of any political party, this seems dubious seeing the discourses he articulates mirror those of AKP. In the train of replies he shows his religious affinities in "May God take you to the true path." Y.Y. also shows his support for AKP through praise for their achievements, such as:

> Not only roads, we have increased our defence production and increased the national products which we offer the market. These all are a success. We should not forget that. This country still gives an independence war.

Though not named in this particular post, Erdoğan is named in previous posts. Here he is credited with economic successes, a central plank to all AKP discourses and one which is drawn upon in many circles. However, comments such as these lead to other comments which again have little to do with the video or the war and more to do with posters expressing their views on recent developments in Turkey.

E.P. seizes upon this comment to ironically make the point that Erdoğan is not a good leader in:

> Of course he is the head commander with those roads we will go for the war, we will fight with the roads, he made roads because of it . . . .

And later on:

> Are you only reading with the black writing, they write with white? Then my brother, have a good night sleep and flirt well with your roads. BECAUSE TURKEY IS NOT EVEN PRODUCING MINDS.

Again, Erdoğan is represented as a despot, this time constructing roads, not to build Turkish infrastructure, but to go to war. E.P. uses irony to counter Y.Y. comments. In the second of these two comments, a secular discourse is drawn upon again, one which equates religious commitment to a lack of intelligence. The first line uses a metaphor of black versus white print to recontextualize the idea that politicians are working behind our backs, manipulating us, telling lies, saying one thing and doing another. The last line, however, in capital letters criticizes Turkish education and society by "not even producing minds." This is a common critique of Turkish education and culture under AKP made by critics who claim that the government is prioritizing religion and religious education while suppressing independent thinking. This draws upon a discourse that AKP and religious commitment are backward, a common discourse seen in Turkish secularism (Way 2012).

Another event articulated in comments about the video is the July 15, 2016, attempted coup. Again, the joker in the palace line from the lyrics is used to articulate another set of politics. Some comments vaguely connect the coup with the song, as in M.E.'s comment, "This song is written for 15 July." This vague reference does not really explain how the two are connected. However, a more detailed connection is made in T.K.'s comment:

> After the failure of the coup they cut the throats of the soldiers and hit them with their belts. Do you know why? They were all a game. They used the military in order to establish the presidential system. Do you want to know who this is? There he is the joker in the palace.

Here, (mostly) AKP supporters who were on the streets in defiance of the coup leader's instructions to stay indoors are named as "they." They are represented acting with agency in "they cut the throats of soldiers and hit them with their belts." These represent the supporters as strong, though people who are nationalists and those who support the army would find these actions negative. At the time, there were images of soldiers being beaten in the street which were displayed proudly by some and repulsed by others. But these actions and the coup itself are represented as "a game."

"They" is used again, but this time to name Erdoğan and his inner circle. Here they are represented negatively in "They used the military in order to establish the presidential system." There was a discourse at the time, especially by those opposed to Erdoğan, that he would do anything to get a presidential system. Some believe this was partly why Erdoğan reignited the conflict between the Turkish army and Turkey's Kurds in 2015 (see Way 2015a). Others believe Erdoğan capitalized on the coup attempt to again argue for a presidential system. There is speculation in some circles that Erdoğan knew about the coup before it happened, fueled by the quickness in which lists and arrests were made of coup suspects and evidence of unusual behavior around his residence days before the coup. The coup has brought about a string of state of emergencies which have given Erdoğan far more powers than he had before the coup. He enjoyed a surge in support immediately after the coup partly due to speeches by AKP and the media representing him as the savior of democracy, despite the power grab. All the same, there is no evidence (at least at the moment) that Erdoğan was behind the coup. However, T.K. uses lyrics to connote that indeed it is Erdoğan who is playing a game on "us," manipulating events for his own advantage in "Do you want to know who this is? There he is the joker in the palace." In the context of Turkish oppositional politics, the joker leader in the palace is Erdoğan.

As this section has shown, politics in music are not determined by musicians alone, confirming established beliefs in popular music studies. What this section has illustrated is how politics from a different time can be used by audiences to act as a springboard for politics and political events which affect them personally. These are not well articulated and well formed, but they point to the political potential in popular music across time.

Good Turk/bad Turk: The Ringo Jets "Spring of War"

Thinking back to the previous chapter, "Spring of War" used a few lines of lyrics, musical sounds, and visuals from Gezi Park to articulate discourses of a non-listening, brutal elite pitted against a knowing and correct "people." The elite, who are unnamed in the lyrics, are represented visually as AKP politicians and police while the "people" are the band, fans, and Gezi Park protesters. The video has received over 200 comments on YouTube, their composition typical of all the videos.[3] I examine comments about the protests which show support for the government and those which do not. I also examine a sequence which takes the form of a more developed interchange to reveal the kinds of discourses that are found and how these discourses interact.

Good Turks dislike AKP: Anti-government comments

Anti-government comments are not unlike the discourses found in the video itself. We have a sense of the knowing people. Consider this comment:

> I open my eyes, I don't jump into the games which are played on us, I read, I don't follow something blindly. I wish our people would lose the blinders and see what is going on.

Although in this case not enough of the people "know," only the protesters. What is to be known is not stated but expressed metaphorically through the removal of "blinders." What is already known once eyes are opened is not expressed in concrete terms but as a "game" being played on the people. Like the video we also find the sense of an "us," a single "people," who are the victims of the game. Pronouns act as an important way of framing the wider events. But in this case there is no agent acting against the people. But that it is a game being played on the people points to something deliberate and malicious.

In a comment further down the same stream we find the "blinders" metaphor taken up in:

> All of this happens because the blinders started to fall. Be careful they only started to fall now. Think about what would happen when they fall completely.

Such a way of talking about gaining vision, clarity, the people no longer being blinded, that the government seeks to blind the people, is typical of the way "what is wrong" is formulated without specific details. A truth is being revealed but its actual nature is not stated.

Many anti-government comments also represent government supporters as being non-thinking, as in "useless herd" below. This is a strategy we have seen in the previous comments analysis. Here, this can also suggest that they may indeed be part of "the people" and are victims. For example:

> What happens if you win elections, you keep sinking. Win the election, it is nothing. What does it mean if crowded, useless herds win? It is good to see you struggle. Now fuck off.

Throughout these comments there is a lack of specificity as regards who may characterize the different sides of the matter. There is a shifting sense of people and of us and them in the fashion described by Fairclough (2003), where sometimes government supporters are blinded at other times part of "crowded, useless herds" and other parts of the self-interested elite. We see this in the following comment:

> You are the one negotiating with PKK, it is your prime minister who is dancing because he made Kurdistan, you have the shoeboxes, you are the thieves, you are the ones who slander people . . . you are the one who are continuing to cut trees which was illegal from the beginning although the court gave a stop order . . . So are we—the ones that are objecting to these—the traitors? Fuck off you are the traitors.

This comment is in response to a pro-AKP comment. "You" here refers to the AKP government and its supporters. Here "you" are the elite represented as powerful, active in a range of verb processes. These all vaguely point to events reported in the press. For example, "you have the shoeboxes" references a corruption case involving millions of dollars found at the manager of the Halk Bank, run by the government. But in no place are issues such as Kurdistan discussed, nor the processes of privatization of which Gezi was a part, nor the huge numbers of unemployed youth, as is characteristic of many contemporary societies across Europe. Important in this comment also is the sense of the "we" who stand apart from "you" and the set of injustices. In populist politics "the people" can easily stand removed from responsibility from any kind of issues, even if at one time such actions were themselves popular and called for by "the people."

What is clear across these comments is rather than analyzing or commenting on the actual events or even on how they are represented in the music video, posters frame events around a set of personal interests flexibly including and excluding through a shifting use of pronouns. This involves, in the fashion described by Georgakopoulou (2014: 532) as to how the Greek crisis was discussed on social media, an exchange of popularized and slightly xenophobic versions of history, what he describes as a process of "homogenization and reduction."

An important part of these anti-government comments is that nationalistic discourses are used to frame the events. For example, in the comment above the government's negotiations with Kurdish leaders are represented as "dancing as he made Kurdistan." In fact, this is part of a discourse which points to Erdoğan being a traitor. This in itself is a complex issue, sometimes interwoven with more far right and xenophobic views. But here it becomes thrown together as part of a list serving to delegitimize. The idea of the "traitor" is also recurrent as a naming strategy. Clearly politicians serve their own ideologies even if we dislike them. Yet the idea of using the concept of traitor, part of a nationalist discourse, is an act of claiming the deeper interests of a coherent and monolithic citizenship and people, rather than constructing these as ideological differences that cut across society at this present time, ones that we need to discuss and understand.

Nationalist discourses can also be found in comments which show their support for Mustafa Kemal Atatürk. For example:

> But your prime minister himself can't say "I am a Turk". He can't even call Atatürk "Atatürk."

In this case patriotism and national identity are called into question. This is partly in reference to Erdoğan and AKP prioritizing Islam as an identity marker over being Turkish. In this sense the argument shifts away from the neoliberal drive to privatization that Gezi first symbolized to issues related to Atatürk, the founder of the modern secular Turkish Republic. Until very recently, it was unthinkable for any public figure to do anything but praise Atatürk. Comments do not make it clear whether or how such identity formulations align with those who are blinded or not.

Clear links are made between those who the protesters are against and religion. For example:

> YouTube shows what the religious gang in the government does to its people, the shoeboxes, the way it benefits some individuals and itself.

It was, of course, not clear that such a religious/secular divide characterized those who protested and those who did not. Conservative Islamic groups such as the radical Muslims and individual women who wore clothes associated with conservative interpretations of Islam were among protesters in Gezi. In this maneuver, religion is connected to the elite, a "gang" who are self-interested and pitted against the knowing people. Choosing to name the government as a gang points not to a democratic body but to a group who use violence and bullying to achieve their aims. This discourse about Erdoğan's rule is common in popular expressions. This is important in the current Turkish political landscape where opposition political parties are based firmly in Kemalism and secularism and where the years of AKP have seen a shift to increasing state control of things like alcohol consumption and women's dress. But these things are not discussed or raised specifically.

In sum these comments represent the government as bullying, a religious gang, self-serving, an elite who act against the interests of and who bully a people with common interests. This elite is also challenged on the grounds of national identity. There is a sense of people being blinded which prevents a more dramatic kind of event. But overall a range of complex issues are hinted at but never fully articulated. Given what Gezi was about in the first place as regards privatization of public property, what this meant for Turkey, the anti-government comments are about what it is to be a good Turk.

Good Turks like AKP: Pro-government comments

What we find in the pro-government comments are a similar lack of specific details about policies—the same homogenization and reduction. There is a similar kind of attempt to frame events in terms of wider interests using pronouns. Here posters try to define just who "the people" are and who the distant, self-serving elite are. As with the anti-government comments these are not actually about the video or Gezi at all, nor privatization, nor specific policies and which sections of the population benefit or not and in which ways. It is more about legitimacy of identity.

In the following comment see how "the people" are to be thought of as government supporters and the government:

> You are "çapulcu" [translation: street person] and . . . . God knows you didn't even leave your village, you wannabe. Wannabe, wannabe, again wannabe. Ahh, ahh you empty-headed çapulcu.

Çapulcu is the name protesters were given by Erdoğan. It is an insult, but it was a strategic way to represent the millions of students, professionals, multi-religious, and secular groups who were protesting for various reasons. They are collectivized as a "you." These people are "empty-headed" and do not understand things represented by them being from a village. In other comments, çapulcu's lack of education is connoted in they "haven't read a decent book in all their life and didn't improve themselves." The value of the protests and protesters' actions are questioned by being called a "wannabe," repeatedly with a sense that they were people looking for their moment of fame.
As with the anti-government discourse the idea of a self-serving elite is also important, though here it is represented by governments that preceded AKP. Pro-government comments often use a sense of past versus future. In some instances the corruption is connected to a wider elite that exists internationally, although the links are never clearly specified. For example:

> Did you start to pay taxes after Erdoğan became prime minister? You paid taxes before Erdoğan, so where did this tax money go? Why are you always biased? But of course the US and Israel were ruling the country before so you didn't raise your voice. We, including our prime minister's voice, were heard like ships . . . Most importantly he paid the debt to the IMF. Why couldn't the previous governments do that? Because they were busy eating and none of them cared about the country.

The elite here include former governments who are represented as corrupt, "busy eating" while "none of them cared," connoting a despotic rule. But this elite also includes the United States and Israel "ruling the country." This is a popular largely anti-American discourse criticizing both former governments and AKP. Presented in this way, it serves to gloss over the complexities of what in some ways has been a mutually beneficial web of relationships, although not without problems. But here it is used to connote that those against the government are somehow in favor of relations with the United States and Israel, represented as them "ruling" Turkey.

Importantly many of the pro-government comments name Erdoğan in ways which connote inclusiveness and respect. While in anti-government comments he is named through abusive terms or as "your prime minister," here he is named not only formally as Erdoğan and Prime Minister, but "our prime minister." The sentence "We, including our prime minister's voice, were heard . . . " makes clear the Prime Minister is a part of "the people," positively acting in unison, opposing corruption and collusion with the United States and Israel. What exactly the people are doing is unclear, but a discourse of populism where the people are pitted against the elite is communicated.

Unsurprisingly the pro-government comments represent AKP positively working for the people, but again never in specific terms. These comments usually are contrasted with negative ones of previous governments. For example:

This country will grow, develop and other countries will shrink. Look at today's Gezi park, not yesterday's. It is better and good people will always win. As long as AK Party exists, my country will be better.

Here, "this country" is conditionally attributed with future growth and development. Gezi Park is "better." Though not directly attributed with these positive attributes, the last line of the comment does just that, by claiming AKP's existence ensures "my country will be better." Overall it is in the co-text of "my country," "grow," "develop," "better," "good people," and "win," connoting more positivity. The AKP government is also represented as leaders of the people, performing positive actions for the people and the country. Again, no details are given, just abstract positive attributes. These positive attributes are contrasted with other countries which "will shrink" and yesterday's Gezi Park, yet another vague reference to the times before AKP's governance.

So in sum what we find is government actions and policies related to Gezi are absent. Police actions, as seen in the visuals of the video, are also absent. Instead, posters concern themselves with constructing the people as AKP and its supporters. AKP works for the good of the country while its supporters are clever. The elite pitted against them are former governments, protesters, and even the United States and Israel.

What characterizes the discourses of both sides are that the events and the video are not commented upon in detail but rather there is an attempt to frame them by setting them into the interests of a shifting notion of a legitimate Turkish people at the mercy of self-interested elites. To accomplish this, popular history and reduced versions of events without connection are thrown together. The pressing sociopolitical issues in Turkish society, even issues like police brutality, or unemployment, are not discussed. What becomes clear is that, like the video, this is populist politics where there is an easy and trustworthy mass public consensus and there are ignorant, self-interested elites.

"You're a bad Turk." "No, you are." An exchange of views

In this section, I want to look at the way pro- and anti-government posters interact on the forum. As stated earlier, many of the comments appear to have little relationship to previous posts, but air an opinion. Arguably it is this tone of a lack of specific details and challenges to the collective other "you" that leads to more comments of this type. As Coffey and Woolworth (2004) point out, such forums tend not to be characterized by attempts at deeper understanding of social relations. But on several occasions there were some clear interactions. Here I examine one of these involving three posters. These provide an opportunity to understand how these discourses interact.

The example starts after poster two claimed that the prime minister is great. Here is how the populist discourses held by each unfold when they meet:

Poster one:	Alright, you are used to being hoodwinked. They are stealing but show you that they are not. When you see reality, you will be shocked.
Poster two:	Actually the ones that came before are the ones that robbed the country. You can't see the service that the government gives, I guess. Investments that are worth billions are made for the country. Go and look at how much money the third bridge which is being built now costs. Talking is not service. They didn't even drive a nail.
Poster three:	Oh leave them alone, they love waiting in the sugar queues.
Poster one:	Is there only Istanbul? The whole of Turkey. I don't live in Istanbul and I don't care about a third bridge. What has the government done as a service to this country? They used the earthquake money to make benefits available to their friends. They made three metres of road. It was ten times more than what it was worth. That money was my taxes. They didn't even deny all these accusations. There isn't a parallel state, is there any proof? What shall I do with this service if the people are not happy?

Poster one is anti-government while poster two and three are pro-government. Poster one begins by constructing an elite who are distinct from "the people," some of whom are "hoodwinked" and some who know. The government is represented through the pronoun "they" who are activated by "stealing." Poster two is accused of being ignorant.

Poster two replies by explaining that it was the former regime which is responsible for present problems. Rather general evidence is given for what the present government is offering in "investments worth billions" and the building of a bridge, which in itself has come under much criticism from environmentalists and for being a poor use of money. Notably this comment begins cordially with "you can't see that . . . "

Poster three throws in a snarky comment drawing on the discourse of the protesters being uneducated peasants. Poster one replies, "I don't live in Istanbul and I don't care about a third bridge," and asks, "What shall I do with this service?" Though this lays out an argument for why he dislikes AKP, this poster personalizes his complaints and gives very few details of the actual problems with AKP. Poster one's comments also include vague references to AKP's clampdown on opposition after the banking scandal in "there isn't a parallel state." AKP's response to the banking scandal was to claim there was a parallel state within Turkey's judiciary, police, and politics headed by Fethullah Gülen which is out to usurp AKP's power. This same discourse has been used after the 2016 coup attempt in order to "cleanse" Turkish politics, education, and other public services of those opposed to the government. This poster's flat denial of the parallel state is backed up with no counterclaims or proof. This same lack of detail and context is seen in "You didn't even deny all these accusations." These serve the purpose of connoting a self-serving arrogant elite.

What is of note in this interaction is that we do find hints and fragments of actual issues which become fuzzy, fused with personalized perspectives and framed in terms of established alignments and prejudices. Here we get a sense of how many people do in fact manage the knowledge they come across about events and persons in civic society and in politics.

Conclusion

In this chapter, I have examined how political discourses in music are used by fans. To do this, I have examined the kinds of political discourses found on YouTube in comments about music videos posted by music audiences. The first case study was of a video production of a concert by Grup Yorum, a band known for its leftist political commitments. The second case study examined recent comments about a video by pop singer Barış Akarsu released nine years earlier. The third case study analyzed comments following a popular music video which recontextualized events around the Gezi Park protests. What have we discovered?

Comments do not deal with the actual events, politics, and issues which are recontextualized in the videos. In fact, these more developed comments I have analyzed rarely deal with the videos at all. Instead, they seek to frame events in terms of wider forms of allegiances to, and betrayal of, entrenched beliefs and in the light of homogenized and reduced forms of history. This applies to events, politics, and issues across time and space. This analysis supports other studies which characterize such forums not as sites of engagement and debate but where comments seek to frame events into preexisting alignments using a populist form of politics. Overall the exchange of ideas is closer to the accounts scholars give of political populism, where the complicities of policy, economics, social, and civic matters are homogenized, reduced, and used to position who is a good national citizen and who is not.

Stuart Hall (1988), writing on the way that the 1980s British working classes voted for a government that appeared completely against their interests, pointed to the way that this government, headed by Margaret Thatcher, understood the processes and the ways that understandings of events were largely reduced and fused with the personal. Fiske (1989) suggested that tabloid newspapers also operate at this level. And perhaps much public debate, that we see here, is more like a poorly informed shouting match than a discussion, unlike a Habermasian coffee shop.

On a positive note, songs and music videos act as a springboard for fans to express their points of view on political matters. Though politics are diluted, these comments and exchanges expose fans to politics not found in mainstream media. Such YouTube forums allow a greater variety of viewpoints to be accessed when the mainstream media is so restricted, exposing audiences to viewpoints, especially those opposed to the government, they would not otherwise be able to express or engage with.

10

Final Notes

I have had the good fortune to live in Turkey for over a decade now. It is a beautiful country with a vibrant array of people, food, cultures, and sounds. Music is a big part of life in Turkey, it being an integral part of most aspects of life. I have learned through listening, observing, and playing a vast amount of music in Turkey. My education in Turkish music has included understanding the long and important tradition of music which is political, some of which criticizes and subverts authorities. It is this political branch of music I have examined in order to consider, more generally, relations between music and politics and how is it done.

What politics does music articulate?

In the introduction and then again in Chapter 3, I went into great detail outlining some of the many ideas and theories about what scholars believe are relations between music and politics. The conclusion we can surmise (in one sentence!) is indeed there are relations and at times it seems that music can be used as a political voice, but just how effective that is seems open to debate. My analysis chapters go some way to add to this body of literature.

Throughout the book, whether in musical political campaign videos, concerts, promotional videos, or social movement songs with cut-and-paste visuals, we find similarities in the political discourses being articulated in music. These common discourses are expressed through the modes of musical sounds, lyrics, and visuals. For the most part, lyrics and visuals focus music's abstract meanings, at times music enhances discourses articulated in the other modes, at other times sounds play a leading role. My close analysis finds the modes of lyrics, visuals, and sounds at times articulate very similar discourses and at other times quite different ones.

My analysis finds that political musings in music are far from coherent, a view shared by many scholars discussed in Chapter 3. MCDS reveals that what we get is politics which are vague, abstract, and lack any particulars and details. Most articulate popular sentiments found in slogans, images, sounds, and chants. There is little in terms of coherent arguments and ideas. In all instances, we find discourses of legitimacy/authenticity, usually of the musician and sometimes of the fans or those being represented. We also find discourses of unity. The unity connoted is based on ideas of community, where some are included and other excluded. Many of these notions are based on populist accounts of events and ideas. I now examine each of these discourses in turn to consider how this is done.

How does music articulate politics?

Authenticity "look at me"

A dominant discourse found in all these analysis is one of authenticity. Echoing Moore (2002), we find first person and second person authenticity throughout this music. Most is aimed at authenticating musicians, representing them as important, sincere, and singing from the heart. For example, camera shots are used in videos to feel close to singer's heartfelt musings, also notable in lyrical choices. In concerts, stage position, facial expressions, and body movement play their parts. Musically, choice in singing styles, song choices, and genre suggest authenticity. But there is also second person authenticity, legitimizing fans and their ideas. In political party videos, lyrics and visuals not only suggest their leaders are important, sincere, and legitimate politicians, but also confirm viewers' political positions of support and unity through the use of inclusive pronouns and visuals. These videos confirm their politicians are "telling it like it is." Fans and their ideas are also legitimized in songs and videos through positive representations of fans, protesters, nonconformists, and others who are represented as sharing their ideas. In all cases, whether through lyrics, visuals, and/or musical sounds, authenticity is a key discourse.

Unity of a community

We see this discourse expressed multimodally in all instances I have examined in the book. Though political campaign videos give political parties a chance to communicate their messages in ways which differ from political speeches, they all connote unity of the nation behind their respective leaders. However, this unity draws upon discourses of division and polarization. In the case of AKP, musical sounds connote a conservative past, visuals emphasize social and religious conservatism in the present, and lyrics suggest a unity of conservative Turks who have suffered. Here all three modes connote unity of conservative Turks, while excluding others. Likewise choosing a music style with connotations of the Left but also the military, the CHP video uses visuals which legitimize the leader and lyrics which draw on populism to connote a despotic AKP who are opposed to the people.

In concerts we also find a discourse of unity. For example, in the Grup Yorum concert, unity of the band and fans with the international political Left is a dominant discourse. This is achieved through a wide array of semiotic resources such as song choices, spoken word, lyrics, communal music making (singing, chanting, clapping), body movement, and visuals displayed on big screens. Though on the surface this community is represented as inclusive, on closer examination we find that it is rather exclusive to those who subscribe to a specific type of Marxism.

The unity in community represented in amateur and professional popular music promotional videos varies, depending on the issues represented in the video. For example, in Duman's video, unity of a community which is suffering under AKP is suggested in visuals and lyrics. Grup Kızılırmak suggests unity with Turkish minorities in lyrics, visuals, and musical choices. Both The Ringo Jets and Marsis construct a united community of protesters and sympathizers. Here fans, bands, and protesters are united in lyrics through the use of pronouns and visually acting together. What is clear is all three modes are used by musicians in a variety of ways to articulate unity within a defined (and exclusive) community.

Populism in community

Though these music commodities offer a sense of unity in a community, they also exclude. There is a simplification of issues and policies, reduced to popular sentiment. Much of this is derived from populist ideas where an "elite" is constructed which are pitted against the "people" who are knowing and in the right. Who are the elite and who are the people change from song to song. This is typical of populist discourse, where "the people" and "the elite" are empty signifiers, dependent on circumstances to gain meaning (Laclau 2005: 7). Depending on the music commodity, the elite may be the police, the government, the West, the American government, or even the media. So, the elite are AKP in Duman's, Hayko Cepkin's, Bariş Akarsu's, Maris's, CHP's, and The Ringo Jets' videos. But so are the police in Marsis's and The Ringo Jets' videos, as is America in Bariş Akarsu's video. In Grup Kızılırmak's video, it is not just AKP, but previous governments with anti-Kurdish and anti-Alevi policies. Ironically, previous governments are represented as the despotic elite in AKP's campaign video, while its supporters are represented as "the people."

Likewise, not only are victims of the elite such as protesters, sympathizers, Iraqi civilians, nonconformists, and minorities represented as "the people," so are bands and musicians. These groupings are represented through positive visuals of "the people" and negative ones of "the elite." Lyrics include the elite acting negatively while the people suffer and/or act positively and united. Musical sounds enhance the idea of negativity of the elite, something we saw in The Ringo Jets, Marsis, and Dev videos. Musical sounds also connote positivity around the people and their actions in videos such as Grup Kızılırmak's and Marsis's offerings.

Though musicians are for the most part well meaning in these songs and videos, by relying on populism issues are simplified and divisions and polarization are amplified. This is by no means conducive to political harmony. In this sense, these songs, concerts, and videos perpetuate the very issues many are trying to challenge, especially in societies as polarized as Turkey. This polarization is clearly illustrated in the comments following on from music videos posted on social media sites such as YouTube. Here we find that though most comments have little to do with the politics articulated in music commodities, some fans do indeed use music and their politics. Songs, concerts, and videos are used as a springboard to communicate fans' personal political ideas. Fans personalize politics presented in music commodities. Posters seem to shout and insult each other, rather than articulate clear precise policies and criticisms. There are a number of mostly polarized views which are expressed in a digital public domain. This public domain seems to be more about shouting and less about listening and exchanging political ideas. In this sense, however limited it is, music commodities are used by fans in political ways.

The state of Turkey at the time of writing

During my years in Turkey, I, along with many, many observers have noticed a severe decline in freedom of speech and freedom of expression. Examples are countless, but include a fourteen-year-old in prison after criticizing Erdoğan in a Facebook post, a doctor on trial after a meme he produced comparing Erdoğan to Gollum from Lord of the Rings, more than 150 journalists in jail, *Zaman* newspaper being put into government hands, and Erdoğan's regime lodging 2,493 requests (more than any other country in the world) for content to be removed from Twitter between January and June 2016.

The pace in the deterioration of freedom of expression has accelerated at an unprecedented rate since the July 15, 2016, failed coup attempt, subsequent state of emergencies, and a referendum campaign designed to boast Erdoğan's powers. Erdoğan's campaign took place in the months after the coup attempt while Turkey endured a state of emergency. He narrowly won the referendum on April 16, 2017, which gives him even more power, described as "unchecked," lacking separation of powers essential for democracy, and "unbalanced." International observers, which include the Organization for Security and Co-operation in Europe and the Council of Europe, criticized the referendum campaign which was conducted on an "uneven playing field." Media coverage of the campaign reflects this unevenness with the "Yes" (to Erdoğan's changes) campaign receiving more than ten times the amount of coverage to the "No" campaign ("Turkish No voices struggling to be heard" 2017). There were also "no" campaigners' complaints of harassment by the police, HDP politicians and leaders put in jail, and the vote count being "marred by late procedural changes that removed key safeguards" ("European Commission urges" 2017). This included reports of "no" voter harassment and charges by the opposition of cheating. This book does not tell this story. However, I offer a taste of the atmosphere in Turkish society at this time.

Immediately after the attempted coup, Erdoğan declared a state of emergency for ninety days, a condition described by Reporters without Borders (RSF) as "draconian." This has been extended numerous times, with no end date in sight at the time of writing. Erdoğan claimed he needed the time to rid Turkish society of Gülenists. Unlike, say, the state of emergency in France after the Paris shootings, in Turkey the powers of the president are unquestionable and far-reaching. Erdoğan and his close circle of advisers or "cabinet" make laws and decrees, bypassing the parliament and the judiciary. There is no recourse or debate to his decisions. As Andrew Gardner, Amnesty International researcher for Turkey, explains, "These are executive orders that should be under scrutiny, but they are rubber stamped by judges and there's no practical way to appeal these decisions" (in Fox-Brewster 2016).

These decrees and laws have affected many in society and touched on all aspects of life here, with critics accusing Erdoğan of using his new powers to silence opponents. In July, 15,200 Ministry of Education personnel were suspended and faced investigation, 4,811 teachers have been removed from their positions, 1,577 university deans were asked to resign, and 2,277 judges and prosecutors were detained. As of December 2016, a total of about 125,000 people had lost their jobs or been suspended, with 37,000 arrests. Those targeted include academics, teachers, journalists, media workers, health workers, prison guards, police, judges, and lawyers. Almost daily, these numbers rise. Erdoğan has granted himself power well beyond his previous (already powerful) position including Erdoğan replacing mayors rather than allowing local elections and deciding on rectors for universities.

These moves by Erdoğan have not gone unnoticed abroad. After visiting Turkey in September 2016, the Council of Europe Commissioner for Human Rights Nils Muižnieks issued a statement which claimed the emergency decrees "created very far-reaching, almost unlimited discretionary powers for administrative authorities and the executive in many areas, by derogation from general principles of rule of law and human rights safeguards ordinarily applicable in a democratic society" (Erkuş 2016). Despite criticisms like these, no foreign government has acted in any concrete way to curb Erdoğan's power.

Opposition politicians are also being arrested. On November 4, nine lawmakers from Kurdish-oriented HDP, including its co-chairs Selahattin Demirtaş and Figen Yüksekdağ, were arrested and detained in jail. Later in the week, the number grew to include party officials. The politicians are held in jail, many in solitary confinement until their trial, with no trial date set at the time of writing. These arrests came at a time when there were consistent reports (including by Amnesty International) of allegations of torture, rape, and ill-treatment. Though protests against the arrests of the HDP politicians were organized, they were short-lived and turnout was lower than would be expected due to a climate of fear and police actions involving water cannons and tear gas. Though the international community condemned the moves, the world's news and politicians were focusing on wars in Iraq and Syria and the US presidential election and its aftermath.

Erdoğan's purge to rid society of those he believes are related in some way or another to the Gülenist coup plotters has included a purge of the media, some with Gülenist connections and some with completely different orientations, though all less government friendly than Erdoğan would like. According to the Committee to Protect Journalists ("Turkey: arrests" 2016), the government has closed more than 100 broadcasters, newspapers, magazines, publishers, and distribution companies. In July, in the second decree law issued under the state of emergency, 102 media outlets were closed, many of whom claimed no affiliation with Gülen, according to RSF ("Turkey: in latest" 2016). The government detained over 100 journalists and media workers in the month of October 2016 alone. At least thirty news-related websites are censored by the courts and regulators acting on Erdoğan's behalf. The government has revoked the press credentials of over 330 journalists. On November 2, 2016, RSF declared Erdoğan an "enemy of press freedom." The report claimed Erdoğan wants the media to be "submissive and docile and sing his praises . . . [hiding] his aggressive dictatorship under a veneer of democracy" (as reported in Hürriyet November 2, 2016).

Turkey's oldest secular newspaper *Cumhürriyet* was one of four winners of the "Alternative Nobel Prize" in October 2016 awarded for "fearless investigative journalism and commitment to freedom of expression in the face of oppression, censorship, imprisonment and death threats" ("Turkey coup" 2016). The Council of Europe also announced it would give *Cumhürriyet* a press freedom award for its opposition to Erdoğan's crackdown. This was awarded two days after eight of its journalists, an editor, and over a dozen of the paper's executives were arrested. One of its editors, Can Dündar, fled into exile. This same week (the last in October 2016) also saw fifteen more media outlets closed (fourteen of which were Kurdish) and 10,000 civil servants dismissed. The week before saw another fifteen Kurdish and left-wing newspapers closed. These actions are despite calls for "an immediate stop to the closure[s], on the basis of a simple administrative decision or an executive order, of legal persons, such as newspapers, TV stations, associations, private companies" (Erkuş 2016).

Musicians have also experienced the wrath of Erdoğan since the coup. Following the coup, on August 7, the government organized a free rally and concert called "Demokrasi ve Şehitler Mitingi/Democracy and Martyrs Meeting" in Istanbul to celebrate the failure of the coup. Pop singer Sıla was invited to perform. She declined the offer saying, "I am against the coup but I cannot be in a show like this." She was chastised by some in the media. Furthermore, she was penalized for her act of defiance by having her shows canceled in the AKP-controlled municipalities of Istanbul, Bursa, Kayseri, and Ankara. Cancellations were announced with negative publicity, such as Ankara's AKP mayor Melih Gökçek writing on Twitter, "The door to Ankara is closed to you [Sıla]. In the future, the Gülenist movement can find you work."

Grup Yorum has also found itself the target of actions by authorities. On November 23, 2016, all seven members of the band were arrested while rehearsing at the Idil Culture Centre. They were accused of assault, resistance, and membership to a terrorist organization. Police cite evidence as traditional dance and folk costumes which they claim are a "monotype costume of an organization," 2,030 Turkish lira (less than £500) deemed as "money of the terrorist organization," a worker's hammer, and a political magazine (Acarer 2016). While they remain in jail, their musical instruments were purposely broken by police actions (see Figure 10.1).[1]

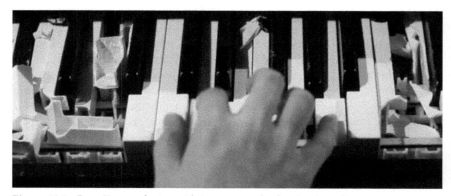

Figure 10.1 Grup Yorum playing with instruments broken by the police

In the virtual world, there have also been repercussions. Many of the Gezi Park songs and videos collected and analyzed in this book have disappeared from the internet. Though this was not uncommon in the past, it is more common since the coup attempt. In the present climate of fear, people are afraid to speak out. This is reflected in social media where people once outspoken in their criticisms of the government and Erdoğan now are fearful and self-censor posts and tweets, myself included. Musicians, as part of this society, no doubt feel the same.

The last, last word

I do not want to finish this book on such a low note. The previous pages have described in great detail a large number of instances how music can be political. Turkey is going through dark days at the moment in terms of democracy, freedom of expression, and freedom of speech. There is a palatable atmosphere of fear and restraint. And it is here I believe music can play a vital role.

Popular music can express subversion multimodally to give people hope for a better future. Here, I am not referring to Adorno's (1941) suggestion that some music (in Adorno's view classical and avant-garde music) offers an implicit critique of society and suggests an alternative, utopian vision through "form" rather than "content." Through detailed analysis, my study has demonstrated how there is politics in music, though this is characterized not as a coherent set of arguments laid down in a clear manner for fans to consider. Instead, music whether live, as part of an election campaign, in music videos, or in social movements all seem to offer personalized and fragmented political experiences. It is highly ambiguous as a political message and draws heavily on a range of connotations and relies on the audience to piece it together. Though this is far from ideal, in a place like Turkey where discourses counter to government ones are few and far between, this can play an important role.

Igor Stravinsky once claimed that "the sole purpose of music is to order sonic phenomena in time such that they can be contemplated in the abstract much as one might contemplate the interplay of architectural forms" (in Zbikowski 2015: 143). I have argued against this idea, describing through a close detailed analysis of music's modes, how music can express meanings. Though there are drawbacks to choosing to use music to express politics, there are also advantages. With music, you get a large number of people who are listening, possibly more so than a speech or a television news report. And unlike political speeches, tirades on television, or political tweets, music can be more subtle, metaphorical, and affective while communicating. This can be an advantage in an oppressive society which is looking for logical arguments and facts in order to confirm a communicative act is indeed subversive. In music, this is more difficult, resulting in some governments dismissing it all together (Street 1988).

Here in Turkey, freedom of expression is in danger while oppositional media are all but nonexistent. However, music thrives. Though most of it is indeed far from politically engaged in Turkey's problems, some of it is engaged. And it is here where hope lies. Through its multimodal nature, popular music can express its opposition to political parties, policies, and ideologies. These oppositional voices do not have to be direct and obvious. Through cultural communion, musicians and fans can oppose what many describe as a dictatorship. Through lyrics, visuals, and musical sounds in songs, videos, and concerts, musicians can contribute to political debate by adding voices to an oppressed public sphere. Jurgen Habermas (1991) spoke of how a healthy democracy depends on a vibrant public sphere where a range of voices are expressed, listened to, and considered. At the moment in Turkey, this is not the case. However, music can contribute to this by offering subversive voices, however subtle and self-serving. And as demonstrated in my analysis of YouTube comments, though comments are more like a shouting match in which nobody is listening than a vibrant public sphere envisioned by Habermas, at least opposing views are being expressed and there lies the political potential of popular music.

Notes

Introduction

1   The permalink for this video is https://youtu.be/Lye7781lliI (accessed May 26, 2017).

Chapter 2

1   The permalink for this video is https://youtu.be/9cVJr3eQfXc (accessed May 26, 2017).
2   The permalink for this video is https://youtu.be/RFhAzSPIJpE (accessed May 26, 2017).

Chapter 5

1   The permalink for this musical advertisement is https://youtu.be/HwEDqIouDdo (accessed May 26, 2017).
2   I am unaware of a link which has the lyrics in full written English. However, the permalink for this video is https://youtube/HwEDqIouDdo (accessed May 26, 2017).
3   The permalink for this musical advertisement is https://youtu.be/nmudoItKA_g (accessed May 26, 2017).
4   I cannot find a link with these lyrics in full in English. However, the permalink to this musical advertisement is https://www.youtube.com/watch?v=nmudoItKA_g (accessed May 26, 2017).

Chapter 6

1   The permalink for a recording of the concert is https://youtu.be/hM9ueSJcKH0 (accessed May 26, 2017).

Chapter 7

1   The permalink for this video is https://youtu.be/YuCOTCcycwE (accessed May 26, 2017).
2   The permalink for this video is https://youtu.be/ah-K6UMjIHA (accessed May 26, 2017).
3   The permalink for this video is constantly changing. One can only suspect that it is being taken off YouTube by some parties only to be put back on by others. The number

of hits is impossible to calculate, though at one point, there were over 152,000 hits, though this has since been removed. If the link does not open the video, I suggest you type in "Duman Iyı de bana ne Tayyip." At the time of writing the permalink is https://youtu.be/v07hy_1AE0E (accessed May 26, 2017).

4 The permalink for this video is https://youtu.be/SQmNhEDAV2Q (accessed May 26, 2017).
5 The permalink for Akarsu's video is https://youtu.be/Lws5Tkk-E4Q (accessed May 26, 2017). I was not given permission to use images from the video. However, in this section I indicate where images I refer to can be found in the link indicated.
6 These actions can be seen throughout the video, though a good example is at 2:28 into the video.
7 Again, these shots can be seen throughout the video. A good example is at 1:49 into the video.
8 This can be seen at 55 seconds into the video.
9 Two good examples of this can be seen at 53 seconds and again at 1:16 into the video.
10 This image can be found at 2:38 into the video.

Chapter 8

1 The permalink for this video is https://youtu.be/oeFUnWBLHbU (accessed May 26, 2017).
2 The permalink for this video is https://youtu.be/1LXNQQ9V8pE (accessed May 26, 2017).

Chapter 9

1 The permalink for this recording of the concert is https://youtu.be/hM9ueSJcKH0 (accessed May 26, 2017).
2 The permalink for this video is https://youtu.be/Lws5Tkk-E4Q (accessed May 26, 2017).
3 The permalink for this video is https://youtu.be/1LXNQQ9V8pE (accessed May 26, 2017).

Chapter 10

1 In an act of defiance, Grup Yorum have released a video with visuals which include them playing instruments broken by police. The permalink for this video is https://youtu.be/9TaBUs0Jznc?list=PL2oJDUzFy_6G7bFsVox4ZcUs1iuLpCMq4 (accessed May 26, 2017).

References

Abousnnouga, G. and D. Machin (2010), "Analysing the language of war monuments," *Visual Communication*, 9(2): 131–149.

Acarer, E. (2016), "Message of support from Joan Baez to arrested members of Grup Yorum of Turkey," *BirGün*. Available online: http://www.birgun.net/haber-detay/message-of-support-from-joan-baez-to-arrested-members-of-grup-yorum-of-turkey-136890.html (accessed December 2, 2016).

Adorno, T. (1941), "On popular music," *Studies in Philosophy and Social Science*, New York: Institute of Social Research, 17–48. Available online: http://www.icce.rug.nl/~soundscapes/DATABASES/SWA/On_popular_music_1.shtml (accessed February 2, 2016).

Adorno, T. (1991), *The Culture Industry: Selected Essays on Mass Culture*, London: Routledge.

"AK Parti: Parti Programı" (2013), *AK Parti*. Available online: http://www.akparti.org.tr/site/akparti/parti-programi (accessed April 25, 2013).

Altunışık, M. (2006), "Turkey's Iraq policy: The war and beyond," *Journal of Contemporary European Studies*, 14(2): 183–196.

Andrejevic, M. (2013), "Estranged free labour," in T. Sholtz (ed.), *Digital Labour: The Internet as Playground and Factory*, 149–164, New York: Routledge.

Androutsopoulos, J. (2010), "Multilingualism, ethnicity and genre in Germany's migrant hip hop," in M. Terkourafi (ed.), *Languages of Global Hip Hop*, 19–43, London: Continuum.

Arnold, M. (1960), *Culture and Anarchy*, London: Cambridge University Press.

Attali, J. (1977), *Noise: The Political Economy of Music*, Minnesota: Minnesota University Press.

Atton, C. (2002), *Alternative Media*, London: Sage.

Atton, C. (2004), *An Alternative Internet: Radical Media, Politics and Creativity*, Edinburgh: Edinburgh University Press.

Auslander, P. (1999), *Liveness: Performance in a Mediatised Culture*, New York: Routledge.

Auslander, P. (2008), *Liveness: Performance in a Mediatized Culture*, 2nd edition, Abingdon, Oxon: Taylor & Francis.

Auslander, P. (2015), "Liveness: Performance in a mediatised culture," in R. Caines and A. Heble (eds), *The Improvisation Studies Reader: Spontaneous Acts*, 357–361, London: Routledge.

Aydin, M. and D. Aras (2005), "Political conditionality of economic relations between paternalist states: Turkey's interaction with Iran, Iraq and Syria," *Arab Studies Quarterly*, 27(1/2): 21–43.

Bahçe, S. and A.H. Köse (2016), "Financialisation/borrowing circle as a solution to an unpleasant conundrum: Observations from the mature neoliberalism in Turkey," *Research and Policy on Turkey*, 1(1): 63–74.

Ballantine, C. (2002), "Music, masculinity and migrancy under early apartheid: Gender and popular song in South Africa, *c.* 1948-1960," in D. Hesmondhalgh and K. Negus (eds), *Popular Music Studies*, 16–32, London: Arnold.

Barış, R. (2010), "Media landscape: Turkey," *European Journalism Centre*. Available online: http://www.ejc.net/media_landscape/article/turkey/ (accessed December 19, 2011).

Barkey H.J. and G.E. Fuller (1998), *Turkey's Kurdish Question*, New York: Rowman & Littlefield Publishers.

Barrett, R. (2017), "Indigenous hip hop as anti-colonial discourse in Guatemala," in L. Way and S. McKerrell (eds), *Music as Multimodal Discourse: Media, Power and Protest*, 179–200, London & New York: Bloomsbury.

"Başbakan Erdoğan: din bir çimentodur ve şu anda en önemli birleştirici unsurumuzdur" (2015), *AK Parti*. Available online: http://www.akparti.org.tr/site/haberler/basbakan-erdogan-din-bir-cimentodur-ve-su-anda-en-onemli-birlestirici-unsur/5641#1 (accessed December 20, 2015).

Başlevent, C. and H. Kirmanoğlu (2016), "Economic voting in Turkey: Perceptions, expectations, and the party choice," *Research and Policy on Turkey*, 1(1): 88–101.

Berger, H. (1999), "Death metal tonality and the act of listening," *Popular Music*, 18(2): 161–178.

Billig, M. (1995), *Banal Nationalism*, London: Sage Publications.

Bishop, H. and A. Jaworski (2003), "We beat 'em: nationalism and the hegemony of homogeneity in the British press reportage of Germany versus England during Euro 2000," *Discourse and Society*, 14(3): 243–271.

Boratav, K. (2016), "The Turkish bourgeoisie under neoliberalism," *Research and Policy on Turkey*, 1(1): 1–10.

Bouvier, G. (2014), "British press photographs and the misrepresentation of the 2011 uprising in Libya: A content analysis," in D. Machin (ed.), *Visual Communication*, 281–299, Berlin: Gruyter Mouton.

Bouvier, G. (2017), "Discourse in clothing: The social semiotics of modesty and chic in hijab fashion," *Gender and Language*, 10(3): 364–385.

Brackett, D. (2002), "(In search of) musical meaning: Genres, categories and crossover," in D. Hesmondhalgh and K. Negus (eds), *Popular Music Studies*, 65–84, London: Arnold.

Brunstad, E., U. Royneland and T. Opsahl (2010), "Hip hop, ethnicity and linguistic practice in rural and urban Norway," in M. Terkourafi (ed.), *Languages of Global Hip Hop*, 223–255, London: Continuum.

Burch, B. and O. Ozbilgin (2013), "Turkey seeks to tighten grip on Twitter after protests," *Reuters*. Available online: www.reuters.com/article/2013/06/26/net-us-turkey-protesters-twitter-idUSBRE95POXC20130626 (accessed December 2, 2013).

Burns, R. (2007), "Continuity, variation, and authenticity in the English folk-rock movement," *Folk Music Journal*, 9(2): 192–218.

Burton, G. (2005), *Media and Society: Critical Perspectives*, Berkshire: Open University Press.

Capple, S. and R. Garofalo (1977), *Rock 'n' Roll Is Here to Pay: The History and Politics of the Music Industry*, Chicago: Nelson-Hall.

Christensen, C. (2005), "Breaking the news concentration of ownership, the fall of unions and government legislation in Turkey," *Global Media and Communication*, 3(2): 179–199.

Coffey, B., and S. Woolworth (2004), "Destroy the scum, and then neuter their families: The web forum as a vehicle for community discourse?" *Social Science Journal*, 41(1): 1–14.

Connell, J. and C. Gibson (2003), *Sound Tracks: Popular Music, Identity, and Place*, London: Routledge.

Cook, N. (1990), *Music, Imagination and Culture*, Oxford: Clarendon Press.

Cook, N. (1994), "Music and meanings in the commercials," *Popular Music*, 13(1): 35–38.

Cook, N. (1998), *Music: A Very Short Introduction*, Oxford: Oxford University Press.

Cook, N. (2008), "We are all (ethno) musicologists now," in H. Stobart (ed.), *The New (Ethno) Musicologies*, 48–70, London: Roman and Littlefield.

Cook, N. and M. Everist (1999), *Rethinking Music*, Oxford: Oxford University Press.

Corn, A. (2011), "Treaty now: Popular music and the indigenous struggle for justice in contemporary Australia," in I. Peddie (ed.), *Popular Music and Human Rights Volume 2: World Music*, 17–26, Surrey: Ashgate.

Dean, J. (2010), *Blog Theory*, Cambridge: Polity Press.

Dearn, L.K. and S.M. Price (2016), "Sharing music: Social and communal aspects of concert-going," *Networking Knowledge*, 9(2): 1–20. Available online: http://ojs.meccsa .org.uk/index.php/netknow/article/view/428/250 (accessed September 29, 2016).

de Bellaigue, C. (2013), "Turkey: Surreal, menacing... pompous," *New York Review of Books*. Available online: www.nybooks.com/articles/archives/2013/dec/19/turkey -surreal-menacing-pompous/ (accessed March 30, 2014).

De Cleen, B. and N. Carpentier (2010), "Contesting the populist claim on 'the People' through popular culture: The 0110 concerts versus the Vlaams Belang," *Social Semiotics*, 20(2): 175–196.

Demirkaya, M. (2013), "İBB'nin stadyumu da yandaşa [IBB's stadium is also for supporters]," *Yurt Gazetesi*. Available online: http://www.yurtgazetesi.com.tr/ekonomi/ ibbnin-stadyumu-da-yandasa-h30527.html (accessed April 21, 2015).

de Zuniga, G. (2012), "Modeling the process of political participation in the EU," in R. Friedman and M. Thiel (eds), *European Identity & Culture: Narratives of Transnational Belonging*, 75–95, Ashgate: New York.

Dowmunt, T. (2007), "Introduction," in K. Coyer, T. Dowmunt and A. Fountain (eds), *The Alternative Media Handbook*, 1–12, Oxon: Taylor and Francis.

Downing, J., V. Ford, G. Gil and L, Stein (2001), *Radical Media: Rebellious Communication and Social Movements*, Thousand Oaks, CA: Sage.

Ensaroğlu, Y. (2013), "Turkey's Kurdish question and the peace process," *Insight Turkey*, 15(2): 7–17.

"Erdoğan 'dindar nesil'i savundu" (2012), *Radical*. Available online: http://www.radikal .com.tr/Radikal.aspx?aType=RadikalDetayV3&ArticleID=1077899&CategoryID=78 (accessed February 21, 2012).

Eriksson, G. and D. Machin (2017), "The role of music in ridiculing the working classes in reality television," in L. Way and S. McKerrell (eds), *Popular Music as Multimodal Discourse: Semiotics, Power and Protest*, 21–45, London: Bloomsbury.

Erkuş, S. (2016), "CoE Commissioner urges Turkey to repeal emergency decrees," *Hürriyet*. Available online: http://www.hurriyetdailynews.com/coe-commissioner -urges-turkey-to-repeal-emergency-decrees.aspx?pageID=238&nID=104706&NewsCat ID=351 (accessed November 11, 2016).

Esen, N. and S. Ciddi (2011), "Turkey's 2011 elections: An emerging dominant party system?," *Rubin Center*. Available online: http://www.rubincenter.org/2011/10/ turkey%E2%80%99s-2011-elections-an-emerging-dominant-party-system/ (accessed December 20, 2015).

"European Commission urges Turkey to launch 'transparent investigations' into referendum results" (2017), *Hurriyet Daily News*. Available online: http://www

.hurriyetdailynews.com/european-commission-urges-turkey-to-launch-transparent
-investigations-into-referendum-results.aspx?pageID=238&nID=112153&NewsCat
ID=510 (accessed April 18, 2017).

Eyerman, R. and A. Jamison (1998), *Music and Social Movements: Mobilising traditions in the Twentieth century*, Cambridge: Cambridge University Press.

Fairclough, N. (1989), *Language and Power*, Harlow: Pearson Education Limited.

Fairclough, N. (1995), *Media Discourse*, London: Edward Arnold.

Fairclough, N. (2003), *Analysing Discourse: Textual Analysis for Social Research*, London: Routledge.

Fairclough, N. and R. Wodak (1997), "Critical discourse analysis," in T. Van Dijk (ed.), *Discourse Studies: A Multidisciplinary Introduction: Vol 2. Discourse as Social Interaction*, 258–284, London: Longman.

Feld, S. and A. Fox (1994), "Music and language," *Annual Review of Anthropology*, 23(1): 25–53.

Filardo-Llamas, L. (2017), "When the fairy tale is over: An analysis of songs and institutional discourse against domestic violence in Spain," in L. Way and S. McKerrell (eds), *Music as Multimodal Discourse: Media, Power and Protest*, 159–178, London & New York: Bloomsbury.

Finkel, A. (2000), "Who guards the Turkish press? A perspective on press corruption in Turkey," *Journal of International Affairs*, 54(1): 147–66.

Finkel, A. (2005), "Fighting the enemy within," *IPI Global Journalist*, 3: 24–5.

Fiske, J. (1989), *Understanding Popular Culture*, London: Routledge.

Flowerdew, J. and S. Leong (2007), "Metaphors in the discursive construction of patriotism: The case of Hong Kong's constitutional reform debate," *Discourse and Society*, 18(3): 273–294.

Fraley, T. (2009), "I got a natural skill…: Hip-hop, authenticity, and whiteness," *Howard Journal of Communications*, 20(1): 37–54.

Forman, M. (2002), *The Hood Comes First: Race, Space, and Place in Rap and Hip-Hop*, Middletown: Wesleyan University Press.

Fowkes, E. and J. Glazer (1973), *Songs of Work and Protest*, New York: Dover Publications.

Fox-Brewster, T. (2016), "Is an American company's technology helping Turkey spy on its citizens?" *Forbes*. Available online: http://www.forbes.com/sites/thomasbrewster/2016/10/25/procera-francisco-partners-turkey-surveillance-erdogan/#4726de0175ce (accessed October 27, 2016).

"Freedom of the press: 2016" (2016), *Freedom House*. Available online: https://freedomhouse.org/report/freedom-press/freedom-press-2016 (accessed September 5, 2016).

Frith, S. (1981), *Sound Effects: Youth, Leisure and the Politics of Rock'n'roll*, New York: Pantheon.

Frith, S. (1988), *Music for Pleasure: Essays in the Sociology of Pop*, Cambridge: Polity Press.

Frith, S. (1996), *Performing Rites: On the Value of Popular Music*, Cambridge, MA: Harvard University Press.

Frith, S. and J. Street (1992), "Rock against racism and Red Wedge," in R. Garofalo (ed.), *Rockin' the Boat: Mass Music and Mass Movements*, Boston, MA: South End Press.

Garofalo, R. (1986), *Rockin' Out: Popular Music in the U.S.A.*, New York: Pearson.

Gedik, A. (2010), "Turkiye'deki Politik Muziğin Değişimi uzerine Bir Tartişma Cercevesi: Ey Ozgurluk! Gelenek," *Aylik Marksist Dergi*, 107: 61–80.

Georgakopoulou, A. (2014), "Small stories transposition and social media: A micro-perspective on the 'Greek crisis,'" *Discourse and Society*, 25(4): 519–539.

"Gezi Park protests: Brutal denial of the right to peaceful assembly in Turkey" (2013), Amnesty International. Available online: http://www.amnesty.org.uk/news_details .asp?NewsID=20991 (accessed October 12, 2013).

Gilbert, J. and E. Pearson (1999), *Discographies: Dance Music, Culture, and the Politics of Sound*, London: Routledge.

Goodwin, A. (1993), *Dancing in the Distraction Factory: Music Television and Popular Culture*, London: Routledge.

Gracyk, T. (1996), *Rhythm and Noise: An Aesthetic of Rock*, Durham, NC: Duke University Press.

Greene, P. (2011), "Intense emotions and human rights in Nepal's heavy metal scene," in I. Peddie (ed.), *Popular Music and Human Rights Volume 2: World Music*, 27–38, Surrey: Ashgate.

Griffiths, D. (2002), "Cover versions and the sound of identity in motion," in D. Hesmondhalgh and K. Negus (eds), *Popular Music Studies*, 51–64, London: Arnold.

Grossberg, L. (1987), "Rock and roll in search of an audience," in J. Lull (ed.), *Popular Music and Communication*, 175–197, Beverly Hills, CA: Sage.

Grossberg, L. (1992), *We Gotta Get Out of This Place: Popular Conservatism and Postmodern Culture*, New York: Routledge.

"Grup Kızılırmak Biyografi" (2013), *Grup Kızılırmak*. Available online: http://www .ilkayakkaya.com.tr/?page_id=7 (accessed March 21, 2013).

Günlük-Şenesen, G. and H. Kırık (2016), "The AKP Era: Democratization or resecuritization? An assessment of the institutional and budgetary reflections," *Research and Policy on Turkey*, 1(1): 75–87.

Habermas, J. (1991), *The Structural Transformation of the Public Sphere*, Cambridge: Massachusetts Institute of Technology

Hall, S. (1988), *The Hard Road to Renewal: Thatcherism and the Crisis of the Left*, London: Verso.

Hallin, D. and P. Mancini (2004), *Comparing Media Systems: Three Models of Media and Politics*, Cambridge: Cambridge University Press.

Hargittai, E. (2008), "The digital reproduction in inequality," in D. Grusky (ed.), *Social Stratification*, 936–944, Boulder, CO: Westview Press.

"Hasan Kalyoncu Kimdir [Who is Hasan Kolyoncu]" (2008), Biyografi. Available online: http://www.biyografi.net.tr/hasan-kalyoncu-kimdir/ (accessed April 14, 2015).

Hassa, S. (2010), "Kiff my zikmu: Symbolic dimensions of Arabic, English and Verlan in French Rap texts," in M. Terkourafi (ed.), *Languages of Global Hip Hop*, 44–66, London: Continuum.

Hebdige, D. (1979), *Subculture: The Meaning of Style*, Suffolk: Metheun & co.

Hesmondhalgh, D. (2013), *Why Music Matters*, Chichester: Wiley Blackwell.

Hesmondhalgh, D. and K. Negus (2002), *Popular Music Studies*, London: Arnold.

Hess, J.S. (2010), "From American form to Greek performance: The Global Hip-Hop poetics and politics of the Imiskoumbria," in M. Terkourafi (ed.), *Languages of Global Hip Hop*, 162–193, London: Continuum.

Hibbett, R. (2005), "What is indie rock?," *Popular Music and Society*, 28(1): 55–77.

Howard, P. and Hussain, M. (2011), "The upheavals in Egypt and Tunisia: The role of digital media," *Journal of Democracy*, 22(3): 35–48.

Hudson, A. (2013), "Woman in red becomes leitmotif for Istanbul's female protesters," *Reuters*. Available online: http://www.reuters.com/article/us-turkey-protests-women -idUSBRE95217B20130603 (accessed January 22, 2014).

Huq, R. (2002), "Raving not drowning: Authenticity, pleasure and politics in the electronic dance scene," in D. Hesmondhalgh and K. Negus (eds), *Popular Music Studies*, 167–85, London: Arnold.

Işık, G. (2013), "Yeni toplumsal hareketler ve sanal gerçeklik boyutunda gezi parkı eylemleri," *Seçukİletişim*, 8(1): 19–33.

Jenkins, G. (2012), "A house divided against itself: The deteriorating state of media freedom in Turkey," *Central Asia-Caucasus Institute*. Available online: http://www.silkroadstudies.org/new/inside/turkey/2012/120206A.html (accessed February 1, 2013).

Jenkins, H. (2006), *Fans, Bloggers and Gamers: Media Consumers in a Digital Age*, New York: New York University Press.

Johansson, O. and T. Bell (2009), "Introduction," in O. Johansson and T. Bell (eds), *Sound, Society and the Geography of Popular Music*, 1–6, Farnham: Ashgate.

Karaman, M.L. and B. Aras (2000), "The crisis of civil society in Turkey," *Journal of Economic and Social Research*, 2(2): 39–58.

Karatepe, İ.D. (2016), "The state, Islamists, discourses, and bourgeoisie: The construction industry in Turkey," *Research and Policy on Turkey*, 1(1): 46–62.

Karip, M. (2013), "Big institutions privatized in the last 10 years," *Milliyet*. Available online: http://blog.milliyet.com.tr/son-on-yilda-ozellestirilen-buyuk-kuruluslar/Blog/?BlogNo=395556 (accessed January 2, 2016).

Keen, A. (2007), *The Cult of the Amateur*, New York: Doubleday.

Keleş, H. (2015), "Erdoğan's presidential system either chaos or dictatorship, says academic," *BGN News*. Available online: http://politics.bgnnews.com/erdogans-presidential-system-either-chaosor-dictatorship-says-academic-haberi/3899 (accessed July 15, 2015).

Korczynski, M. (2014), *Songs of the factory: Pop Music, Culture and Resistance*, New York: Cornell University Press.

Kotsev, V. (2014), "Turkey has one of world's worst mining safety records, and experts say privatization is part of the problem," *International Business Times*. Available online: http://www.ibtimes.com/turkey-has-one-worlds-worst-mining-safety-records-experts-say-privatization-part-1585775 (accessed August 9, 2016).

Köylü, H. (2015), "Seçimlerde AKP-HDP savaşı [AKP-HDP election wars]," *Deutsche Welle*. Available online: http://www.dw.com/tr/se%C3%A7imlerde-akp-hdp-sava%C5%9F%C4%B1/a-18489323 (accessed June 25, 2015).

Kress, G. (1985), *Linguistic Processes in Sociocultural Practice*, Victoria, Australia: Deakin University Press.

Kress, G. (1989), *Linguistic Processes in Sociocultural Practice*, 2nd edition, Oxford: Oxford University Press.

Kress, G. (2010), *Multimodality: A Semiotic Approach to Contemporary Communication*, London: Taylor and Francis.

Kress, G. and R. Hodge (1979), *Language as Ideology*, London: Routledge.

Kress, G. and T. van Leeuwen (1996), *Reading Images: The Grammar of Visual Design*, Oxon: Routledge.

Kress, G. and T. van Leeuwen (2001), *Multimodal Discourse*, London: Hodder Education.

Laclau, E. (2005), *On Populist Reason*, London: Verso.

Lakoff, G. and M. Johnson (1980), *Metaphors We Live By*, London: University of Chicago.

Leavis, F.R. and B. Thompson (1977), *Culture and Environment*, Westport, CT: Greenwood Press.

Lee, F. (2010), "Globalizing keepin' it real: South Korean Hip-Hop Playas," in M. Terkourafi (ed.), *Languages of Global Hip Hop*, 139–161, London: Continuum.

Leppert, R. (1995), *The Sight of Sound: Music, Representation, and the History of the Body*, London: University of California Press.

Letsch, C. (2011), "Recep Erdogan wins by landslide in Turkey's general election," *The Guardian*, June 13. Available online: http://www.theguardian.com/world/2011/jun/13/recep-erdogan-turkey-general-election (accessed June 13, 2015).

LeVine, M. (2011), "How a music about death reaffirms life: Middle Eastern Metal and the return of music's aura," in I. Peddie (ed.), *Popular Music and Human Rights Volume 2: World Music*, 53–72, Surrey: Ashgate.

Lindgren, S. (2010), "At the nexus of destruction and creation: Pirate and anti-pirate discourse in Swedish online media," in Uğur Dai (ed.), *New media and interactivity [NMIC2010 proceedings]*, 229–236. Istanbul: Marmara University.

Lorraine, L. (2006), "Music and national culture: Pop music and resistance in Brazil," *Portuguese Cultural Studies*, 1(1): 36–44.

Lynskey, D. (2010), *33 Revolutions per Minute: A History of Protest Songs*, London: Faber.

Machin, D. (2007), *Introduction to Multimodal Analysis*, London: Hodder Education.

Machin, D. (2010), *Analysing Popular Music*, London: Sage.

Machin, D. (2013), "What is multimodal critical discourse studies?" *Critical Discourse Studies*, 10(4): 347–355.

Machin, D. and A. Mayr (2012), *How to Do Critical Discourse Analysis: A Multimodal Introduction*, London: Sage.

Machin, D. and J.E. Richardson (2012), "Discourses of unity and purpose in the sounds of fascist music: A multimodal approach," *Critical Discourse Studies*, 9(4): 329–345.

Machin, D. and T. van Leeuwen (2005), "Computer games as political discourse: The case of Black Hawk Down," *Journal of Language and Politics*, 4(1): 119–141.

Mango, A. (1999), *Atatürk: The Biography of the Founder of Modern Turkey*, London: John Murray.

McKerrell, S. (2012), "Hearing sectarianism: Understanding Scottish sectarianism as song," *Critical Discourse Studies*, 9(4): 1–12.

McKerrell, S. (2015), "Social distance and the multimodal construction of the other in sectarian song," *Social Semiotics*, 25(5): 1–19.

McKerrell, S. and L. Way (2017), "Understanding music as multimodal discourse," in L. Way and S. McKerrell (eds), *Music as Multimodal Discourse: Media, Power and Protest*, London & New York: Bloomsbury.

"Michelangelo's David: Humanism at its finest" (2014), *Wordpress*, June 13. Available online: https://bhcruickshanks.wordpress.com/2014/06/13/michelangelos-david-humanism-at-its-finest/ (accessed July 2, 2015).

Middleton, R. (1990), *Studying Popular Music*, Buckingham: Open University Press.

Moore, A. (2002), "Authenticity as authentication," *Popular Music*, 21(2): 209–223.

Moore, A. (2013), *Song Means: Analysing and Interpreting Recorded Popular Song*, Farnham: Ashgate.

Morozov, E. (2009), "The brave new world of slacktivism," *Foreign policy*. Available online: http://neteffect.foreignpolicy.com/posts/2009/05/19/the_brave_new_world_of_slacktivism (accessed April 6, 2013).

Mottier, V. (2008), "Metaphors, mini-narratives and Foucauldian discourse theory," in T. Carver and J. Pikalo (eds), *Political Language and Metaphor*, 182–194, London: Routledge.

Muktuavel, V. (2011), "The 'Dangerous' folksongs: The neo-folklore movement of occupied Latvia in the 1980s," in I. Peddie (ed.), *Popular Music and Human Rights Volume 2: World Music*, 73–90, Surrey: Ashgate.

Norris, S. (2004), *Analyzing Multimodal Interaction*, Abingdon, Oxon: Routledge Falmer.

Öğret, Ö. (2016), "Failed coup speeds Turkey crackdown," *Committee to protect journalists*, August update. Available online: https://www.cpj.org/europe/turkey/ (accessed August 5, 2016).

Öncü, A. and E. Balkan (2016), "Nouveaux riches of the city of minarets and skyscrapers: Neoliberalism and the reproduction of the Islamic middle class in İstanbul," *Research and Policy on Turkey*, 1(1): 29–45.

Ord, M. (2017), "Song, sonic metaphor, and countercultural discourse in British folk-rock recordings," in L. Way and S. McKerrell (eds), *Music as Multimodal Discourse: Media, Power and Protest*, 201–222, London & New York: Bloomsbury.

Özbudun, E. and W. Hale (2010), *Islamism, Democracy and Liberalism in Turkey: The Case of the AKP*, London: Routledge.

Özgenç, M. (2013), "RTÜK'ten Halk Tv ve Ulusal Kanal'a Ceza," *Hurriyet*, June 12. Available online: http://www.hurriyet.com.tr/gundem/23486445.asp (accessed June 12, 2016).

Özguneş, N. and G. Terzis (2000), "Constraints and remedies for journalists reporting national conflict: The case of Greece and Turkey," *Journalism Studies*, 1(3): 405–426.

Papathanassopoulos, S. (2000), "Election campaigning in the television age: The case of contemporary Greece," *Political Communication*, 17: 47–60.

Peddie, I. (2011), *Popular Music and Human Rights Volume 2: World Music*. Farnham: Ashgate.

Pennycook, A. (2007), *Global Englishes and Transcultural Flows*, New York: Routledge.

Power, M., A. Dillane and E. Devereux (2012), "A push and a shove and the land is ours: Morrissey's counter-hegemonic stance(s) on social class," *Critical Discourse Studies*, 9(4): 375–392.

Pusane, K. (2014), "Turkey's Kurdish opening: Long awaited achievements and failed expectations," *Turkish Studies*, 15(1): 81–99.

Railton, D. and P. Watson (2011), *Music Video and the Politics of Representation*, Edinburgh: Edinburgh University Press.

Redhead, S. and J. Street (1989), "Have I the right? Legitimacy, authenticity and community in folk's politics," *Popular Music*, 8(2): 177–184.

Renan, E. (1992), "Qu'est-ce qu'une nation?" [What is a Nation?], translated by Ethan Rundell, Paris: Presses-Pocket. Available online: http://ucparis.fr/files/9313/6549/9943/What_is_a_Nation.pdf (accessed June 20, 2016).

Richardson, J.E. (2007), *Analysing Newspapers: An Approach from Critical Discourse Analysis*, London: Palgrave Macmillan.

Richardson, J.E. (2017), "Recontextualization and fascist Music," in L. Way and S. McKerrell (eds), *Music as Multimodal Discourse: Media, Power and Protest*, 71–94, London & New York: Bloomsbury.

Roderick, I. (2013), "Representing robots as living labour in advertisements: The new discourse of worker–employer power relations," *Critical Discourse Studies*, 10(4): 392–405.

'RTÜK'ten Halk TV ve Ulusal Kanal'a Ceza' (2013), *Hürriyet Gazetesi*. Available online: http://www.hurriyet.com.tr/gundem/23486445.asp (accessed June 24, 2013).

Scott, T. (2007), "Analyzing political conversation on the Howard Dean candidate blog," in M. Tremayne (ed.), *Blogging, Citizenship and the Future of Media*, New York: Routledge.

Shank, B. (2014), *The Political Force of Musical Beauty*, New York: Duke University Press.

Shuker, R. (2001), *Understanding Popular Music*, 2nd edition, London: Routledge.

Solomon, T. (2005), "Living underground is tough: Authenticity and locality in the hip-hop community in Istanbul, Turkey," *Popular Music*, 24(1): 1–20.

Sönmez, M. (2015), *Ak faşizmin İnşaat İskelesi* [The Scaffolding of AK Fascism], Ankara: Notabene.

Stokes, M. (2003), "Globalisation and the politics of world music," in Martin Clayton, Trevor Herbert and Richard Middleton (eds), *The Cultural Study of Music: A Critical Introduction*, London: Routledge

Stokes, M. (2010), *The Republic of Love: Cultural Intimacy in Turkish Popular Music*, London: University of Chicago Press.

Storey, J. (2001), *Cultural Theory and Popular Culture: An Introduction*, 3rd edition, Harlow: Pearson.

Stravinsky, I. (1935), *Chroniques de ma vie*, Paris, Denoël et Stael; (English translation: Igor Stravinsky. An Autobiography second edition), New York: Norton, 1962.

Street, J. (1988), *Rebel Rock: The Politics of Popular Music*, Oxford: Basil Blackwood.

Street, J. (2013), "The sound of geopolitics: Popular music and political rights," *Popular Communication: The International Journal of Media and Culture*, 11(1): 47–57.

Stylianou, E. (2010), "Keeping it native (?): The conflicts and contradictions of Cypriot Hip Hop," in M. Terkourafi (ed.), *Languages of Global Hip Hop*, 194–222, London: Continuum.

Sümer, Ç. and F. Yaşlı (2010), *Hegemonyadan Diktoryaya AKP ve Liberal-Muhafazakar İttifak* [From hegemony to dictatorship AKP and Liberal conservatism], Ankara: Tan Kitapevi Yayınları.

Tagg, P. (1979), "Kojak: 50 seconds of television music, toward the analysis of affect in popular music." Available online: <http://search.ebscohost.com/login .aspx?direct=true&db=rih&AN=1979-01928&site=ehost-live80> (accessed April 21, 2016).

Tagg, P. (1982), Nature as a musical mood category. Nordens working paper series. http://www.tagg.org/articles/xpdfs/nature.pdf.

Tagg, P. (1983), *Nature as a Musical Mood Category*, Goteborg: IASPM Internal Publications.

Tagg, P. (1984), "Understanding musical time sense: Concepts, sketches and consequences." Available online: http://www.tagg.org/articles/xpdfs/timesens.pdf (accessed March 3, 2013).

Tagg, P. (1990), "Music in mass media studies. Reading sounds for example," in K. Roe and U. Carlsson (eds), *Popular Music Research*, Sweden: Nordicom.

Tagg, P. (2012), *Music's Meanings, a Modern Musicology for Non-Musos*, New York: Mass Media Music Scholars' Press.

Tatit, L. (2002), "Analyzing popular songs," in D. Hesmondhalgh and K. Negus (eds), *Popular Music Studies*, 33–50, London: Arnold.

Tenzer, M. and J. Roeder (2011), *Analytical and Cross-Cultural Studies in World Music*, Oxford: Oxford University Press.

Terkourafi, M. (2010), *Languages of Global Hip Hop*, London: Continuum.

Traynor, I. and C. Letsch (2013), "Locked in a fateful embrace: Turkey's PM and his Kurdish prisoner," *The Guardian*, March 1. Available online: https://www.theguardian .com/world/2013/mar/01/turkey-pm-kurdish-prisoner-peace (accessed April 12, 2013).

Tremblay, P. (2015), "Why is AKP losing the Kurds?" *Al Monitor*. Available online: http://www.almonitor.com/pulse/originals/2015/05/turkey-elections-akp-losing-kurdish -support.html# (accessed July 20, 2015).

Tunç, A. (2003), "Faustian acts in Turkish style: Structural change in national newspapers as an obstacle to quality journalism in 1990–2003," in O. Spassov (ed.), *Quality Press in Southeast Europe*, Sofia, Bulgaria: SOEMZ/Sofia University.

"Turkey: Arrests, closures censorship persist, week of 13 November" (2016), *Committee to Protect Journalists*. Available online: https://www.cpj.org/europe/turkey/ (accessed November 16, 2016).

"Turkey clashes: Why are Gezi Park and Taksim Square so important?" (2013), BBC. Available at: http://www.bbc.com/news/world-europe-22753752 (accessed June 20, 2015).

"Turkey coup aftermath: Pro-Kurdish Istanbul protests broken up" (2016), BBC, October 31. Available online: http://www.bbc.com/news/world-europe-37820442?SThisFB (accessed October 31, 2016).

"Turkey: In latest escalation, 102 media outlets closed by decree" (2016), *Reporters without Borders*. Available online: https://rsf.org/en/news/turkey-latest-escalation-102-media-outlets-closed-decree (accessed July 28, 2016).

"Turkey ruling party wins election with reduced majority" (2011), BBC, June 12. Available online: http://www.bbc.com/news/world-europe-13740147 (accessed December 20, 2015).

"Turkish no voices struggling to be heard" (2017), BBC, April 8. Available online: http://www.bbc.com/news/world-europe-39518180 (accessed April 8, 2017).

"UNICEF in Turkey: Country profile" (2010), UNICEF. Available online: http://www.unicef.org/turkey/ut/ut2_2010.html (accessed May 27, 2014).

Uzgel, İ. and B. Duru (2010), *AKP Kitabı Bir Dönüşümün Bilançosu*, Ankara: Pheoenix Yayınevi.

Vatikiotis, P. (2014), "New media, democracy, participation and the political," *Interactions: Studies in Communication and Culture*, 5(3): 293–307.

van Dijk, T. (1998), "Opinions and ideologies in the press," in A. Bell and P. Garrett (eds), *Approaches to Media Discourse*, Oxford: Blackwell.

Van Leeuwen, T. (1993), "Genre and field in critical discourse analysis: a synopsis," *Discourse and Society*, 4(2): 193–223.

Van Leeuwen, T. (1995), "Representing social action," *Discourse and Society*, 6(1): 81–106.

van Leeuwen, T. (1996), "The representation of social actors," in C. Caldas-Coulthard and M. Coulthard (eds), *Texts and Practices – Readings in Critical Discourse Analysis*, 32–70, London: Routledge.

van Leeuwen, T. (1999), *Speech, Music, Sound*, London: Macmillan Press.

van Leeuwen, T. (2005), *Introducing Social Semiotics*, London: Routledge.

van Leeuwen, T. (2017), "Sonic Logos," in L. Way and S. McKerrell (eds), *Music as Multimodal Discourse: Media, Power and Protest*, 119–134, London and New York: Bloomsbury.

van Leeuwen, T. and R. Wodak (1999), "Legitimising immigration: A discourse historical approach," *Discourse Studies*, 1(1): 83–118.

Von Hippel, E. (2005), *Democratising Innovation*, Cambridge, MA: MIT Press.

Walser, R. (1995), "Rhythm, rhyme, and rhetoric in the music of public enemy," *Ethnomusicology*, 39(2): 193–217.

"WAN-IFRA calls on Turkish gov't to respect pluralism in media" (2015), *Hurriyet*, June 1. Available online: http://www.hurriyetdailynews.com/wan-ifra-calls-on-turkish-govt-to-respect-pluralism-in-media.aspx?pageID=238&nID=83262&NewsCatID=339 (accessed February 21, 2016).

Way, L. (2012), "Turkish popular music videos as a multi-modal site of resistance," *Multimodal Communication*, 1(3): 251–275.

Way, L. (2013), "Discourses of popular politics, war and authenticity in Turkish pop music," *Social Semiotics*, 23(5): 715–734.

Way, L. (2015a), "YouTube as a site of debate through populist politics: The case of a Turkish protest pop video," *Journal of Multicultural Discourse*, 10(2): 180–196.

Way, L. (2015b), "Spaces of protest in Turkish popular music," in E. Mazierska and G. Gregory (eds), *Relocating Popular Music*, 27–43, London: Palgrave.

Way, L. (2016a), "Protest music, populism, politics and authenticity: The limits and potential of popular music's articulation of subversive politics," *Journal of Language and Politics*, 15(4): 422–446.

Way, L. (2016b), "Visual images in Turkish pop: The subversive role of cultural hybrids," *Visual Communication*, 15(2): 147–165.

Way, L. (2016c), "The punks, the web, local concerns and global appeal: Cultural hybridity in Turkish hardcore punk," *Punk and Post Punk*, 5(2): 111–130.

Way, L. (2017), "Authenticity and subversion: Protest music in videos' struggle with countercultural politics and authenticity," in L. Way and S. McKerrell (eds), *Music as Multimodal Discourse: Media, Power and Protest*, 47–70, London & New York: Bloomsbury.

Way, L. and A. Gedik (2013), "Music and image: Popular music's resistance to conservative politics," paper presented at *Ege University 14th cultural studies symposium – Confinement, Resistance, Freedom*, İzmir, Turkey, May 8–10.

Way, L. and E. Kaya (2015), "Turkish Newspapers' role in winning votes and exasperating Turkish-Kurdish relations: The Ağrı shootings," *Discourse and Communication*, 10(1): 82–100.

Way, L. and S. McKerrell (2017), *Music as Multimodal Discourse: Media, Power and Protest*, Bloomsbury.

"Who are we" (2016), *People's Democratic Party*. Available online: https://hdpenglish .wordpress.com/about/ (accessed June 13, 2016).

Williams, A. (2010), "We ain't terrorists but we Droppin' Bombs': Language use and localization in Egyptian hip hop," in M. Terkourafi (ed.), *Languages of Global Hip Hop*, 67–95, London: Continuum.

Williams, R. (1963), *Culture and Society*, Harmondsworth: Penguin.

Williams, R. (1988), *Key Words*, London: Fontana Press.

Wingstedt, J. (2017), "If You Have Nothing to Say – Sing It!': On the interplay of music, voice and lyrics in the advertising jingle," in L. Way and S. McKerrell (eds), *Music as Multimodal Discourse: Media, Power and protest*, 135–158, London and New York: Bloomsbury.

Winsted, J., Brandström, S. and J. Berg (2010), "Narrative music, visuals and meaning in film," *Visual Communication*, 9(2): 193–210.

Wodak, R. (2001), "What CDA is about – a summary of its history, important concepts and its development," in R. Wodak and M. Meyer (eds), *Methods of Critical Discourse Analysis*, 1–13, London: Sage.

Wodak, R., R. de Cillia, M. Reisigl, and K. Leibhart (1999), *The Discursive Construction of National Identity*, Edinburgh: Edinburgh University Press.

Wodak, R. and G. Weiss (2005), "Analysing European Union discourses: Theories and applications," in R. Wodak and P. Chilton (eds), *A New Agenda in (Critical) Discourse Analysis: Theory, Methodology and Interdisciplinarity*, 121–136, Amsterdam: John Benjamins Publishing.

Wright, W. (1975), *Six Guns and Society: A Structural Study of the Western*, Berkeley: University of California Press.

Yavuz, M. and N. Özcan (2006), "The Kurdish question and Turkey's justice and development party," *Middle East Policy*, 13(1): 103–119.

Yeğen, M. (1999), "The Kurdish question in Turkish state discourse," *Journal of Contemporary History*, 34(4): 555–568.

Yeşiltas, M. (2009), "Soft balancing in Turkish foreign policy: The case of the 2003 Iraq War," *Perceptions*, 14(1): 25–51.

Yıldız, A. (2001), *Ne Mutlu Türküm Diyebilene*, Ankara: İletişim Yayınları.

Zbikowski, L. (2009), "Music, language, and multimodal metaphor," in C. Forceville and E. Urios-Aparisi (eds), *Multimodal Metaphor*, 359–381, Berlin: Mouton de Gruyter.

Zbikowski, L. (2015), "Words, music, and meaning," in P.A. Brandt and J.R. do Carmo, Jr. (eds), *Semiotic de la musique*, 143–164, Liège: Presses universitaires de Liège–Sciences humaines.

Zeidan, D. (1999), "The Alevi of Anatolia," *Middle East Review of International Affairs*, 3(4): 74–89.

Zhang, Y. and O'Halloran, K. (2012), "The gate of the gateway: A hypermodal approach to university homepages," *Semiotica*, 190(1/4): 203–225.

Index